Business and Financial Concepts for Insurance Professionals

ONLINE COURSE PORTAL

The LOMA 307 Course Portal, available online at www.LOMANET.org via your "My Learning" page, includes numerous multi-media features designed to reinforce and enhance your learning experience and help you prepare for the exam. Among these features are numerous "Learning Aids" that illustrate key concepts presented in the assigned course materials; the Test Preparation Guide's popular interactive Practice Questions and Sample Exam with answer feedback, and the "Top 10 Tough Topics" review of the most challenging topics in this course. If you are not already using the online Course Portal but would like access to the many additional study resources for this course, please follow the log-in instructions provided in your Enrollment Confirmation e-mail, or call 1-800-ASK-LOMA or e-mail education@loma.org for assistance.

www.loma.org

LOMA (Life Office Management Association, Inc.)—an LL Global, Inc. company—is an international association founded in 1924. LOMA is committed to a business partnership with the worldwide members in the insurance and financial services industry to improve their management and operations through quality employee development, research, information sharing, and related products and services. Among LOMA's activities is the sponsorship of several self-study education programs leading to professional designations. These programs include the Fellow, Life Management Institute (FLMI) program and the Fellow, Financial Services Institute (FFSI) program. For more information on all of LOMA's education programs, please visit www.loma.org.

Statement of Purpose: LOMA Educational Programs Testing and Designations.

Examinations described in the LOMA Education and Training Catalog are designed solely to measure whether students have successfully completed the relevant assigned curriculum, and the attainment of the FLMI and other LOMA designations indicates only that all examinations in the given curriculum have been successfully completed. In no way shall a student's completion of a given LOMA course or attainment of the FLMI or other LOMA designation be construed to mean that LOMA in any way certifies that student's competence, training, or ability to perform any given task. LOMA's examinations are to be used solely for general educational purposes, and no other use of the examinations or programs is authorized or intended by LOMA. Furthermore, it is in no way the intention of the LOMA Curriculum and Examinations staff to describe the standard of appropriate conduct in any field of the insurance and financial services industry, and LOMA expressly repudiates any attempt to so use the curriculum and examinations. Any such assessment of student competence or industry standards of conduct should instead be based on independent professional inquiry and the advice of competent professional counsel.

Business and Financial Concepts for Insurance Professionals

Lisa M. Kozlowski, FLMI, FFSI, CLU, ChFC, AIAA, AIRC, ARA, FLHC, AAPA, ACS
Patsy Leeuwenburg, Ph.D., FLMI, FLHC, AIAA, ARA, AIRC, AAPA, ACS

LOMA Education and Training
Atlanta, Georgia
www.loma.org

Information in this text may have changed or been updated since its publication date. For current updates visit www.loma.org.

PROJECT TEAM:

Authors:	Lisa M. Kozlowski, FLMI, FFSI, CLU, ChFC, AIAA, AIRC, ARA, FLHC, AAPA, ACS
	Patsy Leeuwenburg, Ph.D., FLMI, FLHC, AIAA, ARA, AIRC, AAPA, ACS
Manuscript Editor:	Harriett E. Jones, J.D., FLMI, ACS, AIRC
Examinations Editor:	Sean Schaeffer Gilley, FLMI, ACS, HIA, CEBS, AIAA, MHP, AIRC, AAPA, ARA, FLHC
Project Manager:	Robert R. Hartley, FLMI, FFSI, ALHC, ACS, CLU, ChFC, RHU
Copy Editor:	Sally Farnham
Indexer:	Robert D. Land, FLMI, ACS
AVP, Marketing:	Paul Wilson
Lead Graphic Designer:	Marlene McAuley
Typesetters:	Allison Ayers-Molette
	Amy Stailey
Production Coordinator:	Amy Stailey
Product Sourcing Manager:	Carol Wiessner, ACS
Administrative Support:	Mamunah Carter
Cover Design	Marlene McAuley

ISBN 978-1-57974-349-9

www.loma.org

Contents

Business and Financial Concepts for Insurance Professionals delivers information about basic economic, financial, and business concepts and about financial practices that are specific to the insurance industry. We present this information in an understandable format that uses real-world insurance examples to convey important concepts. Although this text focuses primarily on the United States, the underlying principles and practices we describe generally apply worldwide. Where appropriate, we include examples of practices in other countries.

Acknowledgments

LOMA's texts always are the result of a joint effort between industry experts and LOMA's own staff. Both groups made invaluable contributions to the success of the *Business and Financial Concepts for Insurance Professionals* text.

Textbook Development Panel and Additional Contributors

Industry experts served as our review panel prior to publication and made the writing of this text possible. During the review process, these individuals reviewed the course outline and every chapter, making many substantive comments on the content of the course, providing suggestions for examples, submitting relevant research materials, and answering numerous questions from the authors. We are deeply grateful for the efforts of our reviewers, who cared enough about the educational needs of current and future industry employees to volunteer their time and expertise to this project. They improved the accuracy, clarity, and relevance of the text, although the authors claim responsibility for any errors.

The following individuals devoted countless hours to reviewing *Business and Financial Concepts for Insurance Professionals*:

Colleen J. Atkins, FLMI, FFSI, ACS, AAPA, AIRC, ARA
Compliance Administrator
Alfa Life Insurance Corporation

Sharon Bartels, CPA, CIA, FLMI
Manager of Auditing
Berkshire Life Insurance Company of America

Pamela J. Brooks, FLMI, AIAF, ACS
SOX Compliance Analyst
Boston Mutual Life Insurance Company

Thad Dawson, FSA, MAAA
Associate Actuary-Pricing
The Principal Financial Group

Tiffany T. King, CPA
Vice President & Controller
The Baltimore Life Insurance Company

J. David Madsen, CPA, FLMI, FFSI, AIAF
Manager, Investment Accounting
Illinois Mutual Life Insurance Company

Ronald T. Menty, FLMI/M, FFSI, CLU, ChFC, CIA, CISA
Audit Consultant
Phoenix Companies

Carrie McCain Morton, FSA, MAAA
Actuary
The Principal Financial Group

Kimberly K. Rasmusson, FLMI, AFSI, ACS
Accounting Coordinator
ING

Jeffery P. Watson, CPA, FLMI, ARA
Manager, Quality Assurance
Blackman Kallick, LLP

John W. Wells, CLU, CPA, FLMI, ACS
Chair Emeritus
LOMA Education Council

We also wish to thank the following individuals, who reviewed portions of the text and provided other assistance with this project: Warren A. Carter, ASA, MAAA, Second Vice President, TIAA-CREF, Retired; Elizabeth Clark, FLMI, ACS, Operations Manager, Forms & Filings, Balboa Insurance Group; Karen M. Roberts, AAPA, ACS, FLMI, Senior Product & Financial Analyst, Allstate Life Insurance Company; and Rachel E. Underwood, CPA, FFSI, FLMI, ACS, Manager of Financial Controls and Statutory Reporting, The Union Central Life Insurance Company.

LOMA Staff/Consultants

LOMA has talented staff members who contribute in many ways to ensure LOMA's products meet the highest possible standards for education and information about the financial services industry.

Our heartfelt thanks go out to Harriett E. Jones, J.D., FLMI, ACS, AIRC, Senior Associate, Designation Programs, who served as our manuscript editor and brought the writing styles of multiple authors into a cohesive whole for this text. We also thank Susan Conant, FLMI, HIA, CEBS, Senior Associate, Designation Programs, and Elizabeth A. Mulligan, FLMI, FLHC, ACS, PAHM, AAPA, AIRC, ARA, AIAA, Senior Associate, Designation Programs, who contributed to the development of the course.

Thanks go to all of the people at LOMA and LIMRA who contributed to the design and development of the Course Portal for the LOMA 307 text. LOMA staff contributors included Kelly Neeley, FLMI, ALHC, ACS, AIAA, PAHM, Senior Associate, Training Programs; Kristen L. Falk, FLMI, FFSI, AAPA, ACS, AIAA, AIRC, ARA, Senior Associate, Training Programs; David A. Lewis, FLMI, ACS, Senior Associate, Learning and Development Services; Sean Schaeffer Gilley, FLMI, ACS, HIA, CEBS, AIAA, MHP, AIRC, AAPA, ARA, FLHC, Senior Associate, Designation Programs; Brad Kimmel, Associate, Learning Technology; Marlene McCauley, Lead Graphic Designer, Production and Graphics; Kathryn H. Brown, PCS, Marketing Associate; Nick Desoutter, FLMI, AAPA, PCS, Senior Associate, Training Programs; and Gene Stone, FLMI, ACS, CLU, Senior Associate, Training Programs. LIMRA staff contributors included Bill Maura, Assistant Vice President, Marketing; Anthony Leathers, Multi-Media Assistant; Frank Robinson, Jr., Multi-Media Technical Specialist; and John Rocchetti, Multi-Media Technical Specialist Assistant.

Additional thanks go to the LOMA staff members who were responsible for examinations and related study materials for the course. These included Melanie R. Green, FLMI, ACS, AIAA, Senior Associate, Designation Programs; Sean Schaeffer Gilley, FLMI, ACS, HIA, CEBS, AIAA, MHP, AIRC, AAPA, ARA, FLHC, Senior Associate, Designation Programs; David A. Lewis, FLMI, ACS, Senior Associate, Learning and Development Services; and Yanhua Xun, Ph.D., FLMI, FFSI, AIAA, ARA, AAPA, PCS, Senior Associate, Designation Programs. Thanks also to Mamunah Carter, Administrative Assistant II, Education & Training Division, who provided administrative support.

In LOMA's Production Department, thanks go to Carol A. Wiessner, ACS, Product Sourcing Manager, who coordinated the printing of the text and associated study materials; Amy Stailey, Production Coordinator II/Scheduling Coordinator, who managed the production of the text; and Allison Ayers-Molette, who typeset the text. In addition, we thank Sally Farnham, a consultant, for her work as copy editor, and Robert D. Land, FLMI, ACS, a consultant, who created the index for the text.

We extend a very special thank you to Robert R. Hartley, FLMI, FFSI, ALHC, ACS, CLU, ChFC, RHU, Assistant Vice President, Designation Programs, who served as Project Manager and provided guidance and support throughout the project; Julia K. Wooley, FLMI, ACS, ALHC, HIA, MHP, Assistant Vice President, Designation Programs, who reviewed preliminary text chapters; and Katherine C. Milligan, FLMI, ACS, ALHC, Vice President, Education and Training Division, who provided leadership, guidance, resources, support, and encouragement for this project.

Lisa M. Kozlowski, FLMI, FFSI, CLU, ChFC,
AIAA, AIRC, ARA, FLHC, AAPA, ACS
Patsy Leeuwenburg, Ph.D., FLMI, FLHC, AIAA, ARA,
AIRC, AAPA, ACS

Introduction

The purpose of *Business and Financial Concepts for Insurance Professionals* is to provide an overview of the general business and financial concepts involved in the insurance business. To enhance your learning experience, LOMA has developed a Course Portal for this course that is accessible upon enrollment in LOMANET. A LOMA Course Portal is an online resource from which learners access everything they need to study and prepare for the course examination. The 307 Course Portal contains an array of blended learning resources, including some multimedia features. The Course Portal provides access to:

- An introductory course video

- Protected PDFs of the assigned study materials, which can be printed or read online

- The interactive Practice Questions and Sample Exam

- Recommended study assignments to help you set goals and manage your learning experience

- Review tools, including a "Top Ten Tough Topics" review

Students preparing to take the examination for LOMA 307—*Business and Financial Concepts for Insurance Professionals*—which is part of the Fellow, Life Management Institute (FLMI) program, will find that the course materials include many features designed to help learners more easily understand the course content, organize their study, and help them prepare for the examination. These features include chapter outlines, learning objectives, key terms, figures containing real-world examples of course content, and a comprehensive glossary. As we describe each of these features, we give you suggestions for studying the material.

- **Chapter Outline.** Each chapter contains an outline of the chapter. Review this outline to gain an overview of the major topics that will be covered; then scan through the chapter to become familiar with how the information is presented. By looking at the headings, you can gain a preview of how various subjects in each chapter relate to each other.

- **Learning Objectives.** The first page of each chapter contains a list of learning objectives to help you focus your studies. Before reading each chapter, review these learning objectives. Then, as you read the chapter, look for material that will help you meet the learning objectives.

- **Key Terms.** This text explains new business, financial, and insurance industry terms that apply to the text material and, where appropriate, reviews key terms previously presented in LOMA courses. Each key term is highlighted with *bold italic type* when the term is defined and is included in a list of key terms at the end of each chapter. All key terms also appear in a comprehensive glossary at the end of the text and are accessible from the Course Portal. As you read each chapter, pay special attention to the key terms.

- **Figures.** We include figures throughout the text to illustrate and bring a real-world perspective to the text's discussion of selected topics. Information contained in figures may be tested on the examination for the course.

- **Glossary.** A comprehensive glossary that contains definitions of all key terms appears at the end of the text and is accessible from the Course Portal. Following each glossary entry is a number in brackets that indicates the chapter in which the key term is defined. The glossary also references important equivalent terms, acronyms, and contrasting terms.

LOMA may periodically revise the course materials and study aids for this course. To ensure that you are studying from the correct materials, check the current LOMA *Education and Training Catalog* available at www.loma.org/ StudentServices.asp or the Course Portal for LOMA 307 for a description of the materials and study aids assigned for the examination for which you are preparing.

Using the LOMA Study Aid

LOMA has prepared a study aid—the *Test Preparation Guide for LOMA 307*—designed to help students prepare for the LOMA 307 examination. LOMA recommends that you use this study aid. **Studies indicate that students who use LOMA study aids consistently perform significantly better on LOMA examinations than students who do not use these study aids.**

LOMA's *Test Preparation Guide for LOMA 307* is assigned reading for students preparing for the LOMA 307 examination. Used along with the text, the Test Preparation Guide (TPG) will help you master the course material. The TPG is accessible from the Course Portal and can be used online or printed as a PDF. It contains practice exam questions and a full-scale sample examination, along with answer explanations to every question in the TPG.

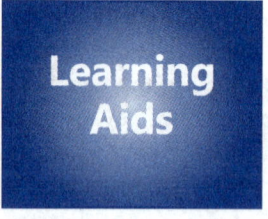
Learning Aids

The LOMA 307 Course Portal, available online at www.LOMANET. org, includes several Learning Aids designed to reinforce concepts covered in the assigned text. If you are not already using the online Course Portal but would like access to the Learning Aids for this course, please follow the log-in instructions provided in your enrollment confirmation email, or call 1-800-ASK-LOMA or email education@loma.org for assistance. **PLEASE NOTE:** Examination questions will be based only on content presented in the assigned text.

Module 1

- ✓ Markets and Market Participants
- ✓ Flow of Funds
- ✓ Insurers as Corporations
- ✓ Planning
- ✓ The Control Cycle

Module 2

- ✓ Basic Risk Management Techniques
- ✓ The Risk-Return Trade-off
- ✓ The Required Rate of Return
- ✓ Evaluating Product Performance
- ✓ The Time Value of Money
- ✓ Expenses
- ✓ Commissions

Module 3

- ✓ The Business Cycle
- ✓ How Changes in Market Interest Rates Affect Insurers
- ✓ Inflation & Disintermediation
- ✓ Revenues and Expenses, Profit and Loss
- ✓ Basic Accounting Equation and the Balance Sheet
- ✓ Linking the Balance Sheet and Income Statement
- ✓ Annual Statement vs. Annual Report
- ✓ Budgeting Approaches
- ✓ Ratio Analysis in Action

Module 4

- ✓ PERT Networks and Critical Paths
- ✓ Performance Dashboards
- ✓ Gantt Chart
- ✓ Normal Distributions
- ✓ Law of Large Numbers
- ✓ Sampling

Chapter 1

The Role of Insurance in the Economy

Objectives:

After studying this chapter, you should be able to

- Define economics and describe the primary sectors that make up local, national, and global economies

- Explain the three primary functions of money in an economy

- Identify the major participants in the marketplace and describe the types of markets in which exchanges among participants occur

- Describe how funds flow between buyers and sellers and between borrowers and lenders during marketplace exchanges

- Describe the types of financial institutions and explain their role in an economy

- Describe the four basic financial needs customers have and identify the kinds of financial products that help satisfy those needs

Outline

The Economy
- Economic Sectors
- The Role of Money in the Economy
- Market Participants
- Markets
- Flow of Funds

The Role of Financial Institutions in the Economy
- Depository Institutions
- Contractual Savings Institutions
- Investment Institutions

Financial Needs of Households and Businesses
- Cash Management and Credit
- Asset Accumulation
- Asset Protection
- Asset Distribution

Changes in the Financial Services Industry

> The Federal Reserve says output rose 0.7% in September versus a fore-casted 0.2% rise ... The better-than-expected figures suggest that economic growth in the third quarter could be stronger than anticipated... Output for the entire third quarter rose at an annual rate of 5.2%, the first quarterly gain since the first quarter of 2008 and the largest increase since the first quarter of 2005. (Excerpted from Ben Rooney, "Industrial production in surprise jump," CNNMoney.com, http://money.conn.com/2009/10/16/news/economy/industrial_production/index.htm, 11/12/09).

> The National Bureau of Economic Research said Monday that the United States has been in a recession since December 2007, making official what most Americans have already believed about the state of the economy... The current recession will likely prove to be one of the longest downturns since the Great Depression of the 1930s. (Excerpted from "It's a 'recession,'" CNNMoney.com, http://money.cnn.com/galleries/2008/news/0803/gallery.economy_overview. 11/12/09).

We hear about the economy every day—in newspapers, on television and radio, and in conversations with friends and coworkers. Sometimes, the news is good. Other times, it's not. In all cases, though, what's happening in the economy affects everyone, including insurance companies and their employees.

The Economy

In basic terms, an *economy* is the part of the environment that includes all of the elements affecting the production, distribution, and consumption of goods and services. Economies exist at three different levels:

- Local economies include the activities of individual neighborhoods, cities, or states

- National economies include the activities of an entire nation

- Global economies are multinational and include the activities of multiple nations

Figure 1.1 shows the relationships among these types of economies. Insurance companies operate in all of these economies.

> The Prism Life Insurance Company is a U.S. insurer whose home office is located in State A. The company also has regional offices in State B, State C, and State D. Recently, Prism expanded its operations into India and China.

In this example, Prism's home office activities are part of the local economy of State A and its operations in States B, C, and D are part of the local economies of those states. Together, Prism's home office and regional office operations are part of the U.S. economy, and its operations in India and China are part of the multinational, or global, economy. Prism contributes to these local, national, and global economies by selling insurance products, hiring employees, and paying taxes.

In spite of the differences between local, national, and global economies, all economies operate on two basic assumptions:

- Members of an economy have unlimited wants. Wants are not the same as needs. *Needs* are conditions that must be satisfied by products and services in order for individuals, businesses, and governments to survive and function properly. Needs often change over time as personal circumstances change, such as going to school or having a child. *Wants* are desires for particular products or services. For example, a person might need a car to get to and from work, but he might want a particular type of car. Wants usually are learned through personal experience and tend to change over time, depending on what products and services are available.

Figure 1.1. Types of Economies

Local	**National**	**Global**
 British Columbia • Canada	N.W.Territories • Canada	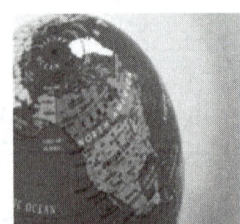
Each of Canada's nine provinces is supported by industries in its cities and neighborhoods. British Columbia's main industries are logging and manufacturing.	Each province's activities are part of Canada's national economy. The nation's most important industries include manufacturing and oil production.	Canada is active in international trade. Its main exports are its natural resources: lumber, oil, and minerals (coal, copper, iron ore, and gold).

■ Members of an economy have limited resources for satisfying their wants. Anyone who has a bank account is familiar with this problem. You may want to take a trip around the world, but you can't do that and still pay your bills. As a result, people and businesses are forced to make choices about how and when to use their resources.

The study of how societies and individuals allocate limited resources among competing, unlimited wants is called *economics*.

Economic Sectors

Economies are generally divided into sectors according to the activities performed by the sector. The four most important of these sectors are

■ **Sector 1: Raw Materials**. This sector, which economists refer to as the *primary sector*, forms the foundation of all economies. It secures the raw materials needed for production, including land, lumber, coal, gas and oil, minerals, and basic foods. The primary activities performed in this sector include agriculture, mining, and forestry. In developing economies, a large percentage of the population may operate in Sector 1. In developed economies, relatively few people are involved.

■ **Sector 2: Manufactured Goods**. This sector—the *secondary sector*—turns raw materials into finished products and makes them available to consumers. The main activities performed in this sector include manufacturing finished goods, processing, and construction.

■ **Sector 3: Services**. The *tertiary* sector provides services—including retail and wholesale sales, transportation, and distribution—that facilitate the transfer of finished goods to end users in the economy. It also provides services that enhance consumers' lives, such as entertainment, media, financial services, healthcare, and law. Insurance companies play an important role in this sector by providing financial security for households and businesses. The services sector is by far the largest economic sector in the United States.

■ **Sector 4: Intellectual Property**. This sector—known as the *quaternary sector*—includes intellectual concerns such as government, culture, education, scientific research, and information technology. The services provided by this sector are designed to improve the quality of life.

Figure 1.2 shows the proportion of the U.S. population employed in each of these sectors of the national economy in 2009.

The Role of Money in the Economy

All economic activities are based on exchanges. An *exchange* is a transaction in which one party gives something of value to another party and receives something of value in return. In an economy, companies hire employees to provide the labor needed to produce products and services. In exchange, they pay wages to those employees. Employees then use their earned wages to buy the products and services they need and want. Money is a key element in all these exchanges.

Figure 1.2. U.S. Employment Distribution by Sector

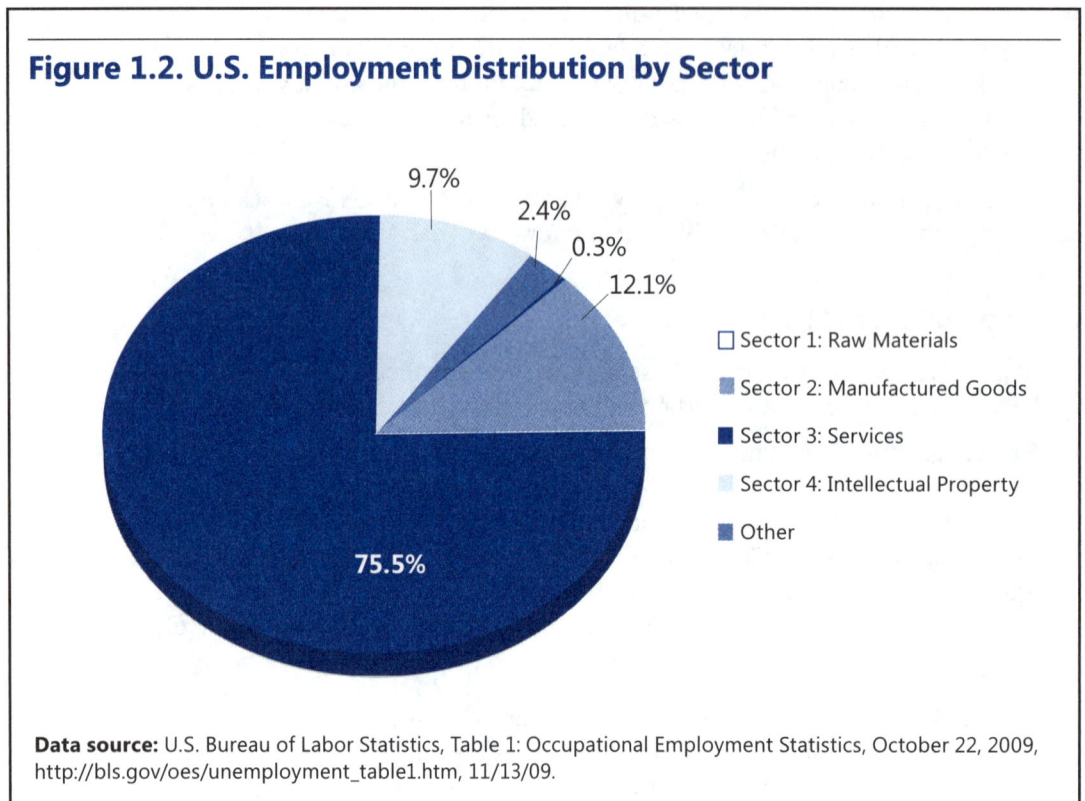

Data source: U.S. Bureau of Labor Statistics, Table 1: Occupational Employment Statistics, October 22, 2009, http://bls.gov/oes/unemployment_table1.htm, 11/13/09.

Unlike other financial instruments, which are designed to help people manage, save, and protect resources, money is designed specifically to facilitate exchanges, by providing a

■ **Standardized medium of exchange**. People usually use money to pay for products and services and accept money as payment for the products and services they provide. Money, in this case, serves as a ***medium of exchange***—a standardized method of making and receiving payments for goods and services. Without money, the exchange process can be cumbersome.

> Suppose that Adam Grant, an accountant, and David Simpson, an electrician, are neighbors. When Adam decided to build a new room on his house, he asked David to help him with the wiring in the new room. In return, Adam offered to help David with his taxes.
>
> As long as Adam and David assign the same value to their services, this kind of exchange can be effective. However, on a large scale, this kind of system is cumbersome. The time and effort needed to negotiate exchanges increase transaction costs; increased transaction costs reduce the volume of exchanges, and fewer exchanges slow down the economy.

■ **Standardized way to measure value**. Before people buy or sell products and services, they need a way to measure the value of those products and services. In most economies, value is expressed in monetary units called ***units of account***. In the United States, the dollar serves as a standard monetary unit of account; in India, the monetary unit of account is the rupee. Value, however, is based on more than monetary amounts. For example, $1,000 in cash and a $1,000 bond that matures in five years represent the same monetary amount, but they may not have the same value to a customer who needs to use the amount to pay his rent in a week. For an exchange to be acceptable, the form as well as the value of payments must meet the trading parties' needs.

- **Store of value**. When people receive payments for products and services, they need to know that those payments will have the same value when they use them to make payments later. Although the value of money fluctuates over long periods of time as economies move through periods of expansion and contraction, it remains relatively stable over the short term.

Figure 1.3 summarizes the three primary functions of money in the economy.

Market Participants

Suppliers (sellers) of products and services and consumers (buyers) of those products and services come together in the marketplace. Market participants can be divided into four basic groups:

- **Households** consist of individuals and families who buy products and services for their personal use. They spend money earned from their labor to buy products or services to satisfy their needs and wants. They also save or invest money to increase their personal wealth.

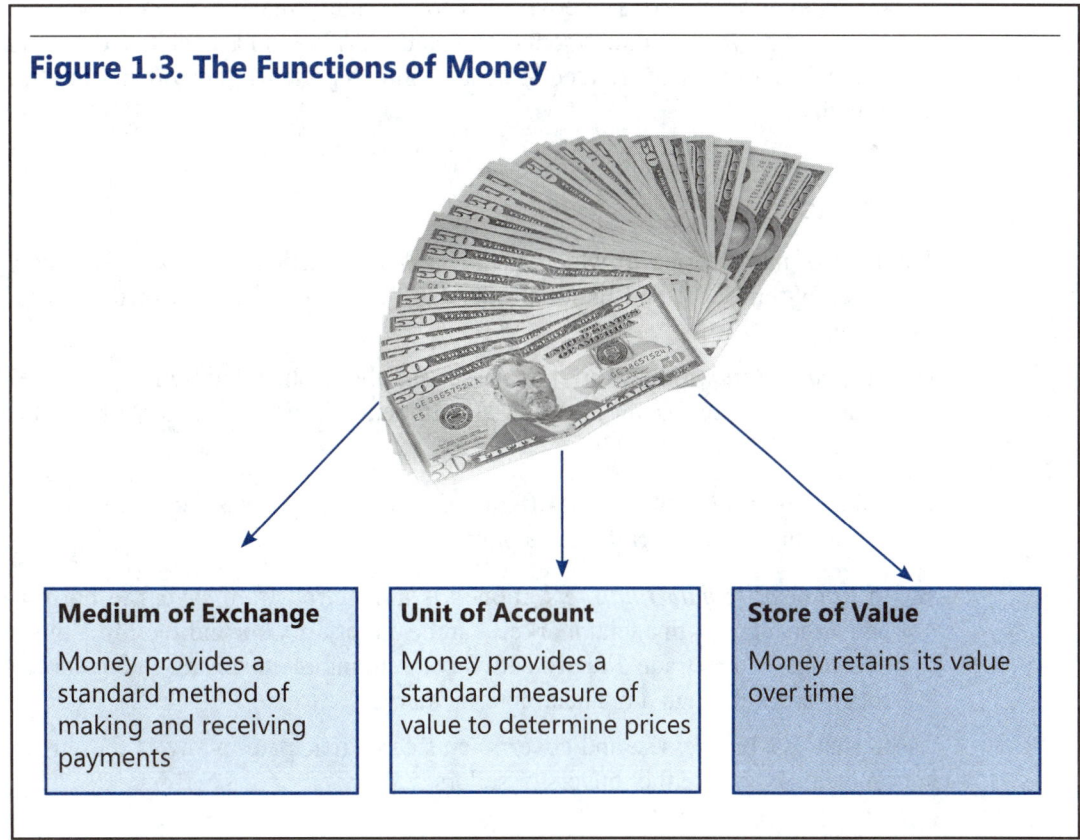

Figure 1.3. The Functions of Money

Medium of Exchange	Unit of Account	Store of Value
Money provides a standard method of making and receiving payments	Money provides a standard measure of value to determine prices	Money retains its value over time

- **Businesses** buy resources or goods and services from producers or intermediaries and secure labor from households. Businesses use these purchased resources, goods and services, and labor to produce other products or provide services, and then sell those new products and services to other intermediaries or end users. Businesses earn money by providing goods and services to buyers. Like households, businesses spend money on products and services to sustain operations and save (invest) money to increase the value of the business.

- **Governments** manage the general operation of the economy. Their primary functions are to (1) purchase, provide, and produce goods and services; (2) set laws and regulations; (3) impose taxes; and (4) make transfer payments to individuals, businesses, and other market participants. *Transfer payments* are payments made by a government for which no goods or services are given in return. For example, in the United States, governments make transfer payments to households in the form of Social Security benefits and unemployment benefits.

- **Financial intermediaries** are organizations that facilitate the movement of funds from buyers to sellers and from households, businesses, and governments that have a surplus of funds (savers) to those that have a shortage of funds (borrowers). The transfer of funds from savers to borrowers through the services of a financial intermediary is known as *intermediation*. For example, each time an individual or business purchases an insurance policy, the purchase transfers funds, in the form of premiums, to the insurer. The insurer invests the premiums it receives in financial markets. The insurer thus serves as an intermediary between customers and financial markets. The insurer also serves as an intermediary when it transfers funds back to a customer in the form of interest credited to the customer's policy and payment of policy benefits.

Markets

The type of marketplace in which exchanges occur depends on what is bought and sold. Within local and national economies, markets fall into three general categories:

- In *product (output) markets*, businesses supply finished goods and services to households, other businesses, and governments. In exchange, buyers pay the prices specified by the seller.

- In *labor markets*, households offer their labor to businesses and governments. In exchange, they receive wages or other compensation.

- In *financial (capital) markets*, money is transferred from savers to borrowers. Exchanges in financial markets can be either direct or indirect. In a direct exchange, sellers trade directly with buyers. In indirect exchanges, buyers and sellers work through a financial intermediary.

Households, businesses, and governments can participate in any of these markets and can serve as either buyers or sellers.

Julie Brenner owns a bakery where she produces homemade breads and pastries. She sells her products to households and businesses through her retail store, which she purchased with money she borrowed from a commercial bank. She also sells products wholesale to local restaurants. Julie employs two full-time store employees and one part-time delivery person.

Analysis: When Julie borrowed money to buy her store, she entered the financial market. In this market, she served as the buyer and the commercial bank that financed her loan served as the seller. Julie obtained the services of her three employees through the labor market. In this market, she also serves as a buyer and the employees function as sellers. Finally, Julie sells her products to retail and wholesale buyers through product market transactions.

In global economies, exchanges often occur across national boundaries and involve multiple currencies. To facilitate multinational exchanges, global economies participate in *foreign exchange markets*, which convert currencies used by buyers into currencies acceptable to the sellers.

Flow of Funds

Every market exchange results in a flow of funds and/or a flow of goods and services from one market participant to another. Economists often use diagrams to illustrate the flow of funds through economies. Because flows tend to be circular, these diagrams are referred to as *circular flow diagrams*. Figure 1.4 shows what the flow of funds through a local or national economy might look like.

As Figure 1.4 illustrates, funds can be tracked from any point in the system. For example, funds from households flow to

- Businesses when goods and services are bought in product (output) markets

- Financial markets through direct investments and through indirect investments managed by financial intermediaries

- Governments in the form of taxes

Similarly, funds from businesses flow to

- Households through labor market transactions

- Financial markets in the form of investments

- Governments in the form of taxes

Funds flow from financial intermediaries to

- Households and businesses in the form of loans/obligations

- Financial markets in the form of investments

Finally, funds from governments flow to

- Households and businesses in the form of transfer payments

- Financial markets in the form of investments

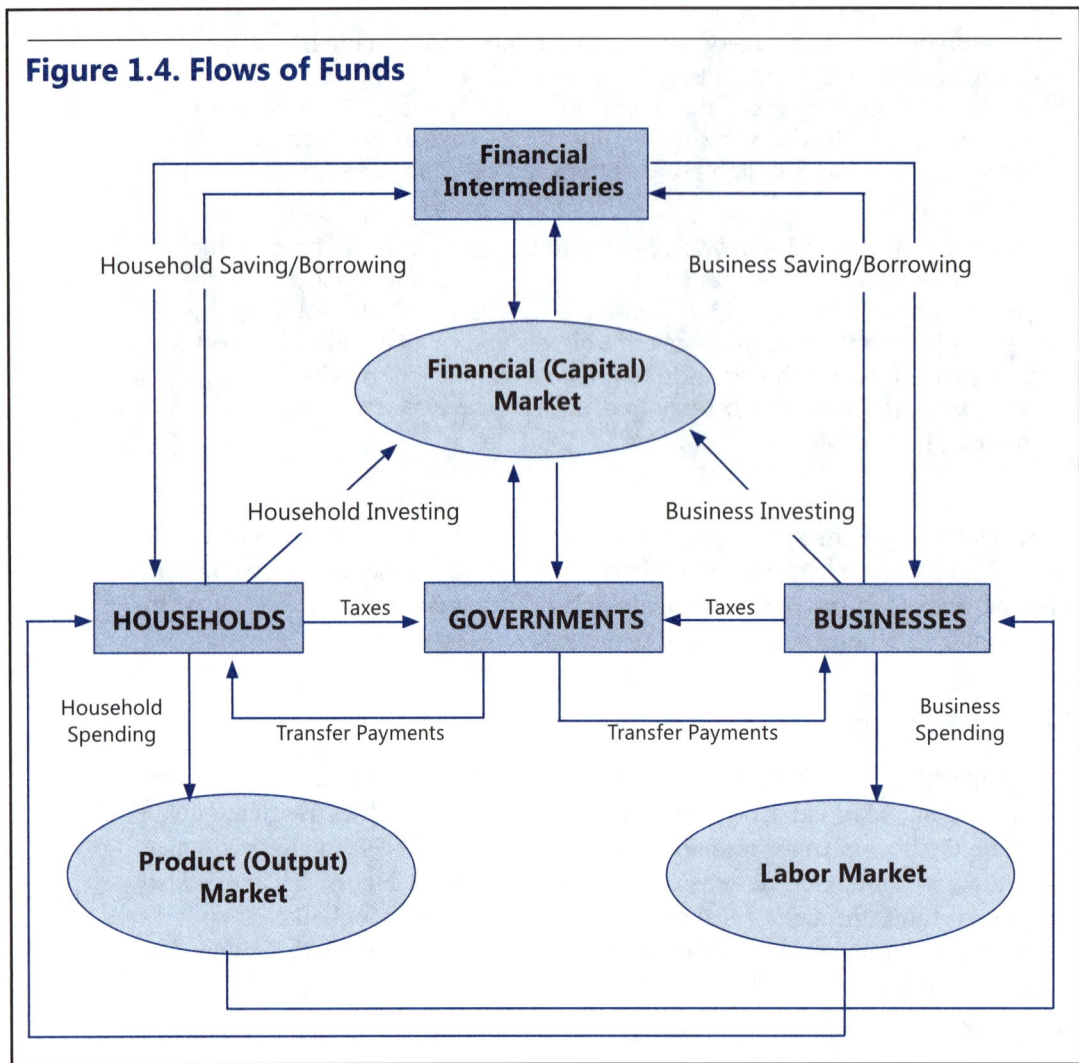

Figure 1.4. Flows of Funds

The flow of goods and services follows this same circular pattern, only in reverse.

If the diagram were expanded to include global transactions, part of the funds spent by households for products and by businesses for labor would be funneled through foreign exchange markets.

The Role of Financial Institutions in the Economy

A *financial institution* is a business that owns financial assets, such as stocks and bonds, rather than fixed assets, such as equipment and raw materials. The primary purpose of financial institutions is to help consumers, businesses, and governments save, borrow, invest, and otherwise manage money. Financial institutions also serve as intermediaries in the marketplace. In this role, they provide significant benefits for market participants. For example, consumers can often reduce investment costs by investing through financial institutions rather than buying securities directly from issuers. Financial institutions also provide risk management and investment planning services.

As financial intermediaries, financial institutions hold a special position of trust among market participants. When households, businesses, and governments entrust financial intermediaries with funds, they trust those intermediaries to act fairly and ethically and to put customers' interests above their own interests when conducting transactions. A financial institution that holds a special position of trust or confidence when handling the affairs of others and who must put the interests of others ahead of its own interests is a *fiduciary*.

Three primary types of financial institutions operate in the economy:

- Depository institutions

- Contractual savings institutions

- Investment institutions

Depository Institutions

A *depository institution* is a financial institution that specializes in accepting deposits and making loans. When a depository institution accepts a deposit from a household or business, it uses the deposited funds to make loans to other households or businesses. In these transactions, the institution pays depositors interest for the use of deposited funds and collects interest from borrowers. *Interest* is a fee that individuals and financial institutions pay (or charge) for the use of borrowed money. Depository institutions also invest deposited funds in financial markets.

In addition to traditional banking products such as checking accounts, savings accounts, and loans, depository institutions now offer a wide variety of other financial products including credit cards, mortgages, investment services, financial counseling services, and trust services. Figure 1.5 describes the primary forms of depository institutions in the United States.

Contractual Savings Institutions

A *contractual savings institution* is a financial institution that acquires funds at periodic intervals on a contractual basis. The primary purpose of contractual savings institutions is to provide financial security and protection for their customers. Insurance companies and pension funds are the two major contractual savings institutions.

Insurance companies offer protection for their customers by providing insurance coverage against financial loss. Insurance companies provide three basic types of insurance protection:

- **Life insurance companies** protect customers against financial loss from death and against the risk of outliving financial resources.

- **Health insurance companies** protect customers against financial loss from disability, illness, and accidents.

- **Property/casualty insurance companies** protect customers against financial loss from property damage, theft, and liability.

In exchange for providing insurance coverage, insurance companies receive periodic premium payments from their customers.

Figure 1.5. Depository Institutions

Type of Institution	Description
Commercial Bank	Commercial banks accept deposits from consumers and businesses and make consumer and business loans. Deposits can be exchanged for currency and can be used to make payments (checkable deposits), for short-term savings (savings deposits), or for long-term asset accumulation (time deposits). Commercial banks are also major distributors of mutual funds and insurance products.
Savings and Loan Associations	The primary function of savings and loan associations (S&Ls) is to provide mortgage loans to consumers. They also accept savings account deposits from households and offer checking services. Together with mutual savings banks and credit unions, S&Ls are often referred to as *thrifts*.
Mutual Savings Banks	Mutual savings banks (MSBs) are cooperative institutions whose depositors own the institutions and share in their earnings. Their primary activities are to accept savings deposits from households and make mortgage loans. Unlike other depository institutions that operate in all states, MSBs are legally allowed only in certain states.
Credit Unions	Credit unions are nonprofit, cooperative institutions owned by their depositors. Originally, owners shared a common bond such as working for the same employer or belonging to the same union. Now, membership is generally open to anyone. The main function of credit unions is to provide consumer loans.

A *pension fund* is a contractual savings institution that provides retirement funds for individuals covered by pension plans. A *pension plan* is an arrangement under which a plan sponsor provides plan participants with a lifetime income benefit that begins at retirement. Pension plans can be private plans or public plans.

A private pension plan is a plan sponsored by an employer for its employees. Private plans are funded by contributions from employers and sometimes employees during the employees' working years. The funds are then used to pay participating employees a lifetime income benefit when they retire. Private pension plans are typically managed by depository institutions, life insurance companies, mutual funds, and securities broker/dealers. A public pension plan is a plan sponsored by a government on behalf of citizens. In the United States, the largest public pension plan is Social Security, which provides specified benefits, including a monthly retirement income benefit, to qualified individuals. To qualify for benefits, individuals must have contributed to the plan during their working years. Governments in other countries also provide pension plans for their citizens.

Investment Institutions

Investment institutions engage primarily in investing and trading *securities*, which are documents or certificates that represent either an ownership interest in a business (stock) or an obligation of indebtedness owed by a business, government, or agency (bond). Investment institutions, which include securities broker/dealers and mutual funds, are key players in financial (capital) markets.

Securities broker/dealers specialize in the purchase and sale of stocks, bonds, commercial paper, and other financial instruments. A *stock* is a security that represents an ownership interest in a company. A *bond* is a security that represents a debt that the borrower (the issuer of the bond) owes to the bondholder (the person or company that buys the bond). Bonds can be issued by governments or by corporations. *Commercial paper* consists of short-term, unsecured promissory notes issued to businesses or governments by corporations as an alternative to short-term bank loans or other forms of borrowing. Commercial paper typically (1) matures in 5 to 45 days, (2) is issued in denominations of $100,000 or more, and (3) is used to fund current transactions.

Securities broker/dealers perform two primary functions. As brokers, these companies match buyers of securities with sellers of those securities. As dealers, they hold an inventory of securities and typically buy and sell securities from their own accounts. Discount broker/dealers focus on executing customer orders to buy and sell securities. Full-service broker/dealers provide investment advice and planning services in addition to handling customer transactions.

A *mutual fund* is an investment company that pools the funds of customers and uses the funds to buy stocks, bonds, and other financial instruments. Figure 1.6 shows the percentage of the total market for the primary types of securities held by mutual fund companies in the United States at year end 2008. Households and businesses that invest in the funds hold shares in those funds. From a customer perspective, the major benefits of mutual funds include

- **Professional management**. Each fund has a fund manager, who chooses securities that best match the fund's investment objectives. For example, some funds focus on generating income; others focus on long-term growth.

- **Diversification of investments**. Because funds are invested in a variety of securities, losses incurred by one security can be offset by gains in another.

- **Wide selection of funds**. Investors can choose from thousands of mutual funds representing a full range of investment objectives.

- **Convenience**. Investors can purchase mutual fund shares directly from the fund company or through a securities broker. Mutual fund companies also offer a variety of shareholder services, including 24-hour online or telephone access to account information and transaction processing.

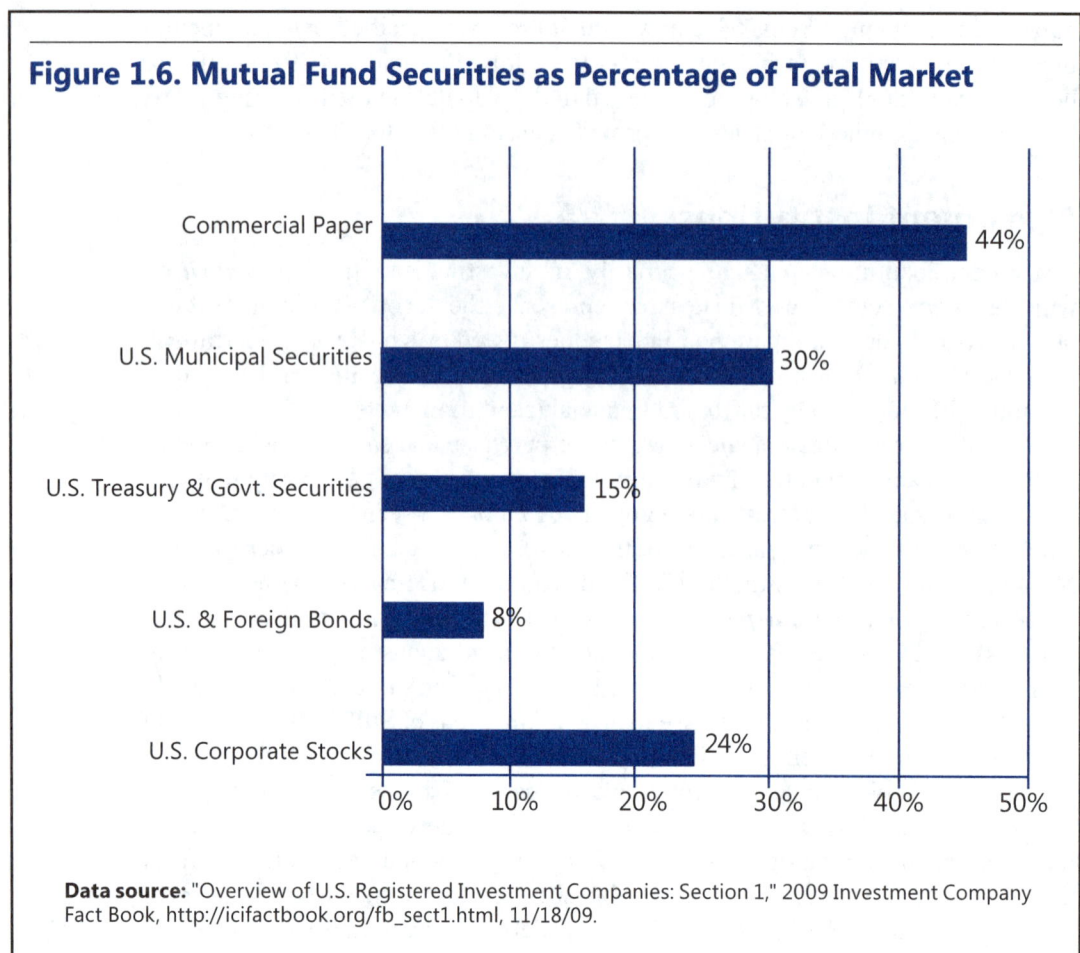

Figure 1.6. Mutual Fund Securities as Percentage of Total Market

Data source: "Overview of U.S. Registered Investment Companies: Section 1," 2009 Investment Company Fact Book, http://icifactbook.org/fb_sect1.html, 11/18/09.

■ **Liquidity**. In the context of financial products, *liquidity* is the ease with which an asset can be converted to cash for an approximation of its underlying value. Investors can quickly and easily redeem mutual fund shares by contacting their broker or the mutual fund company.

Financial Needs of Households and Businesses

Financial products serve a variety of consumer and business needs. Those needs can be divided into four categories:

■ Cash management and credit needs

■ Asset accumulation needs

■ Asset protection needs

■ Asset distribution needs

Cash Management and Credit

Because most people are uncomfortable keeping large amounts of cash on hand to make purchases and pay bills, they need a way to store money for short periods of time and to transfer money from one place to another. Increasingly, people also need a way to purchase products and services even if they don't have the entire purchase price on hand and to either delay payment until funds are available or spread payment over time. Cash management and credit products such as the ones described in Figure 1.7 are designed to satisfy those needs.

Figure 1.7. Cash Management and Credit Products

Cash Management Product	Description
Checking Account	A deposit account that allows customers to write checks for specific amounts against funds on deposit. Account owners can access and transfer funds through checks, debit cards, or electronic funds transfer (EFT).
Share Draft Account	An interest-earning checking account offered by credit unions.
Money Market Deposit Account (MMDA)	A deposit account that invests amounts on deposit in short-term, low-risk investments and then pays interest according to the performance of these investments. MMDAs offer limited check-writing privileges.
Cash Management Account	An account that offers a package of checking services, brokerage services, credit and debit cards, loans, and unified recordkeeping.

Credit Product	Description
Installment Credit	Any loan or credit arrangement that requires the borrower to make periodic repayments on a loan amount or credit balance according to a prearranged schedule. Home mortgages and auto loans, in which the property being financed is pledged as collateral for the loan, are examples of installment credit products.
Non-installment Credit	Any loan or credit arrangement that does not require the borrower to make a series of periodic payments on the loan or credit balance. The borrower typically has flexibility in deciding when and how much to pay, although the lender may establish minimum payment requirements. Credit cards are examples of non-installment credit products.

Cash management products are offered through depository institutions such as commercial banks, savings and loan associations, mutual savings banks, and credit unions. Credit products, which were once available only through depository institutions, are now available from other financial institutions (including insurance companies), credit card companies, and retail businesses. Cash management and credit products satisfy customers' needs for

- **Easy access to funds**. Access to financial products is often measured in terms of liquidity. Products such as checks, check substitutes, debit cards, and credit cards are highly liquid and provide customers with almost immediate access to funds.

- **Protection of funds against loss**. In the United States, bank-issued products are protected against loss, subject to certain requirements, by the Federal Deposit Insurance Corporation (FDIC), a federal agency that guarantees funds deposited in individual accounts in member institutions. Funds in credit union accounts are afforded similar protection through the National Credit Union Association (NCUA). In addition, most credit cards offer protection against loss resulting from unauthorized use of lost or stolen cards.

- **Low transaction costs**. Cash management and credit products generally can be purchased and maintained at minimal cost. Although finance charges and interest rates for credit transactions can be high, they generally apply only to unpaid balances carried over from one billing period to the next. Amounts paid in full when billed generally are not subject to finance charges.

- **Wide acceptance**. Most businesses and many individuals accept checks, debit cards, and credit cards as a form of payment for goods and services.

Asset Accumulation

When people reach the point where their income exceeds their spending, ways to save and accumulate money and other financial assets become important. *Asset accumulation products* enable customers to increase the amount and/or value of their assets over time. Asset accumulation products are especially important for customers who wish to ensure a steady income during retirement, fund a child's education, or provide an inheritance for children or grandchildren.

The financial services industry offers a variety of asset accumulation products, as shown in Figure 1.8. The type of product a customer buys depends on the product's ability to provide an acceptable level of

- **Earning potential**. For the value of an asset to increase over time, the asset must generate returns, or earnings. Most asset accumulation products generate returns in one of three forms: interest, dividends, or capital appreciation. *Interest* is a fee that individuals and financial institutions pay (or charge) for the use of borrowed money. A *dividend* is a share of a company's profits payable to owners of the company's stock. *Capital appreciation* is an increase in the value of invested assets. In general, products that offer guaranteed rates of return—such as certificates of deposit (CDs), savings accounts, and fixed-rate insurance products—have lower earning potential than products whose returns are based on market performance and are not limited to a specified rate—such as stocks and mutual funds.

Figure 1.8. Asset Accumulation Products

Product	Description
Savings Account	A deposit account offered through depository institutions that pays interest on deposited funds. Funds can usually be added to or withdrawn from the account at any time. Savings accounts do not have a maturity date.
Certificate of Deposit (CD)	An interest-earning time deposit held for a specified period of time. Upon maturity, the principal and earnings are paid to the account owner.
Mutual Fund	An investment account offered by investment companies that pools investors' funds and uses those funds to buy a diversified portfolio of securities.
Brokerage Account	An account offered by a brokerage firm that allows investors to buy and sell securities.
Deferred Annuity	An annuity issued by an insurance company under which premiums paid into the contract accumulate interest or investment earnings on a tax-deferred basis until the contract owner withdraws funds or begins receiving periodic income payments from the account.

■ **Risk**. All asset accumulation products carry a certain amount of *risk*, which is defined as the possibility that results will be different than expected. From an investor's perspective, risk is generally associated with the possibility of loss. Risks associated with financial products arise from exposure to unpredictable fluctuations in interest rates, market performance, or inflation rates. Most people base their product purchase decisions on both the amount of risk the products carry and the person's *risk tolerance*, or comfort level with risk. Risk tolerance, for most people, depends on such things as age, financial situation, and personality.

■ **Liquidity**. Eventually, customers will need to convert accumulated assets into cash to meet current financial obligations. The more liquid the asset, the more easily it can be converted to an amount of cash that approximates the underlying value of the asset. For example, shares of stock generally are more liquid than funds in CDs, 401(k) retirement plans, or individual retirement accounts (IRAs), which require that funds be held for a specified period of time or until the owner reaches a specified age. Insurance products, which are designed to provide long-term solutions to customers' financial needs, are generally less liquid than other financial products. However, because insurers know that customers occasionally need immediate access to funds, most cash value insurance policies and deferred annuity contracts allow access to funds in the form of policy loans and/or withdrawals.

■ **Cost**. Many asset accumulation products involve purchase fees in the form of commissions on sales or sales charges. A *commission* is payment for services rendered, and it is usually calculated as a specified percentage of the transaction amount. A sales charge is a fee charged for the purchase or sale of shares in securities. Financial products also assess on-going maintenance charges or expense charges designed to cover an issuing company's or a distributor's operating expenses.

Asset Protection

People who have accumulated assets over time need ways to protect those assets against loss. *Asset protection products* protect owners against the risk of financial loss from unforeseen events such as natural disasters, theft, accidents, illnesses, and death. All asset protection products are forms of insurance. *Insurance* is a mechanism for transferring some or all of the risk of a financial loss from an individual or entity to an insurance company. Figure 1.9 describes the core insurance products that satisfy customers' asset protection needs.

Figure 1.9. Asset Protection Products

Product	Description
Life Insurance	Insurance that provides protection against the economic loss caused by the death of the insured. Term life insurance provides coverage for a specified period of time; permanent life insurance provides protection for the insured's lifetime.
Medical Expense Insurance	Insurance that covers medical expenses resulting from injury or sickness and may also provide coverage for long-term care or supplemental benefits.
Disability Income Insurance	Insurance that covers loss of income resulting from a disabling injury or illness.
Automobile Insurance	Insurance that protects an insured from financial losses arising from the operation of a vehicle. Policies typically cover liability for bodily injury or property damage of others and damage to an automobile caused by a collision or other peril.
Homeowners' Insurance	Insurance that protects an insured from financial losses resulting from damage to a home or its contents or from being held liable for the losses of others suffered while on the insured's property.
Liability Insurance	Insurance that covers individuals from losses they incur as a result of being held liable for losses of others.

Asset Distribution

During retirement, customers need to use the assets they have accumulated in their homes and other property and in savings, investment, and retirement accounts. To do that, they often need to liquidate, or cash in, their assets. In most cases, they receive the cash from these sources in a lump sum. People also receive lump-sum payments from life insurance proceeds, court-ordered awards, large cash prizes, gifts, and bonuses. The retiree is then responsible for managing the money and making sure it lasts through retirement. Without some type of planning, retirees can easily exhaust their resources early. One way customers can reduce the management requirements of lump-sum distributions is to reinvest the proceeds in an annuity. The annuity can then be structured to provide the owner with regular income payments during a specified period or for the owner's lifetime. Annuities are the only financial products that offer guaranteed income for life.

Changes in the Financial Services Industry

Over the past two decades, the financial services industry has moved from clearly segmented sectors, such as banking, insurance, and investments, to a more generalized industry in which different financial institutions compete with each other for business. For example, although insurance companies are still the only companies that can issue (that is, design, develop, underwrite, and administer) insurance products, banks, broker/dealers, and mutual fund companies now actively distribute insurance products to their own customers. Insurance companies, in turn, have entered the banking arena by developing or acquiring thrifts. Broker/dealers and mutual fund companies now compete with commercial banks for customer deposits and with insurance companies for employer-sponsored retirement plans and public retirement savings plans.

This change has come about primarily through

- Regulatory changes, which have removed many of the regulatory barriers that prevented affiliations between different types of financial institutions.

- Advances in technology, which have facilitated the development and delivery of new financial products and services, lowered communication costs, increased understanding of customer behavior and risk, improved the efficiency of work processes, provided faster, more efficient service delivery, and enhanced customers' understanding of products and services.

- Increased globalization of business, which has created competitive pressures from foreign institutions. For example, a large number of U.S. banks and insurance companies have purchased companies in other countries as a way to gain entry into foreign markets.

- An increased demand among consumers for "one-stop shopping." Some institutions have responded to this demand by trying to position themselves as financial "supermarkets." Other institutions have pulled back to focus on core businesses.

The future is likely to bring even more changes, and financial institutions of all kinds, in all economies, will have to find ways to manage their businesses effectively, efficiently, and profitably.

Key Terms

economy
need
want
economics
exchange
medium of exchange
unit of account
transfer payment
intermediation
product (output) market
labor markets
financial (capital) market
foreign exchange market
circular flow diagram
financial institution
fiduciary
depository institution
interest

contractual savings institution
pension fund
pension plan
security
stock
bond
commercial paper
mutual fund
liquidity
asset accumulation product
dividend
capital appreciation
risk
risk tolerance
commission
asset protection product
insurance

Chapter 2

Insurance Company Management

Objectives:

After studying this chapter, you should be able to

- ■ Explain how the corporate structure benefits an insurance company's customers and owners

- ■ Describe the three types of insurance companies: stock companies, mutual companies, and fraternal benefit societies

- ■ Explain why it is important for a business to establish a clear mission statement

- ■ Describe how insurers use information gathered from inside and outside the company to develop corporate objectives and strategies

- ■ Explain how corporate plans are translated into operational plans and describe the focus of an insurance company's operational objectives and strategies

- ■ Describe the four primary ways insurance companies organize their operations and identify the advantages and disadvantages of various organizational designs

- ■ Identify the components included in a company's organizational chart and describe the relationships among these components

- ■ Explain the steps in the control process and describe the important control mechanisms insurance companies use to measure, evaluate, and improve their operational performance

Outline

Insurance Company Structure
- Requirements for Incorporation
- Organizational Form
- The Mission Statement

Managing Insurance Company Business
- Planning
- Organizing Operations
- Controlling Performance

If you're employed by an insurance company, or any other kind of company, you know first-hand how management affects you. The company's managers are responsible for running the company and deciding what activities the company performs. Employees carry out those activities. In an insurance company, management affects employees at all levels, because everyone in the company—even the chief executive officer (CEO)—reports to someone. But did you know that you affect management, too?

Today, successful business operations depend on managers and employees working as a team. As a result, every employee, regardless of level or amount of responsibility, plays a part in determining whether a company succeeds or fails. In other words, management is everybody's business.

Insurance Company Structure

How an insurance company does business is defined, in part, by the way the company is structured. In most industries, a business can be structured as a

- Sole proprietorship

- Partnership

- Corporation

These primary structures are described in Figure 2.1. Sole proprietorships and partnerships are considered *privately held companies* because ownership is restricted to specified individuals. Corporations can be privately held or publicly held. A *publicly held company* is a company that sells ownership shares to the public.

Because the public depends on the financial stability and continued operation of insurance companies, insurance laws in most jurisdictions require that insurance companies organize and operate as corporations. A *corporation* is a legal entity, separate from its owners, that is created by the authority of a government and that continues beyond the death of any or all of its owners. Corporations can sue or be sued, can enter into contracts, and can own property.

The corporate structure offers benefits for both insurance company customers and owners. For insurance company customers, who may not receive benefits from their insurance policies or annuity contracts for many years, corporate structure ensures that the company will continue regardless of the withdrawal, personal misfortune, or death of any or all of the company's owners. For company owners, corporate structure offers the benefit of limited liability. Although an insurer can be a party in legal actions that affect the company's assets and liabilities, legal

Figure 2.1. Basic Organizational Structures

Sole Proprietorship:

■ Owned and operated by one person

■ Owner earns all company profits; is responsible for all company debts

■ Operations cease if owner dies

Partnership:

■ Owned and operated by two or more people (the partners)

■ Partners earn all company profits; are responsible for all company debts

■ Partnership dissolves if a partner dies or withdraws

Corporation:

■ Legal entity created by government authority

■ Corporation is separate from owners; owners can't be held responsible for company debts

■ Continues beyond death or withdrawal of owners

■ Can sue or be sued, can enter into contracts, and can own property

actions don't create personal liability for any of the company's owners—that is, its stockholders or policyowners. If an insurance company fails, the company's owners cannot be legally required to use their personal property to pay the company's debts.

Requirements for Incorporation

Before an insurance company can conduct business, it must be formally incorporated. In most jurisdictions, the incorporation process involves filing information about the proposed company with the appropriate regulatory agency. In the United States, insurance companies are incorporated at the state level. In Canada, insurers can be incorporated at the provincial level or the federal level. In India, corporations are under the direction of the federal government.

To apply for incorporation, companies must provide the appropriate regulatory agency with the following information:

■ A basic description of the company, including the company's name and the names of its original directors, the company's location, and the type of business the company intends to conduct

- The company's business plan and financial projections

- The company's plan for organizing its operations

- The amount of the initial investment being made in the company by stock-holders or policyowners

If a company's application for incorporation is approved, the next step is for the corporation to obtain a *license*, which is a document issued by a regulatory agency that grants an insurer the legal authority to conduct insurance business in a specific jurisdiction. An insurer that intends to conduct business in more than one jurisdiction must be licensed in each jurisdiction. The purpose of licensing is to ensure that an insurance company is (1) financially sound and able to meet its obligations to policyowners and (2) directed by knowledgeable and capable managers.

Organizational Form

Although insurance companies must be structured as corporations, they can be organized as stock companies, mutual companies, or fraternal benefit societies.

Stock Insurance Companies

The majority of life and health insurance companies are established as stock companies. A *stock insurance company* is an insurance company that is owned by the people and organizations that purchase shares of the company's stock. If financial conditions are favorable, stockholders may receive periodic dividends, which represent a return on their investment.

One of the major advantages of organizing as a stock company is that stock companies are relatively easy to establish. The founders of a stock insurance company can raise the funds needed to create the company by selling shares of stock in the proposed company. A stock insurance company can raise additional operating funds by selling more shares of company stock. Another advantage of organizing operations as a stock company is that stock companies can expand their operations relatively quickly and efficiently by acquiring other companies, which then become subsidiaries of the acquiring company, or by establishing affiliations with other companies. For example, a stock insurance company can acquire another stock insurance company or a publicly held corporation by buying most or all of the other company's stock. In the process, the purchasing company obtains the acquired company's products, customers, and distributors.

> The Premier Insurance Company is a stock insurance company that sells individual life insurance and annuity products. Premier recently acquired another insurance company that specializes in group life insurance and pension products. Premier was able to use its subsidiary to expand its business without having to produce new products or increase its marketing efforts.

Insurance companies often enter international markets by acquiring companies operating in those markets.

However, to protect insurance companies, policyowners, and beneficiaries from the possible negative financial effects of affiliations, regulators in many jurisdictions, including the United States, have enacted laws governing how structural affiliations involving insurance companies must be managed.

Mutual Insurance Companies

A *mutual insurance company* is an insurance company that is owned by its policyowners. If financial conditions are favorable, mutual insurance companies may distribute a portion of their operating profits to policyowners in the form of *policy dividends*.

An insurer that chooses to organize as a mutual company must sell a certain number of policies in advance to provide the funds necessary to begin operations. This process can take years, because people are often reluctant to buy products from companies that don't actually exist. As a result, most mutual companies today began operations as stock companies and later converted their operations to mutual companies. The conversion of a stock insurance company to a mutual insurance company is called *mutualization*. One important reason for mutualizing operations is to protect the company from being taken over by another company. In many jurisdictions, mutual insurance companies can't be purchased or controlled by another company. Mutualization also can decrease the filing and reporting requirements imposed on stock companies.

A large number of mutual companies have converted to stock companies through the process of *demutualization*. The primary reason for demutualization is that companies can raise operating funds more easily by selling shares of stock than they can by selling more policies. Stock companies also have greater flexibility than mutual companies in buying and operating other types of companies.

Fraternal Benefit Societies

A *fraternal benefit society* is an organization formed to provide social and insurance benefits to its members. The members of such societies often share a common ethnic, religious, or vocational background, although membership in some societies is open to the general public. One requirement of a fraternal benefit society is that society members must elect the officers. In addition, only society members or their families are eligible to receive benefits, including insurance coverage. Figure 2.2 shows the number of stock companies, mutual companies, and fraternal benefit societies operating in the United States in 2008 and the proportion of premium income they held.

The Mission Statement

Before an insurance company can conduct business, it needs to define the scope of its business activities and its business direction. In other words, the company needs to create a mission statement. A company's *mission statement* sets out, in writing, the company's fundamental purpose or reason for being. It answers two important questions: "Why do we exist?" and "What is our primary purpose?" The answers to these questions affect all company operations and all company employees.

Figure 2.2. Types of Insurance Companies, 2008

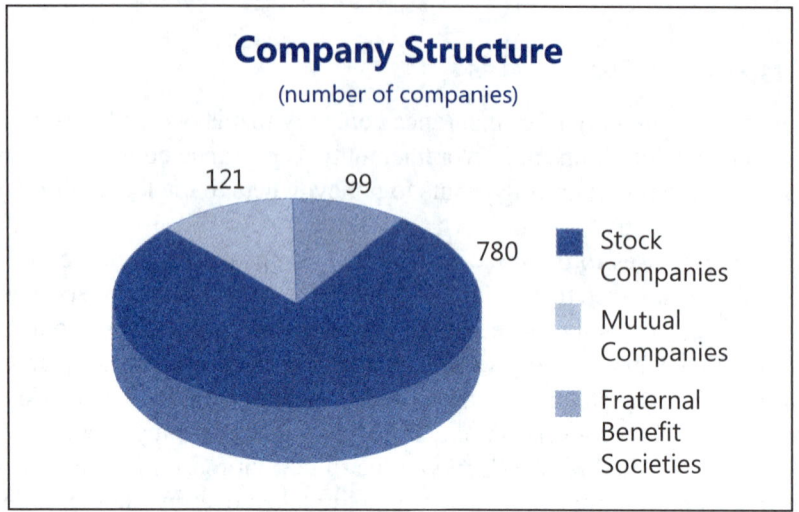

Company Structure
(number of companies)

121   99
780

- Stock Companies
- Mutual Companies
- Fraternal Benefit Societies

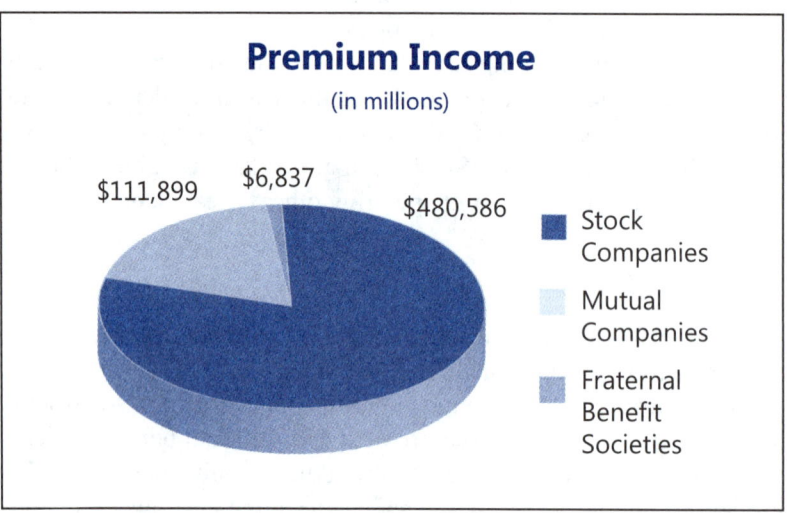

Premium Income
(in millions)

$111,899 $6,837
$480,586

- Stock Companies
- Mutual Companies
- Fraternal Benefit Societies

Data source: American Council of Life Insurers, *Life Insurers Fact Book: 2008*, Industry Overview.

When developing a mission statement, an insurer needs to make sure the statement is broad enough to cover all aspects of the company's business. At the same time, a mission statement should be specific enough to focus on what the company actually does. A mission statement that is too narrow limits what a company can do to expand business. A mission statement that is too broad may be impossible for a company to live up to within the limits of its resources. Failure to accurately describe a company's mission can have disastrous results. Figure 2.3 describes the risks involved in not establishing a clear mission.

Figure 2.3. The Importance of a Clear Mission Statement

The ABC Insurance Company has been in business for 40 years. The company's stated mission is to provide individuals and households with high-quality life insurance products that help customers protect themselves, their families, and their future.

Although ABC's core business consists of individual permanent and term life insurance products and individual annuity products, the company recently added a variety of banking, investment, and advice-based services to its product portfolio. ABC offers its life insurance products exclusively through company-affiliated producers. It offers its banking, investment, and service products online and through direct mail.

ABC's decision to offer an expanded product line and become a company that could answer all its customers' financial needs was based on evidence that

- The demand for advice-based services such as financial planning, tax planning, retirement planning, and estate planning is increasing

- Increases in the number of affluent households indicate a growing demand for multiple types of financial products designed to meet multiple financial needs

- Customers have doubts about the viability of existing government- and employer-sponsored retirement programs and are looking for individual financial products that will help them secure their financial future

- More and more customers are buying products online and through alternate distribution systems

Unfortunately, ABC is not performing as well as expected. Sales of the company's non-insurance products have been low and the company has failed to gain a significant share of the market for financial services products. Sales of the company's core products have also declined.

ABC assigned a task force to identify the possible causes of these problems. In its report to management, the task force stated that the primary reason for ABC's failure to meet its performance expectations is that the company has not accurately defined the business it's in. To support this conclusion, the task force pointed out that

- ABC's mission statement is very narrow. It is also product based. By adding advice-based services such as financial planning, tax planning, retirement planning, and estate planning, the company has stepped outside the boundaries of its stated mission.

- ABC has built its reputation as a provider of high-quality life insurance products. By expanding its focus to include non-insurance products, ABC may have confused its customers and diluted its reputation.

- All of ABC's internal and external communications focus on the company's core products. Customers may not be fully aware that ABC now offers additional products and services.

- Although ABC has developed significant expertise in the life insurance business, it has very little experience outside that business. Adding new products or product lines without the necessary background and planning puts the company at a distinct disadvantage compared to companies with extensive experience.

- Entering more broadly defined markets has increased the number of competitors ABC faces. Some of these competitors have established a strong enough market share in these markets to create barriers for new companies.

- ABC has limited human, financial, and technological resources. To support its new products and services, ABC has been forced to reduce support for its core products, possibly jeopardizing the company's current level and quality of service.

- ABC has historically relied on company-affiliated producers to distribute its life insurance products. Adding new online and direct distribution systems has not only increased ABC's costs, but also may have damaged its relationship with its producers.

By defining its mission too narrowly, the company has limited its ability to successfully expand its business into new areas. In addition, it has potentially put its core business at risk.

Managing Insurance Company Business

Management is the process companies use to plan, organize, and control operations effectively and efficiently. Although planning, organizing, and controlling activities are usually divided into separate stages, management is actually a continuous process in which managers use information developed during one stage to direct the next stage and provide feedback on the previous stage. For example, during planning, management sets objectives and establishes strategies for implementing and controlling the company's activities. These objectives, in turn, help determine the structural framework that will maximize management's ability to execute the company's plans. During the control stage, management analyzes the performance of its plans and programs to determine whether objectives are being achieved. Management then uses performance results to recommend necessary changes in existing business plans or operations. In most cases, planning, organization, and control operate at both the corporate level and the operational level.

Planning

Before an insurance company can begin operations, it needs to determine what it wants to accomplish and how it can best achieve its goals. The process of evaluating business opportunities, assessing resources, determining goals, and developing strategies for implementation and control is called ***planning***. Most insurance companies conduct two types of planning: corporate planning and operational planning. Corporate planning is performed by a company's senior managers and guides the activities of the entire company. Operational planning is performed by division or operational managers and governs the activities of the company's operational units.

In most companies, corporate planning begins at the executive level. Senior management usually begins the process by analyzing the company's current operations to identify strengths and weaknesses. An insurance company's strengths might include

- Its ability to respond quickly to market trends

- The quality of its products and services

- Its effectiveness in managing expenses

   An insurer's weaknesses might include

- The length of time it needs to develop new products and services

- Its narrow range of products and services

- Its limited human or technological resources

Management also analyzes factors outside the company, such as economic, legal, and population trends that may present opportunities for or threats to the company. In general, opportunities are situations in which a company's resources and core competencies allow it to take advantage of emerging trends. For example, the aging of the population and the weakening of government-sponsored and employer-sponsored retirement programs represent opportunities for insurers that offer a wide range of annuity and other retirement products. Threats are situations in which the company's culture, organizational structure, resources, or core competencies prevent the company from responding to emerging trends. For example, passage of new regulations governing insurance products or increased demands to get new products to market quickly can present threats to insurers.

Because this initial analysis weighs company strengths and weaknesses against environmental opportunities and threats, it is often referred to as a ***SWOT analysis***. As Figure 2.4 illustrates, companies use the results of a SWOT analysis to help develop corporate objectives and determine the company's strategic direction.

Corporate Objectives

Senior management uses the information gained from the SWOT analysis to define the company's objectives. ***Corporate objectives*** are statements of the long-term results a company plans to achieve. In most cases, an insurance company's corporate objectives focus on operational efficiency and long-term profitability.

To be effective, objectives should be

- **Clearly stated**. For example, saying that the company wants to "increase sales" doesn't mean much. Stating an objective of "increasing total product sales, as measured by first-year collected premiums" or of "achieving an average increase in total product sales as measured by total revenues" provides clear direction regarding what the company wants to accomplish.

- **Specific and measurable**. Knowing how much a company expects to accomplish and how quickly it expects to accomplish those results also is important. For example, "increasing total customer retention by 10% over four years" or "reducing company operating expenses by 6% within five years" makes it clear what the company expects from its operations and its employees.

- **Realistic.** Improvements in company operations don't happen overnight. They take time and effort. Objectives that conflict with corporate culture may be impossible to achieve. Successful objectives are those that take into account factors in the company's internal and external environment.

- **Actionable.** Even if a corporate objective is stated clearly, is specific and measurable, and is realistic, it won't mean anything if it can't be accomplished either with existing resources or with additional resources that can be obtained easily.

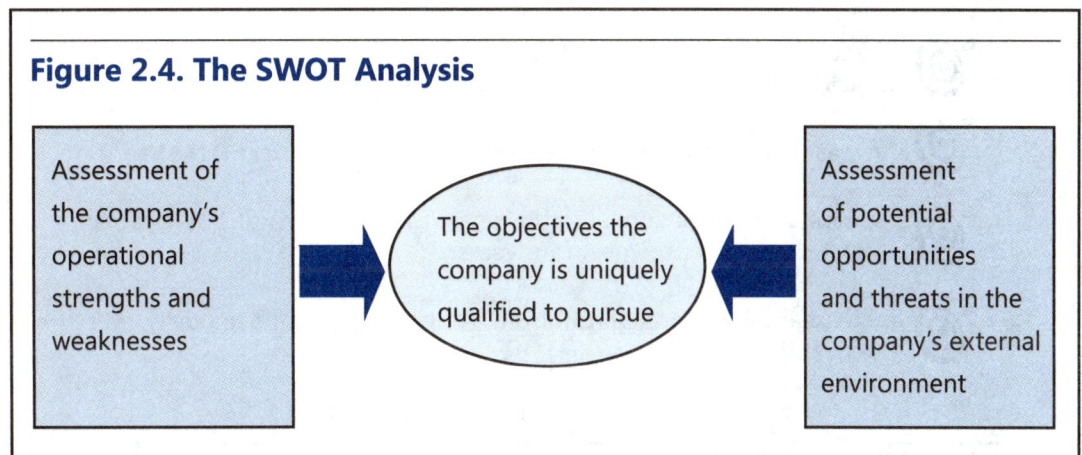

Figure 2.4. The SWOT Analysis

Assessment of the company's operational strengths and weaknesses → The objectives the company is uniquely qualified to pursue ← Assessment of potential opportunities and threats in the company's external environment

Figure 2.5 provides some examples of possible corporate objectives for an insurance company.

Corporate Strategies

Corporate strategies define the long-term methods a company intends to use to achieve its objectives. Companies usually can achieve their objectives in different ways. As a result, corporate strategies vary from company to company, even when the companies are all trying to reach similar goals. Company strategies also vary from time period to time period in response to changing environmental conditions.

Corporate strategies for most insurance companies focus on growing and expanding business. In most cases expanding business is equated with selling more products. Most companies can expand product sales in one of three ways:

- **Increasing sales among existing customers**. An insurance company often can increase sales of existing products by increasing the size of its sales force; by introducing new distribution options, such as direct mail or Internet sales; or by increasing its promotion efforts. An insurer also can increase sales by modifying existing products to better serve customers' existing needs or by introducing new products to address new or unmet needs.

- **Generating sales among new customers or in new markets**. Most insurers limit their marketing efforts to specific markets. For example, most insurance companies operate in only a few states or regions, or they offer products to narrowly defined customer groups, or niche markets. Companies can increase their total product sales by expanding into new states or regions or by offering their products to additional customer groups.

- **Capturing business from competitors**. Customers generally need a reason to switch from one insurance company to another. An insurance company can provide that difference by offering features and benefits that aren't available in other products or by offering services that add value to the company's products or the customer's product experience.

Figure 2.5. Examples of Corporate Objectives for Insurance Companies

Increase total new premium income to $21 million during the next year, to $25 million in the second year, and to $30 million in the third year

Increase the persistency of business by 15% over the next three years

Achieve an average annual return on investment (ROI) of 10% over all business units over the next four years

Increase total corporate profit from all operations by 8% annually over the next 5 years

At the end of the corporate planning process, the company's mission statement, corporate objectives, and corporate strategies are assembled into a preliminary corporate business plan. This plan is then communicated downward to managers in various operational areas.

Operational Planning

Operational planning is designed to help the company meet its established objectives using the fewest human, technological, and financial resources possible. Operational planning consists of the same steps performed during corporate planning: identifying internal strengths and weaknesses and external opportunities and threats, defining objectives, and establishing strategies to achieve those objectives. However, operational planning is narrower in scope than corporate planning and covers a shorter time period. For example, corporate objectives and strategies normally cover a period of one to five years. They are established for the whole company, and they deal with such issues as profit, growth, technology utilization, service quality, and sales and market share. Operational objectives focus on specific areas of company operations, such as claims, underwriting, or marketing, and extend only one to two years into the future. For example, a corporate objective might call for a 4% annual increase in total product sales over the next four years. The corresponding marketing objective might call for an increase in sales of a particular product line by 10% during the coming year.

In addition, operational planning is usually tactical rather than strategic—that is, operational plans describe specific, action-oriented activities that a unit will perform; how, when, and where activities are to be performed; who is responsible for performing each activity; how much each activity will cost; the results (revenue, profit, awareness, attitude change, and so on) expected from the activity; the main elements of uncertainty involved; and how results will be monitored and evaluated.

Operational plans are communicated back up to senior management for review. Senior managers work with operational area managers to make necessary changes in individual operational plans and then incorporate the finalized operational area plans into the company's final overall business plan. Figure 2.6 shows the relationship between corporate and operational planning.

Figure 2.6. Levels of Planning

Organizing Operations

To ensure that business runs smoothly, insurance companies need to organize their operations so that they support company goals.

Organizational Options

Insurance companies have traditionally organized operations by function. Organization by function divides operations according to the work that each division performs, as shown in Figure 2.7.

In a company organized by function, each functional area is a separate unit or division that performs its function for all of the company's products. For example, all underwriting, marketing, accounting, and actuarial functions are performed by separate units. However, functional units don't operate in isolation. In order to evaluate the risk presented by insurance applicants, an insurer's underwriting unit usually depends on computer and technical support provided by the company's IT unit. The company's actuarial unit, in turn, relies on information provided by underwriting to establish the premium rate structures for various products.

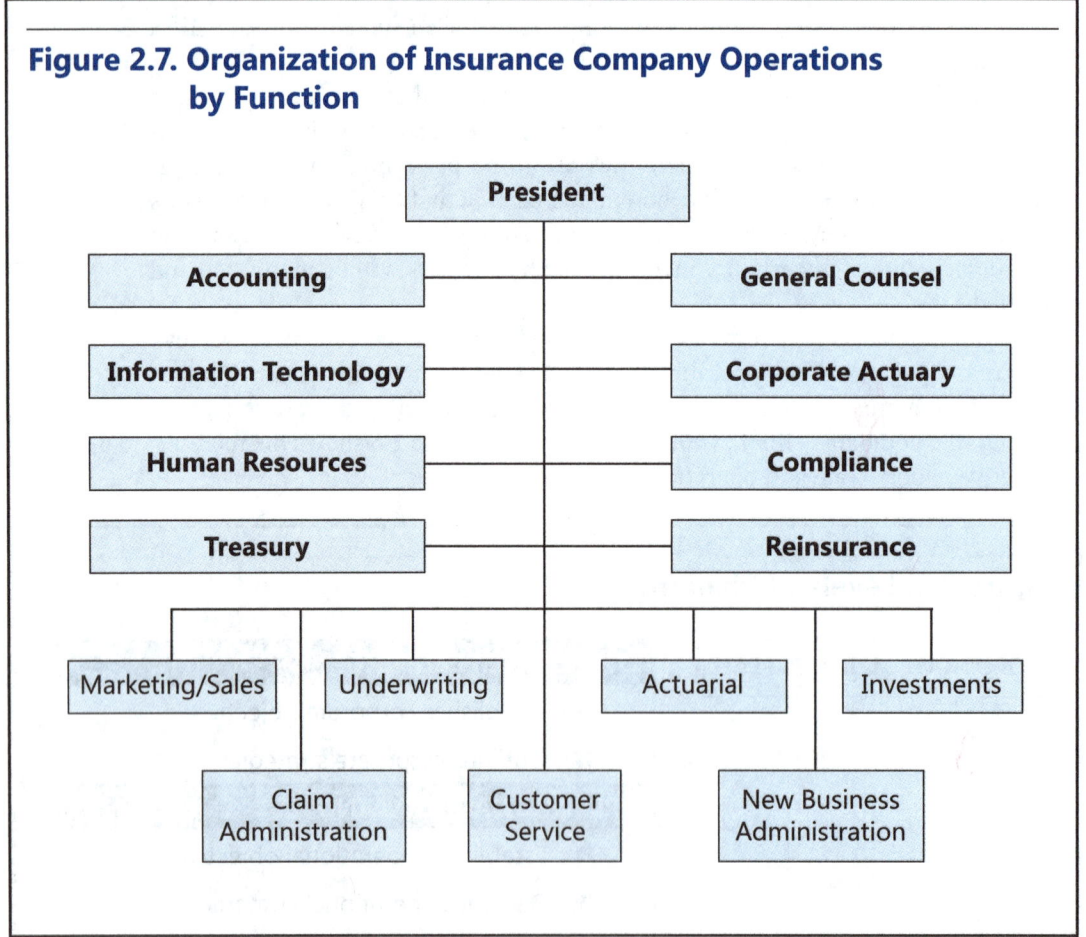

Figure 2.7. Organization of Insurance Company Operations by Function

The major advantages of organizing operations by function are the approach's simplicity and its focus on the development of managerial and technical skills in each functional area. Functional organization usually works well in small companies with centralized operations and in large centralized companies that offer only a few product lines to fairly well-defined customer groups. As the number of different products a company offers and the size and diversity of the company's markets increase, functional organization becomes less effective. For example, in a functional structure, new or specialty products and markets might be neglected because of competing demands for resources from larger product lines or markets.

As an alternative to functional organization, companies can organize operations by product, geographic region, or customer type.

- **Organization by product** divides operations into product lines. Insurance companies often divide operations into individual insurance and group insurance business or into life insurance, health insurance, and annuity product lines. Each division is responsible for performing most of its own product development, underwriting, marketing, and administration. Organization by product allows employees who are most involved with a particular type of product to make decisions related to that product. To organize operations by product, however, each product must be large enough, distinct enough, and profitable enough to support its own separate management.

- **Organization by geographic region** divides operations into territories, and each territory performs all functions for that territory. Insurers that operate in more than one state or more than one country and companies that serve territories with distinctive regulatory or language differences often divide operations geographically.

- **Organization by customer type** divides operations according to specific target markets, such as household markets, corporate markets, and small business markets. In this structure, managers are responsible for all activities for a specific customer group. Organization by customer type increases the company's ability to satisfy distinct customer needs.

A company that organizes operations by product, geographic region, or customer type usually manages each division as a strategic business unit. A *strategic business unit (SBU)* is an area of business distinct from other areas within a company in that it generates its own profits, has its own separate set of customers and competitors, has its own management, and is capable of having its own goals and strategies.

Dividing operations into SBUs tends to increase employees' involvement in decision making because authority over operations is shifted from the company's board of directors and senior managers to division leaders. Using SBUs also allows an insurance company's senior management to evaluate the profitability of each division or line of business and to identify which areas are performing above or below expectations. However, maintaining SBUs can lead to duplication of effort and increased costs. For example, each SBU, of necessity, needs its own management system and its own financial and support functions.

To avoid the inefficiency of maintaining strictly defined SBUs, many insurance companies have established structures in which certain services are shared by multiple divisions. A *shared service* is a functional area that performs specified business processes for multiple SBUs and that shares accountability for the costs, timing, and quality of those processes with the SBUs. The services that most often function as shared services in an insurance company are information technology (IT), accounting, finance, legal, compliance, and human resources (HR). For example, rather than maintaining separate computer systems and IT departments for each division, most insurers have a single IT department that handles systems development and maintenance for all of the company's business units. IT costs are shared by the company and individual business units.

Organizational Charts

Management of an insurance company's operations is documented in its *organizational chart*, which provides a visual display of the various jobs and the formal lines of authority and reporting within the company. The organizational chart for most insurance companies is shaped like a pyramid—narrow at the top and wide at the bottom. Figure 2.8 shows a typical pyramid structure. At the top of the pyramid is the company's *board of directors*, which is elected by the company's owners (the stockholders of a stock company or the policyowners of a mutual company) and serves as the company's primary governing body. Although company owners usually have ultimate authority over company operations, they usually don't appear on organizational charts because they don't participate directly in a company's day-to-day activities.

Figure 2.8. Structure of an Organization

Below the board of directors are various levels of managers, who guide the work of other employees. The major function of managers is to plan company activities, organize human and technical resources to get jobs done, supervise and direct employees' activities, and control the work process so that work is performed successfully. At the bottom of the pyramid are the company's non-managerial employees. These employees are critical to an insurance company because they are the people who keep the company operating by performing the day-to-day activities of the company.

Although they usually aren't shown on an organizational chart, committees are an important part of insurance company operations. A *committee* is a group of people chosen to consider, investigate, or act on specified issues. Insurers generally use committees when a particular problem or task requires the expertise of individuals with specific talents and perspectives. In some cases, committees are composed of members of the company's board of directors. Typical insurance company committees include the

- **Executive committee**, which deals with questions of overall company policy, including what lines of business the company sells, the areas in which it operates, and policies affecting company employees

- **Investment committee**, which determines the company's broad investment goals and strategies

- **Audit committee**, which sets policies for the company's accounting department, reviews all company policies and internal audit plans, and oversees internal and external financial and market conduct audits

- **Tax committee**, which analyzes and evaluates the tax implications of company policies, programs, and regulatory actions

- **Risk committee**, which provides overall guidance and control of an insurer's enterprise risk management (ERM) efforts

Interdepartmental committees guide specific company-wide activities such as product development, underwriting, budgeting, asset-liability management, corporate communications, human resources, and information technology.

Span of Control. Some insurers have a tall organizational structure—one that includes multiple levels of management. For example, a large insurance company might have several categories of vice presidents, such as executive vice presidents, senior vice presidents, vice presidents, and assistant vice presidents. Large companies also can have senior managers, assistant managers, and supervisors. Other insurers have fewer management levels, even though they may have the same number of employees. In this case, the shape of the pyramid is wide rather than tall.

Whether a company's organizational structure is tall or wide depends largely on management's span of control. A manager's *span of control* is the number of people who report directly to the manager. A narrow span of control, in which each manager oversees the activities of a relatively small number of employees, tends to create a tall organization. A wide span of control, in which each manager oversees the activities of a large number of employees, tends to create a wide organization. Figure 2.9 illustrates the difference between narrow and wide spans of control.

In general, narrow spans of control are best when employees work in different locations, when tasks are distinctly different and highly complex, and when employees need focused supervision. For example, insurance companies often maintain functions such as accounting, finance, investments, legal, compliance, and human relations in the company's executive area. They maintain functions such as customer service, new business administration, and claims in one or more separate areas. Functions such as IT may even be performed outside the company entirely. In this situation, a narrow span of control would produce more effective management. However, spans of control that are too narrow are counterproductive. Extremely narrow spans can result in too much supervision, long lines of communication, slow decision-making, minimal employee initiative, and restricted development opportunities for managers. Narrow spans also require a considerable amount of planning and coordination with other managers. More importantly, overly narrow spans of control usually increase administrative costs by adding layers of supervision and increasing the number of managers needed to oversee operations.

Wide spans of control typically are best when employees perform the same simple or repetitive tasks in the same work area and where little or no direction is needed. For example, employees involved in data entry and new business processing typically don't require close supervision because their tasks are well-defined and consistent. Although insurance companies are moving toward wider spans of control, they need to avoid spans that are too wide. An overly wide span may reduce the time needed for planning and coordination, but it can also increase costs. For example, lack of employee training can result in poor employee performance, and lack of supervision and coordination can create behavioral problems. Correcting these problems costs money.

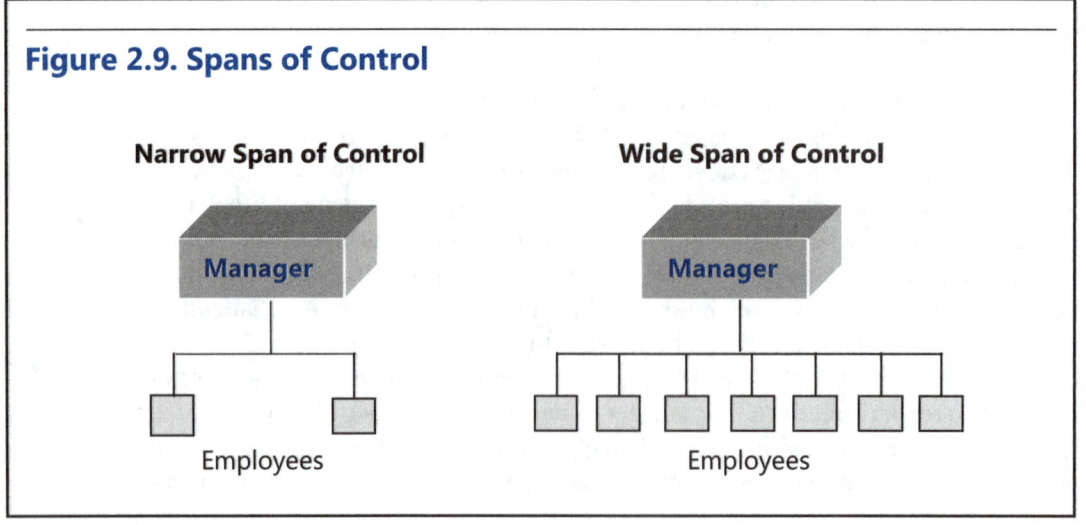

Figure 2.9. Spans of Control

Narrow Span of Control

Wide Span of Control

Manager

Manager

Employees

Employees

Authority and Accountability. An insurance company's organizational chart also defines the relationships among operational levels, including

- **Types of authority.** *Authority* is defined as the right an employee has to make decisions, take action, and direct others. For example, a manager who is responsible for making sure that all policyowner requests are completed within a specified time usually has the authority to hire additional employees, rotate existing employees, or assign overtime to meet assigned deadlines.

- **Levels of authority.** Most companies establish a ***chain of command***, or structure of authority, that travels downward through an organization from higher levels to lower levels. In other words, the chain of command identifies who reports to whom. In general, managers at higher levels in the chain of command have more authority than managers at lower levels.

- **Lines of accountability.** According to the principle of ***unity of command***, each employee should be under the authority of and be accountable to only one person. In today's environment, where projects often require input and expertise from multiple functional areas, few insurance companies adhere strictly to the idea of unity of command.

Controlling Performance

Control is the process of monitoring, evaluating, and regulating how effectively and efficiently a company and its employees are performing the activities necessary for achieving the company's goals. In most companies, the control process consists of four primary steps:

- **Establishing standards of performance against which company performance can be measured.** A *performance standard* is a previously established level of performance against which actual performance can be measured. Performance standards can be internal or external. Internal standards are developed by a company and are based on the company's planned or historical performance. For example, the starting point for establishing performance standards is often the company's corporate objectives. External standards are based on outside information such as published industry-wide averages or best practices. One of the most common external standards used by insurers are *benchmarks*, which are the best outcomes that have been achieved for a specific operational activity and the practices that resulted in those outcomes.

- **Measuring actual performance.** Insurance companies continually monitor and evaluate the performance of all their operational units. For example, insurance companies measure product performance in terms of sales or persistency rates. The ***persistency rate*** is the percentage of an insurer's business in force at the beginning of a specified period that remains in force at the end of the period. Figure 2.10 shows how insurers calculate persistency rates. Customer service performance is often measured by tracking how long it takes for representatives to answer calls or complete transactions. Financial performance can be measured by examining the company's financial statements and accounting records.

Figure 2.10. Calculating Persistency Rates

The Dartmore Insurance Company had a block of 10,000 whole life insurance policies in force on January 1. By the end of the year, 200 of those policies had lapsed because of nonpayment of premium and 300 policies had been surrendered.

To determine the product's persistency rate, Dartmore's product manager first calculated the lapse rate for the block of policies. The lapse rate for a block of policies is equal to the number of policies lapsed or surrendered during the year divided by the total number of policies in force at the beginning of the year.

Using this formula, the product manager determined that the lapse rate for the block of policies was 5%:

Number of policies lapsed or surrendered during the year = 500

Number of policies in force at beginning of year = 10,000

500 ÷ 10,000 = 0.05, or 5%

To find the persistency rate for the block of policies, the product manager subtracted the lapse rate from 100%, or

Persistency rate = 100% - 5% = 95%

■ **Comparing actual performance with established standards.** All insurers establish policies and procedures that govern how staff should carry out their responsibilities. These policies and procedures are backed by an administrative control cycle such as the one shown in Figure 2.11. A ***control cycle*** is a repetitive process designed to ensure that all areas of a company adhere to the company's performance standards. Most control cycles consist of three basic types of controls. ***Steering controls*** are established in advance and describe the company's expectations. Because steering controls focus on future performance, they are often referred to as *feedforward controls*. ***Concurrent controls*** address a company's current activities and systems by continuously monitoring activities as they are performed. ***Feedback controls*** are used to compare actual performance or output with established standards.

■ **Evaluating results and initiating action, if necessary**. Deviations from standards can be produced by a variety of causes, including unrealistic performance standards, inaccurate projections, unanticipated changes in the environment, or exceptionally good or exceptionally poor performance. Most insurers allow deviations that fall within a specified range of established standards. Deviations outside the acceptable range often require corrective action. Companies can generally correct performance by changing the programs used to carry out company strategies, establishing new ways to implement strategies, developing new strategies, modifying the way performance data are collected and analyzed, or re-evaluating the performance standards stated in company objectives to make sure they are valid and realistic.

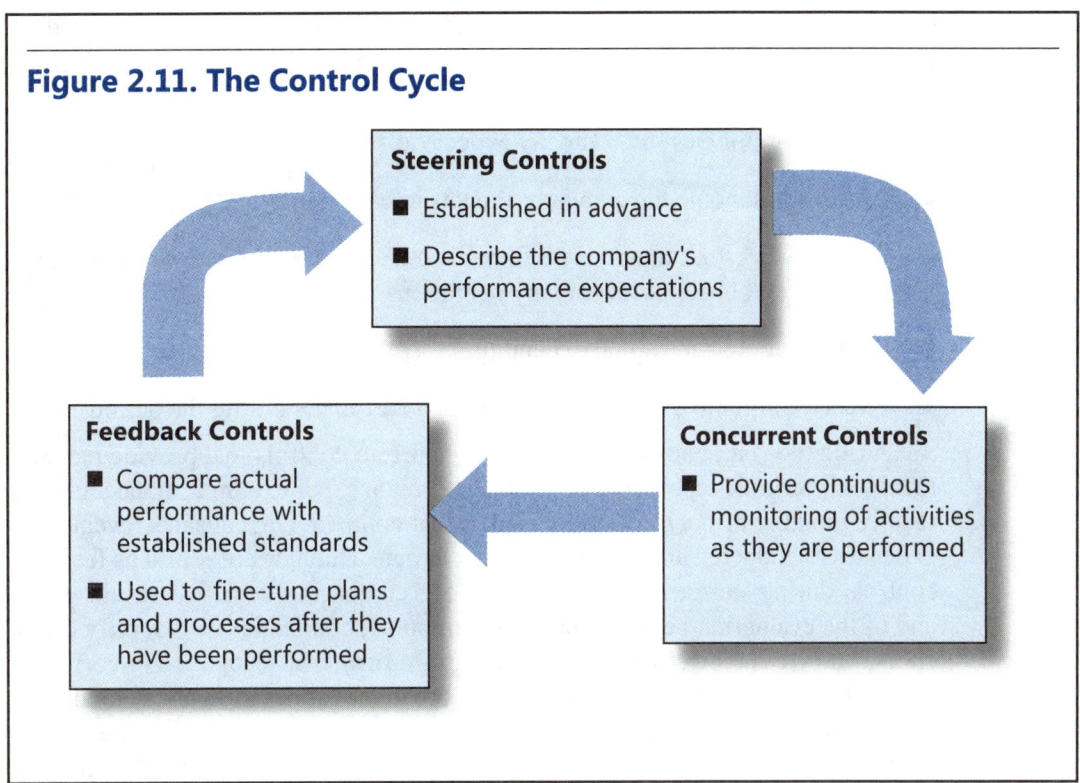

Figure 2.11. The Control Cycle

Steering Controls
- Established in advance
- Describe the company's performance expectations

Concurrent Controls
- Provide continuous monitoring of activities as they are performed

Feedback Controls
- Compare actual performance with established standards
- Used to fine-tune plans and processes after they have been performed

Control Mechanisms

Insurance companies use a variety of control mechanisms to monitor their operational and financial performance. Some of these mechanisms apply only during one phase of the control cycle. Other mechanisms can be used in all phases of the cycle.

Plans, Policies, and Procedures. The corporate business plan and tactical operational plans that companies prepare during the planning process and the company's policies and procedures serve as steering controls. They outline what needs to be done in the company and help employees carry out activities effectively and efficiently. For example, most insurance companies have written policies that describe how the company handles policy replacements. They also have procedures that outline what policy administration or customer service staff need to do if the insurer receives notice that a policyowner intends to replace an existing policy with a new policy. An insurer's underwriting procedures specify how underwriters evaluate the risks presented by insurance applicants. A company's claim administration procedures describe the specific steps analysts must follow to evaluate a life insurance claim and the actions analysts must perform to ensure payment of valid claims or handle denied claims.

Budgets. A *budget* is a financial plan of action expressed in monetary terms that covers a specified time period. Budgets are used during all phases of the control cycle. During the planning process, budgets are used as steering controls that help establish revenue or expense expectations for the company as a whole and for departments, products, or lines of business. In life insurance companies, budgets include forecasts of the

- Number of policies the company expects to sell during the period

- Amount of income the company expects to earn during the period

- Cost of work that must be performed to sell and administer the company's products and to support company operations

- Cost of anticipated capital expenditures

- Expected amount of benefits to be paid to customers during the period

During the year, budgets are used as concurrent controls that provide management with periodic reports of company performance. For example, managers often receive monthly or quarterly sales reports that compare current sales revenue and expenses to budgeted amounts for the year to date. Budgets are useful as feedback controls during performance evaluation. By comparing achieved results at the end of the evaluation period to budgeted amounts, companies can identify differences, known as budget variances, that warrant further investigation or corrective action. Insurers regularly prepare reports on budget variances as a way to identify substandard performance or problem areas, such as higher-than-expected costs or lower-than-expected revenue. Large budget variances may require changing the company's operating procedures.

Audits. An *audit* is a systematic examination and evaluation of a company's records, procedures, and controls. Audits can be performed at regular intervals, in which case they serve as concurrent controls, or they can be performed at the end of a specified performance period, in which case they serve primarily as feedback controls. The most common form of audit is a *financial audit*, which is an evaluation of whether a company's financial information, financial statements, and source documents comply with accounting standards and are a fair and consistent depiction of the company's financial condition and performance. Audits also cover non-financial conditions, such as operating procedures, management efficiency, market conduct, and regulatory compliance.

Audits can be conducted internally or externally. In an internal audit, company employees conduct the review. External audits are conducted by an auditor who is employed by a public accounting firm and who is not associated with the insurer. External audits are used primarily to (1) present an independent opinion as to whether an insurer's financial statements fairly present the company's operations, (2) recommend changes to the company's internal systems, and (3) prepare reports of audit findings for the benefit of interested parties such as stockholders, policyowners, and regulators. Most jurisdictions also require insurers to undergo periodic external audits of their financial statements.

Exception Reports. A company's actual performance rarely matches its expected performance. But differences between actual performance and expected performance don't necessarily mean that a company wasn't successful in meeting its objectives. Because a company's performance can be affected by conditions that are outside the company's control—such as changes in interest rates or customer behavior—managers in most operational areas of an insurance company establish a range of acceptable performance on either side of the standard. For example, a company that set a goal of generating $1 million in first-year premiums for a new product might be satisfied if actual premium income was between $900,000 and $1,100,000. Managers generally tolerate differences between actual and expected performance that fall within the established range. Differences outside the acceptable range, however, usually require investigation.

Most insurance companies today maintain management information systems that help track company performance. A ***management information system (MIS)*** is a computerized system that provides information about a company's daily operations. A company's MIS helps managers make decisions and control routine activities. An MIS usually provides a variety of reports automatically, including sales reports, budget reports, benefit payment reports, lapse reports, commission reports, and financial reports. Managers can also program an MIS to provide exception reports. An ***exception report*** is a report produced automatically by an insurance company's MIS when certain predetermined conditions or exceptions in operating performance occur. Exception reports provide immediate feedback about a company's operations and its risk exposures. For example, an exception report might indicate that a company's commissions were higher than expected. Although high commission levels probably mean that producers are doing a good job of selling products, it also means that the company's expenses are higher than anticipated, and adjustments may be necessary.

Managing the business of insurance is not a static, one-time activity, but a continuous process of planning, organizing, and controlling a company's operations and finances. It is also not a task restricted to managers. Every employee contributes to management by ensuring that company policies and procedures are followed, that plans are carried out effectively and efficiently, and that performance meets established goals and objectives.

Key Terms

privately held company
publicly held company
corporation
license
stock insurance company
mutual insurance company
policy dividend
mutualization
demutualization
fraternal benefit society
mission statement
management
planning
SWOT analysis
corporate objective
corporate strategy
strategic business unit (SBU)
shared service
organizational chart

board of directors
committee
span of control
authority
chain of command
unity of command
control
performance standard
persistency rate
control cycle
steering control
concurrent control
feedback control
budget
audit
financial audit
management information system (MIS)
exception report

Chapter 3

Managing Solvency and Profitability

Objectives:

After studying this chapter, you should be able to

- Explain the goals of solvency and profitability for an insurance company
- Define risk management and explain the four basic approaches to managing risks
- Explain how regulators use minimum reserve requirements and minimum capital standards to ensure that insurers remain solvent
- Define return and investment, and identify the major categories of life insurer investments
- Explain the risk-return trade-off
- Define the required rate of return, the risk-free rate of return, and the risk premium, and be able to explain the relationship between these terms
- Describe the types of risks that insurers face and identify examples of each
- Describe insurers' use of asset-liability management (ALM) and enterprise risk management (ERM)

Outline

Basic Risk Management Techniques
- Avoiding Risk
- Controlling Risk
- Accepting Risk
- Transferring Risk

Insurance Regulation and Solvency
- Minimum Reserve Requirements
- Minimum Capital Standards

Managing Risks for Profitability
- Investments for Life Insurers
- The Risk-Return Trade-Off
- The Required Rate of Return
- Typical Risks that Insurers Manage
- Return and Diversification
- Asset-Liability Management (ALM)
- Enterprise Risk Management (ERM)

> When Riley Nugent purchased a life insurance policy from the Steadfast Life Insurance Company, he submitted his initial premium payment to the producer who sold him the policy. "I'm just curious," Riley said. "What exactly does Steadfast do with my premium?"

It's not surprising that Riley asked this question. Most customers understand that insurers have to charge premiums to fund the benefits on products. But most customers don't know what happens to those premiums in the meantime. That's the business side of insurance.

When Steadfast receives a premium payment from Riley, it uses part of the premium to cover the expenses that it incurs in selling and supporting the product. Steadfast invests the remainder of the premium. The portion of the premium that is invested—along with the investment income earned on the investments—will be used to pay benefits on Riley's policy in the event that he dies. After Steadfast has covered its expenses and funded the benefits for its policyowners, any remaining money will provide profits for the owners.

This example illustrates the twin goals of all insurance companies: to remain solvent and profitable at the same time. *Solvency* is an insurance company's ability to meet its financial obligations on time. *Profitability* is a company's overall success in generating returns to its owners and increasing the value of the company. Customers are concerned with company solvency because they need to know that the company will be around to keep its promises under their policies. Company owners are concerned with the company's long-term profitability because they want to earn a return on their investment.

To achieve the goals of solvency and profitability, insurance companies must be able to manage the many risks to which they are exposed. Although risk can produce negative or positive outcomes, our discussion generally assumes that the outcomes are negative. Fortunately for customers—and company owners—insurance companies are experts at *risk management*, which is the practice of systematically identifying, assessing, and minimizing the negative impact of risk.

Basic Risk Management Techniques

Four basic strategies can be used to eliminate or reduce exposures to risk: (1) avoiding risk; (2) controlling risk; (3) accepting risk; and (4) transferring risk. Individuals and insurance companies can use these strategies.

Avoiding Risk

One method of managing risk is to avoid it altogether.

> Steadfast was thinking about marketing an existing product in a new geographic area, but its preliminary research indicated that the risks associated with this venture would outweigh any of the benefits. Therefore, Steadfast chose not to pursue this venture.

> Another way that Steadfast avoids risks is by rejecting applications for life insurance if the proposed insured does not meet insurability standards.

Because insurance companies are in the business of risk, avoiding risk is not always an effective risk management option for them.

Controlling Risk

Controlling risk involves reducing or mitigating the actual losses from a given risk exposure. For example, insurers can reduce their overall losses on high-risk products by making adjustments to those products.

> Steadfast offers annuity contracts that pay a guaranteed minimum interest-crediting rate to customers. When Steadfast sold these contracts ten years ago, they had guaranteed minimum interest-crediting rates of 4% or higher. When market interest rates dropped, Steadfast redesigned these contracts with lower guaranteed rates of 3%. By reducing the guaranteed minimum interest-crediting rates on new business, Steadfast was able to reduce its overall exposure to the risk that interest rates will drop.

Another way that insurers control risk is through their underwriting guidelines.

> Steadfast's underwriters classify proposed insureds according to the risk they present to the company. If a proposed insured represents a higher than average risk, Steadfast attempts to control this risk by charging a higher premium than it would charge a similar proposed insured who represents an average risk.

Accepting Risk

A third method of managing risk is to accept, or *retain*, risk. To retain risk is to recognize the existence of a risk and accept the financial responsibility for that risk.

> Any time Steadfast issues a life insurance policy, it is accepting the risk posed by the policy. Steadfast charges a premium that it believes is adequate for accepting this risk.

Note that simply choosing to ignore the existence of a risk is not risk acceptance. Risk acceptance requires recognition of a risk and the explicit choice not to avoid, control, or transfer it.

Transferring Risk

But what do you do when a risk is impossible to avoid or control, and the financial consequences of accepting it would be devastating?

> For Riley, dying prematurely poses just such a risk. His death is unavoidable, is unpredictable in terms of timing, and would be financially catastrophic for his family.

For most people, the only way to manage the potential loss associated with this type of risk is to transfer some or all of the risk to someone else. Insurance plays a vital role here because the most common way for most individuals to transfer risk is to buy insurance.

> Riley purchased a life insurance policy from Steadfast to transfer the risk of his premature death to Steadfast.

When insurers issue insurance and annuity contracts, they can reduce their exposure to risk by transferring some or all of the risks to another insurer. *Reinsurance* is a type of insurance that one insurance company, known as the *direct writer*, or *ceding company*, purchases from another insurance company, known as the *reinsurer*, or *assuming company*.

> If Steadfast chose to obtain reinsurance to cover part of the death benefit for Riley's policy, then Steadfast would be transferring part of its risk on this policy.

Using reinsurance doesn't necessarily eliminate all exposure to risk, however, because there is still a risk that the reinsurer will fail to perform its part of the agreement. In the event that the reinsurer fails to meet its obligations, the direct writer is still responsible for paying benefits to the customer.

It's important to note that, when an insurer uses reinsurance to transfer part of the risk on a life insurance policy or annuity contract, the insurer is also *controlling* its risk exposure. In other words, controlling risk and transferring risk are not always mutually exclusive techniques.

Steadfast issued an individual life insurance policy to Jeremy Wilkie. Jeremy's policy included a two-year suicide exclusion provision. According to the terms of this provision, Steadfast will not pay the policy proceeds if Jeremy commits suicide within two years of policy issue—instead, the company will refund the premium payments to the beneficiary of Jeremy's policy. By including a suicide exclusion provision, Steadfast is both controlling and transferring risk on this policy: Steadfast controls its exposure to paying a claim for suicide by transferring the risk of death (through suicide) back to the policyowner.

Insurance Regulation and Solvency

If you buy an insurance policy or an annuity, you want and should expect some assurance that your company will remain in business over the long term. You want to know that your company won't fall into *insolvency*, which is a condition in which a company is unable to meet its financial obligations on time.

Minimum Reserve Requirements

Because the financial stability of insurance companies is important to so many people, governments in most jurisdictions actively regulate insurance company operations to make sure that companies remain solvent. Much of this regulation focuses on contractual reserves, which are also known as policy reserves. For most people, reserves are extra sources of funds that are available in case of an emergency or special need. In the context of insurance, however, contractual reserves are a bit different; they represent money that the company needs to cover its expected financial obligations, not extra money to cover emergencies. For an insurer, *contractual reserves* represent the amount that, together with future premiums and investment earnings, the insurer estimates it needs to pay benefits on in-force policies as they come due. To satisfy regulatory requirements, insurance companies must maintain at least a minimum amount of contractual reserves.

Because contractual reserves represent the amount that an insurer owes in policy benefits, reserves are a liability. A *liability* is a debt or future obligation of a company. The insurer must maintain assets that exceed its contractual reserve liabilities so that it has the funds to pay claims when they come due. An *asset* is any item of value owned by a company.

Minimum Capital Standards

The assets backing an insurer's contractual reserves go a long way toward ensuring that enough money will be available to pay claims on time. But sometimes those assets aren't enough. That's where capital comes in. In the context of minimum capital standards, *capital* refers to the excess of an insurer's assets over its liabilities. Most jurisdictions require insurers to maintain at least a minimum amount, or standard, of capital.

The minimum standard of capital varies from insurer to insurer and is related to the degree of risk associated with an insurer's products and its investments. For example, an insurer that holds riskier investments has a higher minimum standard of capital than does a comparable insurer that holds less risky investments. By establishing such risk-based minimum standards of capital along with minimum requirements for contractual reserves, insurance regulators attempt to ensure that each insurer has sufficient resources to pay contractual benefits and other financial obligations on time.

Although an insurance company's customers are concerned with the company's solvency, they aren't the only people who want the company to remain viable as a business. An insurance company's employees want the company to remain solvent because otherwise they would lose their jobs; the company's creditors want the company to be able to pay them back. Because an insolvent company is no longer an attractive investment option, company owners are concerned with solvency as well. They have a slightly different take on the company's overall condition, however: they want solvency, but they also want a good return on their investment in the company. That's where profitability comes in.

Managing Risks for Profitability

A *return* is any reward, profit, or compensation an investor hopes to earn in exchange for taking a risk. Any time a company invests its funds with the expectation of earning a return, the company is taking the financial risk that the investment may fail to generate the expected level of return or even that the insurer will lose money. In this sense, an *investment* is any use of a company's resources that is intended to generate a positive return of some type.

Investments for Life Insurers

The most important categories of investments for life insurance companies are bonds, stocks, mortgages, and cash and cash equivalents.

Bonds

On a worldwide basis, the greatest portion of life insurer investments is in bonds. A *bond* is a debt security—it represents a debt that the borrower, or issuer of the bond, owes to the *bondholder*, the investor who owns the bond. The bond issuer must pay the bondholder a specified amount of money on a specified date, known as the *maturity date*. The amount owed on the maturity date is specified in the bond and is known as the bond's *par value*, *face value*, or *maturity value*. Typically, bonds are issued with par values of $1,000, $10,000, or $100,000.

In addition to repaying the bond's par value, the bond issuer is usually obligated to make periodic—typically semiannual—interest payments to the bondholder. Such interest payments are called *coupon payments* because the amount of the interest payments is based on an interest rate, known as the *coupon rate*, specified in the bond.

The following is a simple example of how insurers invest in bonds.

The Kalavinka Corporation issued $1 million worth of bonds. These bonds were issued with par values of $100,000, a 10-year term to maturity, and a 5% annual coupon rate.

Steadfast purchased five of the $100,000 bonds at par value. For each bond, Kalavinka was obligated to pay Steadfast interest of $5,000 ($100,000 par value x 0.05 coupon rate) each year for ten years. Interest payments were due semiannually, so Kalavinka paid Steadfast $2,500 for each bond every six months. On the bonds' maturity date, Kalavinka made the last of the interest payments and repaid each bond's $100,000 par value to Steadfast.

Because Steadfast purchased these bonds at par value and held them to maturity, its sole return on these bonds was the interest payments. The total interest that Steadfast received on these bonds can be calculated as follows: 10 years x 5 bonds x ($100,000 x 0.05) = $250,000.

In the United States, life insurers invest heavily in *corporate bonds*, which are issued by corporations. Life insurance companies in all countries also invest in *government bonds*, which are issued by national, state, provincial, or city governments.

Stocks

Stocks are an important investment category for all life insurers. As a type of equity security, stocks represent an ownership interest in the issuing company. Life insurers invest in both common stock and preferred stock. *Common stock* entitles its owner to share in the issuing corporation's dividends and provides its owner with the right to vote on certain matters, such as voting for the company's board of directors. *Preferred stock* entitles its owner to certain privileges that common stockholders do not have. For example, preferred stockholders have the first right in receiving dividends; thus, any profits available for payment to stockholders must be paid to preferred stockholders before they may be paid to common stockholders. Preferred stockholders generally do not have the right to vote for the company's board of directors, but they may have the right to vote on other matters, such as the sale of substantially all of the company's assets.

Life insurers earn returns on their stock investments through (1) any increase in the price of the stock when they sell it and (2) any dividends paid by the issuing company.

Five years ago, Steadfast purchased 10,000 shares of common stock in the Minotaur Corporation. Each share of Minotaur stock was $50. For each of the past five years, the Minotaur stock paid dividends of $2 per share. Steadfast recently sold the stock for $75 a share. In this situation, Steadfast earned a return on the appreciation in the stock's price, as well as a return in the form of dividends. Steadfast's total return can be calculated as follows:

[($75 - $50) x 10,000] + ($2 x 10,000 x 5 years) = ($25 x 10,000) + ($2 x 50,000) = $250,000 + $100,000 = $350,000.

Mortgages

Mortgages are a type of debt security. A *mortgage* is a loan, typically long term, secured by a pledge of specified real estate. The borrower pays off the loan through the process of *amortization*, which is the reduction of a debt by regular payments of principal and interest that result in full payment of the debt by the maturity date.

Life insurers have always been an important source of mortgage loans in the United States. The greatest share of the mortgages held by U.S. life insurers is in commercial mortgages and collateralized mortgage obligations (CMOs). *Commercial mortgages* are loans secured by commercial real estate, such as shopping centers, office buildings, hospitals, factories, and retail stores. *Collateralized mortgage obligations (CMOs)* are bonds secured by a pool of residential mortgage loans. *Residential mortgages* are loans secured by single-family homes. Insurers favor CMOs because they can be bought and sold like bonds and thus are relatively liquid.

Although mortgages are an important investment category for U.S. life insurers, they are generally not as common for insurers in Brazil, China, Hong Kong, Mexico, and Taiwan.

Cash and Cash Equivalents

Cash and cash equivalents are both examples of short-term assets, which are assets that a company expects to readily convert into cash or consume within the current accounting period, typically one year. *Cash* is the amount of currency on hand or on deposit at an insurer's bank. *Cash equivalents* are not cash but can be converted to cash within 90 days with little or no risk of losing value. Cash and cash equivalents provide an important source of liquidity for insurers.

The Risk-Return Trade-Off

Investments play a critical role in generating earnings and building value for company owners. To generate earnings, however, the insurer must take risks. For any investor, the ideal situation would be to earn returns while avoiding risk entirely. In practice, though, this situation doesn't exist. Therefore, insurers seek to earn returns while limiting risk to an acceptable level. In general, the greater the risk associated with an investment, the greater the expected return on the investment. Conversely, the lower the risk associated with an investment, then, generally, the lower the expected return. This interplay between risk and return is known as the *risk-return trade-off*. Virtually every financial decision is subject to the risk-return trade-off.

> Any time Steadfast considers purchasing a bond, it must weigh the expected return from the bond against the risk incurred by investing in the bond. If it buys a given bond, Steadfast risks losing some or all of the money invested in the bond. The level of risk varies from issuer to issuer, depending on the issuer's financial stability. For this reason, a bond issuer with a poor credit rating will typically need to pay an investor such as Steadfast a higher interest rate than would a bond issuer with a better credit rating. Otherwise, Steadfast would simply buy the bond with the better credit rating.

The characteristics of a given investment transaction affect that investment's potential risk and return, as shown in Figure 3.1.

Life insurers must be especially careful about the risks they take when making investments.

> Steadfast is considering the purchase of common stock issued by a company that recently began operations. This company is also in a very risky industry, so its stock is a high-risk investment. Because it is so risky, though, this stock could provide Steadfast with some very high returns on its investment.

Although high-risk investments offer the potential to earn high returns, they have a similarly great potential for incurring losses. In the example above, Steadfast could earn a high return if market conditions are favorable and the price of the stock rises. On the other hand, Steadfast could lose some or all of its investment if market conditions worsen and stock prices fall. If an insurer's total investment losses are great enough, they could threaten the insurer's solvency.

Figure 3.1. Risk and Return in Investment Transactions

Lower risks with *lower* expected returns	Higher risks with *higher* expected returns
Owning a short-term asset	Owning a long-term asset
Lending to a borrower with a good credit rating	Lending to a borrower with a poor credit rating
Owning an investment with good liquidity or marketability—one that is easy to sell at a fair value	Owning an investment with poor liquidity or poor marketability—one that is difficult to sell at a fair value
Issuing a new product that has low initial costs	Issuing a new product that has high initial costs
Introducing a product in a familiar market	Introducing a product in an unfamiliar market
Owning a loan that requires the borrower to repay the lender on a specified due date	Owning a loan that a borrower can choose to repay at any time
Issuing a mortgage loan with a prepayment penalty	Issuing a mortgage loan with no prepayment penalty
Owning an investment that pays returns in the investor's domestic currency	Owning an investment that pays returns in a currency that is foreign to the investor

The Required Rate of Return

Like all investors, insurance companies require a sufficient return on their investments. Otherwise, there would be no point in investing—they'd be better off just holding on to their money. For a given investment, the **required rate of return** can be expressed as the sum of the risk-free rate of return and the risk premium.

> Required rate of return = Risk-free rate of return + Risk premium

As its name suggests, the **risk-free rate of return** is the return on a risk-free investment. In most countries, this return is the yield on a short-term, highly rated issue of the government. Historically, in the United States, the risk-free rate of return has been the return on a **U.S. Treasury bill**, which is an obligation issued by the U.S. Treasury as part of its ongoing process of funding the national debt. Because these bills have virtually no risk of default, they are considered the safest of all investments. For a country that does not have a risk-free investment, the risk-free rate of return can be estimated by using the average long-term growth rate of the economy. For example, if a country's economy is growing at an average annual rate of 3%, then the risk-free rate of return is 3%.

The **risk premium** is the compensation that investors demand for taking on the risk associated with a specific investment. Without a risk premium, investors would be better off investing in a risk-free investment; therefore, the risk premium serves as the incentive for an investor to pursue a specific investment opportunity. For a given investment, the risk premium includes risks such as credit risk (default risk), liquidity risk, interest-rate risk, and currency risk.

> Steadfast is determining the required rate of return for one of its bond investments. Because U.S. Treasury bills are currently providing a 4% return, Steadfast uses a risk-free rate of return of 4%. After evaluating the investment's risk, Steadfast assigns a risk premium of 6%. Steadfast's required rate of return for this investment, therefore, is 10%, found by adding 4% and 6%.
>
> Steadfast is also evaluating the required rate of return for a stock investment in a foreign company. This foreign company is located in a country that doesn't have a risk-free investment. The economy for this country, however, has been booming in recent years, growing at about 5% a year. Therefore, Steadfast will use 5% as the risk-free rate for this investment. After evaluating the stock's risk, Steadfast derives a risk premium of 7%. The required rate of return on this investment would be 12%, found by adding 5% and 7%.

Typical Risks that Insurers Manage

Now we're ready to talk about the most important risks that insurers face. The risks that have the greatest priority for life insurers generally are the financial risks of (1) losing some or all of an original investment and (2) failing to earn some or all of an expected return. Financial risks that are priority risks for insurers include credit risk and market risk.

Credit Risk

Credit risk is the possibility that a borrower could be late with payments or could entirely fail to pay its obligations. A failure to meet a financial obligation is known as a *default*. Therefore, credit risk is sometimes called *default risk*.

> Three years ago, Steadfast purchased bonds issued by the Origami Corporation. Recently, Origami ran into financial difficulties and ended up defaulting on these bonds—that is, it failed to pay bondholders like Steadfast the money that it owed them.

Market Risk

Market risk is the risk arising from movements in the direction of an entire financial market. Market risk takes many forms, such as equity risk, interest-rate risk, reinvestment-rate risk, liquidity risk, and currency risk.

- When market risk applies to the stock market, it is known as *equity risk*.

> Steadfast doesn't invest heavily in the stock market, but it does have some stock investments. By owning stock investments, Steadfast is exposed to equity risk. However, Steadfast limits its exposure to equity risk by limiting the amount of stock that it owns.

- *Interest-rate risk* is the uncertainty arising from fluctuations in market interest rates. Because this risk is so significant for insurers, we discuss it in detail in a later chapter.

- *Reinvestment-rate risk* is the risk that a decline in interest rates will lead to lower income when bonds are paid off and the insurer must reinvest the funds. In general, when a bond matures, the bond issuer must pay the bondholder the par value. However, the bond issuer may be permitted to pay off a bond early. If early repayment occurs at a time when market interest rates have fallen, the bondholder will be reinvesting the funds at this lower interest rate. Because they invest fairly heavily in bonds, insurers are exposed to a significant amount of reinvestment-rate risk.

> Five years ago, when Steadfast purchased bonds issued by the Sunflower Corporation, market interest rates were 5%. Although these bonds had a maturity date of ten years, the bonds were callable—meaning, Sunflower was permitted to pay them off early. When Sunflower paid off the bonds two years ago, market interest rates had fallen to 3%. Therefore, when Steadfast reinvested the funds from the bonds, it wasn't able to make as much money as it had planned.

- *Currency risk* is the risk arising from changes in currency exchange rates. Insurers that operate in more than one country or that invest in securities that are denominated in a foreign currency have exposure to currency risk.

> Steadfast operates in a single economy—the United States. It is planning to begin operating in Asia, however. By operating overseas, Steadfast will have to manage currency risk for the first time.

■ *Liquidity risk* is the risk of not having adequate liquidity to meet obligations as they come due. Liquidity risk is important for insurers because they must have enough cash and liquid assets on hand at all times to pay benefits on their products.

> Steadfast carefully manages its liquidity because it does not want to face a situation where it could be forced to sell long-term assets to meet current cash needs.

Operational Risk

Insurers also face risks that derive from their operations. *Operational risk* is the risk of financial losses resulting from (1) inadequate or failed internal processes and controls, people, or systems or (2) external events. As its name implies, operational risk occurs in the various operational areas of an insurance company—such as marketing, claim administration, information technology, and underwriting.

One challenge that insurers face in managing operational risks is that these risks are often difficult to categorize. For example, a situation might involve more than one type of operational risk, such as distribution risk, human resources risk, technology risk, business process risk, and event risk.

> At Steadfast, long turnaround times on customer service requests are causing customers to terminate their policies with the company. Steadfast determined that this problem was caused in part by using outdated technology in the customer service department—a type of operational risk known as technology, or systems, risk. A further problem that Steadfast identified was that some of the processes used in the customer service department were inefficient—an operational risk known as business process risk. In addition, several employees in the customer service department ended up leaving the company because of their frustrations with these problems—in this case, the operational risk category was human resources risk.

Another challenge is that the effects of operational risk can be difficult to measure.

> Some of Steadfast's sales producers violated market conduct requirements by selling inappropriate products to seniors—a type of operational risk known as distribution risk. As a result, Steadfast became involved in several lawsuits. The negative publicity from these lawsuits created financial difficulties for the company. Although they couldn't assign a dollar amount to their losses, producers found that many customers, especially seniors, no longer trusted Steadfast and refused to buy products from the company.

Although operational risks can be difficult to identify and measure, it is essential that insurers attempt to manage them. The first line of defense against these risks should be an effective system of internal controls.

Business Risk

Insurers also face business risk. *Business risk*, which is sometimes called *marketplace risk*, is the risk that changes in a company's external environment will affect its operations. Two types of business risk are competition risk and regulatory risk.

- *Competition risk* includes any risks posed by direct competitors of a company, changes in an industry's structure, or changes in an industry's standards for the use of technology.

> A company recently introduced new software that results in faster and better claims processing. Steadfast decided to purchase this software because failure to do so could mean losing customers to companies who are using this new technology.

- *Regulatory risk* is the risk that arises from changes in the regulatory environment.

> One of Steadfast's most popular products is its indexed annuity product. Although indexed annuities are currently considered to be fixed products under U.S. laws, a movement is underway to change the way these products are regulated. Steadfast must monitor this situation because a change in the product's regulation would affect the company's sales of the product.

Pricing Risk

All types of businesses face the foregoing risks. In addition, insurance companies face risks that are unique to the insurance business, such as pricing risk. *Pricing risk* is the risk that an insurer's actual experience will be significantly worse than expectations, causing the insurer to lose money on its products. Three types of pricing risk are mortality risk, expense risk, and policyholder behavior risk:

- *Mortality risk* is the risk that actual mortality will differ from expectations, causing the insurer to lose money on its products.

> Any time that Steadfast designs a life insurance product, it assumes that a certain number of insureds will die each year. If more insureds die than the company has anticipated, Steadfast will have to pay out more in death benefits than it has planned.

- *Expense risk* is the risk that actual expenses will be higher than expectations, causing the insurer to lose money on its products.

■ *Policyholder behavior risk*, sometimes called *customer behavior risk*, refers to the risk that a company faces as a result of the choices made by policyholders. This type of risk can affect the persistency of an insurer's products. *Persistency* refers to the amount of an insurer's products that remain in force. Life insurance and annuity products can cover long periods of time, and sometimes customers stop paying their premiums—causing their policies to lapse—or customers may surrender their policies. A *surrender* occurs when the owner of a cash value life insurance policy or deferred annuity contract chooses to receive the contract's monetary value before the contract reaches maturity. Lapses and surrenders can be costly to insurers. First, they eliminate future income streams because premium payments stop; in addition, in the case of surrenders, the insurer has to pay the policyowner the surrender value, which could result in a monetary loss for the insurer. Second, because a typical insurance policy must remain in force for several years before the policy becomes profitable for the insurer, a lapse or surrender may prevent the insurer from recovering its costs on the policy.

> To manage the risks of lapses and surrenders on contracts, Steadfast has come up with a number of strategies. First of all, for any new product it develops, Steadfast assumes that a certain number of lapses and surrenders will occur over time. In this way, Steadfast can protect itself against these two types of policyholder behavior. Of course, if a high number of lapses and surrenders occur—especially if they occur around the same time—they could exceed the number that Steadfast estimated, causing the company to lose money on its products.
>
> Steadfast also lessens the impact of surrenders by assessing a charge whenever a policy or contract is surrendered. This charge is designed to discourage surrenders and to help Steadfast recover its costs when surrenders do occur.

Return and Diversification

One of the most important techniques that insurers use for managing their investment risks is diversification. *Diversification* is a technique for spreading risk by investing in different assets with different characteristics. To diversify their investments, insurers carefully spread their investment selection among the securities of different issuers in different business categories. By diversifying, insurers hope to avoid *asset concentration risk*, which is the risk of the excessive concentration of assets in any single category.

> Steadfast invests heavily in bonds. It diversifies these investments, however, by investing in different kinds of bonds—some are corporate bonds, while others are government bonds. Then, for its corporate bonds, Steadfast selects bonds that represent a wide variety of industries.
>
> The company also invests in stocks, mortgages, and real estate to provide even greater diversification.

Insurers also view their products as investments and attempt to diversify the risks they represent. To diversify product risks, companies issue a variety of product types, such as both life insurance and annuity products; issue contracts to geographically dispersed customers; and issue contracts to diverse types of customers.

Diversification is so important that risk managers talk about whether a given risk is diversifiable or nondiversifiable. A ***diversifiable risk***, also known as a *nonsystematic risk*, is a risk that is specific to an individual asset or issuer. Most of the financial risks associated with investing are diversifiable risks. For example, the risk of a bond issuer defaulting is a diversifiable risk because an insurer can diversify this risk by investing in bonds from a wide variety of issuers. A ***nondiversifiable risk***, also known as a *systematic risk*, is a risk that affects all assets in an economy and is therefore not specific to an individual asset or issuer. The risk of an economic depression is an example of a nondiversifiable risk.

Asset-Liability Management (ALM)

Insurers generally take a portfolio approach to managing the risks associated with the company's assets and liabilities. A ***portfolio*** is a collection of various risky assets, usually assembled to meet a defined set of goals.

Insurers group their risk exposures into two types of portfolios:

- An ***asset portfolio***, which holds the insurer's securities and other invested assets

- A ***liability portfolio***, or *product portfolio*, which represents the insurer's obligations to customers

In coordinating the risk interactions between these portfolios, insurers combine these two portfolios into a composite asset-liability portfolio.

Asset-liability management (ALM) is the practice of coordinating the administration of an insurer's asset portfolio (its investments) with the administration of its liability portfolio (its obligations to customers) so as to manage risk and still earn an adequate level of return. One important goal of ALM is to ensure that the value of a company's assets always exceeds the value of its liabilities. The basic concept of ALM is straightforward, but ALM applications are extremely complex. Nevertheless, ALM has become a day-to-day risk management activity for many insurance companies.

Enterprise Risk Management (ERM)

If you're getting the impression that risk management is complicated for insurers, you're right—it is. Fortunately, insurance companies hire experts, such as actuaries and investment specialists, to handle this area. You don't have to become an expert in this area, but you should be aware of some recent changes.

For example, an important innovation in the way that insurers manage risk is enterprise risk management. In technical terms, ***enterprise risk management (ERM)*** is a system that identifies and quantifies risks from both potential threats and potential opportunities and manages these risks in a coordinated approach that supports the organization's strategic objectives. ERM is a holistic approach to managing *all* of the significant risks that an organization faces. Think of all the risks we've covered in this chapter—and we haven't even covered every risk that insurers face. Every one of these risks would be managed under ERM.

In addition to integrating all the types of risk into one framework, ERM differs from traditional risk management approaches by expanding the definition of risk to include opportunities. In other words, ERM targets not only risks that threaten an organization's viability but those that have the potential to enhance a company's profitability.

Critical Components of an ERM Program

According to the Society of Actuaries, an ERM program should include the following four components:

- A **risk control process**, in which the organization implements processes and practices that support specific risk control.

- A **strategic risk management process**, in which risks are reflected in the company's strategic choices.

- A **process for managing catastrophic risk**, in which extreme events that could destroy the organization's viability are addressed.

- A **risk management culture**, in which risk management approaches are automatically incorporated into all decision making.[1]

Although each of these components is necessary for an effective ERM program, we will focus here on the risk control process.

A Risk Control Process

As a crucial component of a successful ERM program, a risk control process gathers information and then evaluates, monitors, and limits risk exposures. The typical steps in this process are as follows:

Identify risk exposures throughout the organization.

Evaluate the organization's risk exposures and prioritize each one. Assign top priority to selected risks.

Create managerial accountability for monitoring and actively managing each risk and a formal reporting system for communicating the status of each top priority risk.

Assign risk limits and implement an action plan for each priority risk. Action plans can include avoiding, controlling, accepting, or transferring risk.

Companies differ in the ways that they classify their risk exposures. In an operating environment, though, the framework itself is far less important than the effort to ensure that all significant risk exposures are addressed. Figure 3.2 presents one way in which a life insurance company can categorize its risk exposures. This list is not meant to be exhaustive, but it covers the major risks discussed in this chapter.

Most insurers practice ERM at some level, although some are more advanced than others in this area. ERM is likely to gain in importance over time, as it provides insurance companies with an integrated approach to managing all of their significant risks.

Figure 3.2. Risks Monitored for ERM

The following chart shows some of the major risks addressed by ERM.

Credit Risk

Market Risk

- Equity risk
- Interest-rate risk
- Reinvestment-rate risk
- Currency risk
- Liquidity risk

Operational Risk

- Distribution risk
- Human resources risk
- Technology (systems) risk
- Business process risk
- Event risk

Business Risk (Marketplace Risk)

- Competition risk
- Regulatory risk

Pricing Risk

- Mortality risk
- Expense risk
- Policyholder behavior risk

Key Terms

solvency

profitability

risk management

insolvency

contractual reserve

liability

asset

capital

return

investment

maturity date

par value

coupon rate

corporate bond

government bond

common stock

preferred stock

mortgage

amortization

commercial mortgage

collateralized mortgage obligation (CMO)

residential mortgage

cash

cash equivalent

risk-return trade-off

required rate of return

risk-free rate of return

U.S. Treasury bill

risk premium

credit risk

default

market risk

equity risk

interest-rate risk

reinvestment-rate risk

currency risk

liquidity risk

operational risk

business risk

competition risk

regulatory risk

pricing risk

mortality risk

expense risk

policyholder behavior risk

surrender

diversification

asset concentration risk

diversifiable risk

nondiversifiable risk

portfolio

asset portfolio

liability portfolio

asset-liability management (ALM)

enterprise risk management (ERM)

Endnote

1.   *Enterprise Risk Management Specialty Guide*, (Schaumburg, IL: Society of Actuaries, © 2006), 26.

Chapter 4
Product Design and the Time Value of Money

Objectives:

After studying this chapter, you should be able to

- Describe the important components of technical product design, such as the cost of benefits, operating expenses, and investment earnings

- Describe the testing of product designs and explain how changes to a given model can improve the model's financial results

- Recognize examples of adverse and favorable deviations in product evaluation

- Describe the difference between simple interest and compound interest and be able to calculate interest earnings using each type of interest

- Explain the Rule of 72 and how it is used, and distinguish between a nominal and an effective interest rate

- Perform future value calculations and explain how the future value of an annuity is calculated

- Differentiate between an ordinary annuity and an annuity due and provide examples of each

- Perform present value calculations, explain how the present value of an annuity is calculated, and describe insurer applications of present value

- Explain the general rules that govern future values and present values

Outline

Financial Aspects of Product Development
- Technical Product Design
- Evaluating Product Performance

Interest
- Interest Rates
- Types of Interest
- The Investment Period

The Time Value of Money
- Calculating Future Values
- Calculating Present Values
- General Rules Governing Future Values and Present Values

In the last chapter, Riley Nugent had a question about what happens to his premium payment after he submits it to the Steadfast Life Insurance Company. Another piece of this puzzle concerns how Steadfast came up with the amount of Riley's premium payment. Customers probably don't realize how much time and effort it takes for an insurance company to design an insurance product that meets customer—and company—needs. Actuaries are experts in the mathematics of insurance, and one of their most important job duties is to design insurance and annuity products so that these products are financially sound right from the start—meaning, the insurer always has enough funds to provide the benefits owed under a product and the product contributes to the company's profitability. In addition to ensuring that products are financially sound, actuaries also need to make sure that premiums are competitive with those of other companies.

Financial Aspects of Product Development

Actuaries focus on the financial aspects of products during the phase of product development known as technical product design. The financial results of a product are also evaluated in the final stage of product development—the stage known as monitoring, evaluation, and feedback.

Technical Product Design

Technical product design, also known as *financial design* or simply *product design*, is the phase in the product development process in which a product's financial structure is created. Figure 4.1 presents a typical product development process and shows where technical product design falls in this process.

As you can see from Figure 4.1, technical product design includes a number of activities and requires the efforts of people from all areas of the company. This chapter focuses on the product design activities performed by actuaries: creating a product's financial structure and testing the product design. One objective of product design is to establish a premium rate that will enable the company to both cover its costs of developing and administering the product and generate a reasonable profit for the company and its owners. To ensure that a product's design meets this dual objective, insurers focus on three primary components of the product's premium rate structure: (1) the cost of benefits, (2) operating expenses, and (3) investment earnings. Let's take a closer look at each of these components.

Figure 4.1. Product Development Process

You should keep in mind that the product development process differs in details from one company to another, and companies may use their own terms for the activities of product development. For educational purposes, we describe customary industry practice and rely on terminology that is widely used in the industry.

Idea Generation

The insurer gathers ideas for new product concepts that will meet the company's needs and the needs of specific market segments.

Idea Screening

The insurer evaluates new product ideas quickly and inexpensively to separate workable ideas from those that have little or no potential.

Comprehensive Business Analysis

The insurer prepares a number of studies designed to thoroughly analyze the feasibility of a proposed product. The insurer also identifies the investment strategy that optimizes results and evaluates whether the product can meet all proposed regulatory requirements.

Technical Product Design

The insurer develops a contract form for the product, sets the product's financial structure, models and tests the product design, and prepares schedules and budgets for the new product.

Product Introduction

The insurer files the contract form and related documents with the appropriate regulatory authorities and obtains any required approvals of the product. The insurer also establishes the administrative structures and processes necessary to sell the product and then offers the product for sale.

Monitoring, Evaluation, and Feedback

After the product has been introduced, the insurer evaluates its performance.

Cost of Benefits

The premiums an insurer receives for a product must be large enough so that, when they're invested, they will fund the benefits the insurer promises to pay out under the product. Thus, in pricing the product, the insurer must estimate the cost of providing those benefits. A product's *cost of benefits*, also known as the *cost of insurance*, is the value of the contractually required benefits that the product promises to pay. Under life and annuity contracts, important examples of contractual benefits paid to customers include

- Death benefits upon the death of an insured or annuitant

- Cash surrender values

- Partial withdrawals of the account balance of a cash value life insurance policy or a deferred annuity contract prior to the scheduled maturity date

- Policyholder dividends

- Annuity payments under payout annuities

- Secondary benefit guarantees payable under variable annuities

For a given life insurance or annuity contract, the projected cost of benefits generally equals the sum of all the potential benefit payments under the contract times the expected probability that the benefits will be payable. We can express the projected cost of a given benefit as follows:

> Projected cost of a given benefit = Potential benefit amount payable × Probability that the benefit will be payable

A single product may offer one benefit or numerous benefits, and the product's financial design must anticipate the costs of each of these benefits throughout the life of the product. For a given product, the projected cost of *all* benefits is the sum of the individual benefit costs.

Mortality—the incidence of death in a specified group of people—is an important element of the cost of benefits for all life insurance and some annuity products. For example, for a given life insurance product, the insurer's death benefit obligations for a specific policy year are equal to the death benefit amount times the number of insureds expected to die during that year.

Another important element of the cost of benefits is the lapse rate. As you may recall, the *lapse rate* for a block of policies is the number of policies that lapse or surrender during a policy year divided by the total number of policies in force at the beginning of the year. Lapse rates determine the amount of surrender benefits that a company has to pay out. In addition, for life insurance products, the lapse rate will determine how many customers remain to collect death benefits.

Operating Expenses in Product Design

Some of an insurer's operating expenses must be paid by a new product's premiums. In setting the premium rate, the insurer must estimate the costs associated with supporting the product over the years it is expected to remain in force. Examples of operating expenses that are included in such an estimate are the costs of

- Commissions paid to producers

- Underwriting applications

- Actuarial services

- New administrative software

- Product approval

- Claims settlement

- Customer service support

The assumed expenses built into a product's premium rates are designed to reflect the actual pattern of the insurer's operating expenditures. Some components of a product's price are restricted by state regulations. For example, a state may limit the amount of the commission that can be paid on a product. Actuaries have to factor this information into their calculations.

After an insurer has described the expenses attributable to a product, it must incorporate those expenses into the financial design of the product. For many products, insurers offset at least some operating expenses by means of explicit charges to customers. These charges can be classified as transaction charges or periodic charges that are assessed at regular intervals, such as every month or every year.

In designing a fixed deferred annuity product for the Steadfast Life Insurance Company, Steadfast's actuaries included a transaction charge known as a *surrender charge*. This charge, which applies only during the first eight years of the contract, is imposed when a contract owner surrenders a deferred annuity contract or withdraws funds from the contract in excess of a specified amount. The charge is 8% of the amount withdrawn for the first year and decreases by 1% each year until the charge disappears. Steadfast's surrender charge is both a preventive measure and a defensive measure. It imposes the charge to discourage annuity contract owners from surrendering their contracts. However, when a surrender does occur, the charge is Steadfast's way of recovering the costs it incurred in developing and issuing the contract.

Steadfast's actuaries also included a type of periodic charge known as an administrative charge. An *administrative charge* is designed to cover the costs of issuing a contract, making administrative changes to the contract, preparing contract owner statements, and performing general maintenance activities. This charge is assessed once a year and is based on the amount of the annuity's accumulated value.

Investment Earnings

In pricing a new product, an insurer must estimate the investment income it will earn from the product's premiums. In general, the larger the investment earnings the insurer expects to receive, the lower the premium rate the insurer must charge for the product.

The insurer must also evaluate whether the new product is a good fit with the company's existing investment strategies and investment expertise. If not, the company must acquire new competencies, expertise, consulting services, support software, or other accommodations for investing the product's premiums.

For fixed life insurance and annuity products, the **interest spread**, or *interest margin*, represents the element of profit that insurers hope to earn from their investment operations. For these products, the interest rate credited to products on behalf of customers is called the *interest-crediting rate*. The relationship between the interest spread, the interest rate earned, and the interest-crediting rate can be expressed as follows:

Interest spread = Interest rate earned – Interest-crediting rate

In general, insurers try to earn an interest spread on their fixed products by earning a higher rate of return on their investments than the rates they credit for their products. The interest spread is, in effect, part of the price the customer pays for the product.

> Last quarter, for its fixed deferred annuity product, Steadfast credited interest to customers at a rate of 4%, and it earned 6% on the investments supporting this product. Therefore, Steadfast's interest spread for this product last quarter was equal to 6% − 4%, or 2%.

It's important to realize that, if an insurer's investments perform worse than expected, the insurer will still have to pay the interest-crediting rate on its fixed products. In this situation, the spread could be negative, meaning the insurer has lost money on the product.

> This quarter, Steadfast earned only 3% on the investments supporting its fixed deferred annuity product. The company still had to credit interest to customers at a rate of 4%. Therefore, for this quarter, Steadfast's interest spread for this product was equal to 3% − 4%, or -1%.

Variable life insurance and annuity products don't have interest spreads; instead, insurers earn a profit on the investment component of these products by charging periodic management fees. These fees are typically applied to the product's account value and are assessed in basis points. A **basis point (bp)** is 1/100th of a percent, or 0.0001. Therefore, 100 basis points equal 1 percent or 0.01. Ten basis points equal 0.10 percent or 0.001.

> For its variable annuity products, Steadfast assesses periodic management fees of 60 bp. Therefore, if a variable annuity issued by Steadfast has an account value of $100,000, then the fee charged would be equal to:
>
> $$\$100,000 \times 0.006 = \$600$$

Testing New Product Designs

Creating a new product requires testing and validating the product design. Testing a product's design consists of modeling the financial results for one or multiple sets of estimated values and comparing the results to the established objectives for the product. Generally, a **model** can be defined as a system that simulates something else—in this case, an insurance or annuity product. Product development software uses mathematical modeling to simulate the financial processes that occur over the time that contracts are in force for a given product. In testing a product design, actuaries typically examine whether the product's profitability, assets, reserves, and cash flows are adequate.

If initial testing of a product design produces unsatisfactory results, actuaries can change some of the product features or assumptions—provided the new values are realistic and financially sound. During product design and testing for a given life or annuity product, examples of changes that would ordinarily improve a product model's profitability, all other factors remaining the same, would be to:

- Increase charges to customers

- Decrease product expenses

- Decrease benefit costs

- Increase investment earnings

Any design adjustments that an actuary makes to the product design must be supported by the company's real-world operations.

> Lowering expense assumptions in a product model must be supported in the real world by finding new, more efficient ways to do business so that actual business expenses are reduced.
>
> Similarly, increasing an investment income assumption in a product design must be supported in the real world by new investment strategies that are likely to produce greater investment income.

It's also not unusual for actuaries to go through several iterations of a product model before they are satisfied with the results.

> Steadfast's actuaries are developing a new term life insurance product. They assigned the product a profit target of 14%, and they created an initial set of premium rates to support this target. To test this design, they ran a pricing model that calculates the product's profit. After the model's first run, the profit was only 12%. The actuaries then changed the product's features and re-ran the model. They repeated this process until they arrived at a combination of premium and product features that produced their target of 14%.

Evaluating Product Performance

Once a product has been introduced, the company must evaluate the product's performance. This evaluation typically takes place during the final stage of product development—the stage known as monitoring, evaluation, and feedback. In evaluating a product's results, insurers compare the product's actual values against the assumed values used in product design. In such comparisons, insurers consider any difference between the values to be a *deviation*. Deviations can be adverse or favorable. In product operations, an **adverse deviation** produces a decrease in actual product profitability relative to assumed product profitability. An adverse deviation arises whenever a specific product result differs from the modeled assumptions so that

- Product revenue is *lower* than assumed

- Benefit payments are *greater* than assumed

- Product expenses are *greater* than assumed

Steadfast had a life insurance product for which the assumed mortality built into product design was 90% of the mortality rates in a specific mortality table. Actual mortality proved to be 98% of the rates in this table. In this situation, Steadfast's product had an adverse deviation because the actual mortality rates were 8% higher than the assumed mortality rates. More insureds died than expected, resulting in greater benefit payments than expected.

If large adverse deviations occur, then the insurer must try to identify reasons for them and, if possible, take corrective action, such as cutting operating expenses. If the results from a product are unsatisfactory, the company has a range of options to explore, from slightly adjusting the product to completely abandoning future sales of the product.

A *favorable deviation* is a difference between actual and assumed product values that produces an increase in actual product profitability relative to assumed product profitability. A favorable deviation occurs whenever a specific product result differs from the assumptions used in product design so that

- Product revenue is *greater* than assumed

- Benefit payments are *lower* than assumed

- Product expenses are *lower* than assumed

Steadfast had a life insurance product for which the assumed mortality built into product design was 90% of the mortality rates in a specific mortality table. Actual mortality proved to be 84% of the rates in this table. In this situation, Steadfast's product had a favorable deviation because the actual mortality rates were 6% lower than the assumed mortality rates. Fewer insureds died than expected, resulting in lower benefit payments than expected.

Figure 4.2 summarizes the sources of adverse deviations and favorable deviations in product evaluation.

Interest

In product design, investment earnings—whether for a fixed or variable product—are represented by an interest rate. In fact, earnings can take forms other than interest. Conveniently, though, any form of investment earnings can be expressed as a percentage of the original amount invested. When a return is expressed as a percentage of the original investment, it's called a rate of return. For our purposes, a rate of return is equivalent to an interest rate. When insurers earn interest on their investments, three primary factors affect the growth of investments: (1) the interest rate, (2) the type of interest, and (3) the time period during which the invested principal earns interest.

Interest Rates

You may recall that *interest* is a fee that individuals and financial institutions pay (or charge) for the use of borrowed money. In the case of interest earnings, the

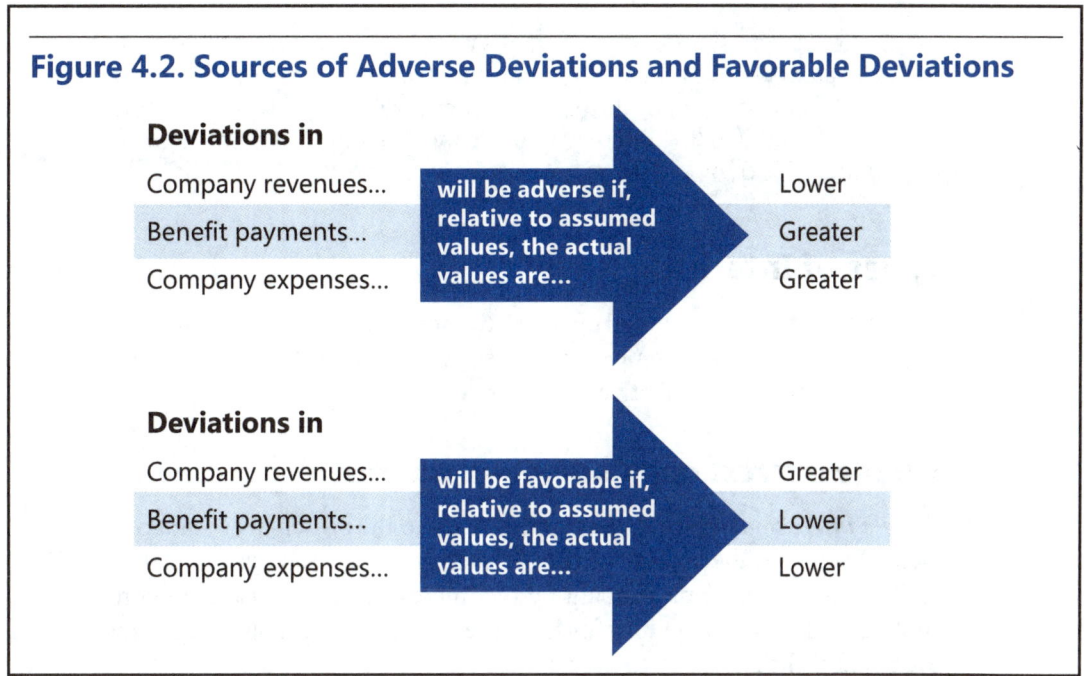

Figure 4.2. Sources of Adverse Deviations and Favorable Deviations

Deviations in

	will be adverse if, relative to assumed values, the actual values are...	
Company revenues...		Lower
Benefit payments...		Greater
Company expenses...		Greater

Deviations in

	will be favorable if, relative to assumed values, the actual values are...	
Company revenues...		Greater
Benefit payments...		Lower
Company expenses...		Lower

amount of the earnings depends on the interest rate. An *interest rate* is the percentage by which an amount of money is multiplied to derive the amount that is paid for the use of that money. The original amount of money upon which interest is calculated is known as the *principal*.

In calculations, interest rates are usually expressed in decimal form.

> A 5 percent interest rate can be expressed as 5% or 0.05 and a 2.5 percent interest rate can be expressed as 2.5% or 0.025.

An investor can calculate the interest amount earned on an initial sum of money invested for one year at a specified interest rate by multiplying the principal by the interest rate, expressed in decimal form:

> Principal × Interest rate = Interest earned

> Suppose Steadfast purchased a 10-year bond at its par value of $100,000. In this situation, the par value of the bond is the principal amount of the investment. This bond also has a coupon rate of 5%. At the end of the first year, Steadfast would receive $5,000 in interest payments on this bond, calculated as follows: $100,000 (principal) × 0.05 (interest rate) = $5,000.

An investor who knows the amount of an investment and the amount of interest earned can find the interest rate by dividing the interest amount by the principal amount.

> Interest amount ÷ Principal = Interest rate

One of Steadfast's investments had a principal amount of $1,500,000. One year later, the investment had earned $60,000 in interest. The interest rate that Steadfast earned on this investment for last year can be found by dividing $60,000 (the interest amount) by $1,500,000 (the principal), which equals 0.04, or 4%.

Types of Interest

The amount of interest earned on an investment also depends on whether the interest is simple interest or compound interest and whether the interest rate is a nominal interest rate or an effective interest rate.

Simple Interest and Compound Interest

Simple interest is interest that is applied only to the principal amount of an investment. Therefore, the amount of simple interest earned each year is determined by multiplying the principal amount by the interest rate. Because the interest rate is applied to the same amount of principal each year, the amount of interest earned each year is the same.

Steadfast invested $100,000 for five years at 3% simple interest, calculated annually. If Steadfast made no withdrawals during the five-year period, then the total interest on this investment would be equal to $15,000, as shown in the table below:

Year	Beginning of year balance	+	Interest earned (Principal × 3%)	=	End of year balance
1	$100,000.00	+	$3,000.00	=	$103,000.00
2	$103,000.00	+	$3,000.00	=	$106,000.00
3	$106,000.00	+	$3,000.00	=	$109,000.00
4	$109,000.00	+	$3,000.00	=	$112,000.00
5	$112,000.00	+	$3,000.00	=	$115,000.00

Compound interest is interest earned on both the principal *and* accumulated interest. Today, the interest on most loans and investments is compound interest. When interest is compounded, the interest earned each investment period is equal to the accumulated balance at the beginning of the period multiplied by the interest rate. The amount of interest earned that period is then added to the accumulated balance to determine the beginning balance on which interest will be paid during the next period. In this way, interest is earned on both the original principal and on all accumulated interest.

Steadfast placed $100,000 in an account that earns 3% interest, compounded annually. Steadfast left the money in the account for five years and made no withdrawals. At the end of the five-year period, the value of Steadfast's investment was equal to $115,927.41, as shown in the table below:

Year	Beginning of year balance	+	Interest earned (Beginning of year balance × 3%)	=	End of year balance
1	$100,000.00	+	$3,000.00	=	$103,000.00
2	$103,000.00	+	$3,090.00	=	$106,090.00
3	$106,090.00	+	$3,182.70	=	$109,272.70
4	$109,272.70	+	$3,278.18	=	$112,550.88
5	$112,550.88	+	$3,376.53	=	$115,927.41

The difference in the amount of interest earned by Steadfast with these two investments was $927.41 ($15,927.41 - $15,000.00). Over a long period of time, the difference can be significant.

Suppose that 100 years ago someone had placed $10 in an interest-bearing account. The columns below show how the growth in the value of this account would differ for simple interest and compound interest.

Simple interest	Compound interest
At a constant annual rate of 5% simple interest, after 100 years the $10 account would have earned $50 in interest (100 x $0.50) and the total value of the investment would be $60.00.	At a constant annual rate of 5% compound interest, after 100 years the $10 investment would have earned $1,305.01 in interest and the total value of the investment would be $1,315.01.

The difference in interest earned from compound interest rather than simple interest would be $1,255.01 ($1,305.01 - $50.00).

The Rule of 72

Insurers can use a simple rule of thumb known as the Rule of 72 to estimate how fast a principal sum doubles at a specified compound interest rate. The Rule of 72 states that, for a known interest rate, under annual compounding, the approximate number of years for a principal sum to double is equal to 72 divided by the interest rate. The formula for using the Rule of 72 is shown below:

$$\text{Years to double} = 72 \div \text{Interest rate}$$

Suppose Steadfast deposits $100,000 into a money market account earning 10% interest, compounded annually. To find the approximate number of years it will take to double this investment, Steadfast divides 72 by 10, which is equal to 7.2 years.

If, instead of 10% interest, this investment earns 6% interest, compounded annually, it will take approximately 12 years (72 ÷ 6) for the investment to double.

The Rule of 72 can also help determine the rate of interest a principal sum must earn to double in a certain number of years. Manipulating the previous formula produces the following formula for the interest rate:

Interest rate = 72 ÷ Years to double

Steadfast doubled a principal sum in nine years. Using the formula for calculating the interest rate, Steadfast found that the investment had earned approximately 8% interest:

Interest rate = 72 ÷ 9 = 8.

The following table shows examples of Rule of 72 calculations for various rates of interest:

Interest rate, compounded annually	Approximate number of years to double a principal sum
2%	36.0
3%	24.0
4%	18.0
5%	14.4
6%	12.0
7%	10.3
8%	9.0
9%	8.0
10%	7.2

Nominal Interest and Effective Interest

Most investments quote interest rates without the effects of compounding. This kind of interest rate is known as a *nominal interest rate* because it is the named interest rate for a particular investment (nominal means "in name only"). In our discussion, when we specify an interest rate, we mean a nominal rate, unless otherwise noted. The type of interest rate that includes the effects of compounding is the *effective interest rate*. Because compounding produces greater interest earnings, the effective interest rate for a given investment is greater than the nominal interest rate if interest is compounded more frequently than annually. As Figure 4.3 illustrates, the more frequently the same interest rate is compounded for a given term, the greater the interest amount and the greater the corresponding effective interest rate.

The Investment Period

The longer an investment accumulates interest or other earnings, the greater the total value of the investment will be. Insurers rely heavily on this rule. Many insurance products are in force for years, and insurers invest the premiums from these products. Over a number of years, these investments can grow significantly.

The Time Value of Money

The relationships among payment amounts, interest, and time are explained by a concept known as the *time value of money*, which states that the value of a sum of money will change over time as a result of the effects of interest. According to the time value of money concept, a sum of money has both a present value and a future value.

- The *present value (PV)* of a sum of money is defined as the amount that, if invested at a specified interest rate on a specified date, would grow to equal a specified future amount. In simple terms, the present value of an investment is the principal—that is, the original amount invested before it is affected by interest.

- The *future value (FV)* of a sum of money is the amount that an original sum is expected to be worth at a specified future date, given a specified interest rate. In other words, the future value of an investment is the invested principal plus the accumulated earnings generated by the investment.

Figure 4.3. Effect of Compounding Frequency

Steadfast is considering investing $100,000 in one of several interest-bearing accounts. Each account offers a nominal interest rate of 10 percent, but each account uses a different compounding period. The effect of different compounding periods on the effective interest rate of this investment is shown below:

Account	Compounding Period	Times Compounded in One Year	Effective Interest Rate
A	Year	1	10.00000%
B	Quarter	4	10.38129%
C	Month	12	10.47131%
D	Week	52	10.50648%
E	Day	365	10.51558%
F	Hour	8,760	10.51703%
G	Minute	525,600	10.51709%

Account E, which offers daily compounding, has an effective interest rate that is more than half a percentage point higher than the effective interest rate for Account A, which offers annual compounding. In one year, therefore, Account E would credit Steadfast's investment of $100,000 with $515.58 more in interest than it would have earned from Account A.

Although all businesses use the concept of the time value of money, insurance companies depend to an unusual degree on accurate time value of money calculations. Life insurance and annuity products, after all, involve a legal promise of a financial benefit in the future in exchange for a customer's payment of a premium. In life insurance companies, the time value of money is applied to such decisions as whether to introduce a new product, lease equipment, purchase real estate, or invest in financial assets.

Calculating Future Values

Future values can be calculated for a single amount or for multiple amounts and for a single interest period or for multiple periods. Because interest is compounded, the interest periods used in future value calculations are called *compounding periods*.

Calculating the Future Value of a Single Amount for One Period

The simplest application of future values is an investment of a single amount for a single compounding period, which is equal to the principal plus the interest earned for one period. Analysts typically substitute present value (*PV*) for principal because, like principal, present value represents a sum of money before it is affected by interest. Therefore, the formula for calculating the future value (*FV*) of a single amount for one period is

$$FV = PV + \text{Interest earned}$$

For a one-year period, the amount of interest earned is equal to the present value multiplied by the interest rate, *i*. Because compounding only occurs when money is held for more than one period, a value for the number of interest periods, *n*, is not specified. The formula for the interest earned on a one-year investment can be expressed as follows:

$$\text{Interest earned} = PV \times i$$

Incorporating the formula for interest into the basic future value formula results in the following equation:

$$\text{Future value} = \text{Present value} + \text{Interest earned}$$
$$FV = PV + (PV \times i)$$

We can simplify that equation by factoring out the common multiplier *PV* on the right-hand side.

$$FV = PV \times (1 + i)$$

> Steadfast deposited $100,000 into an account that earns 5% interest, compounded annually, for one year. The future value of this investment is found as follows:
>
> $$\begin{aligned} FV &= PV \times (1 + i) \\ &= \$100{,}000 \times (1 + 0.05) \\ &= \$100{,}000 \times (1.05) \\ &= \$105{,}000 \end{aligned}$$

Calculating the Future Value of a Single Amount for Multiple Periods

When a single amount is invested for more than one interest period, the interest is compounded—that is, the present value is multiplied by one plus the interest rate for each interest period n. The general formula for finding the future value of an investment earning compound interest, i, for n periods, can be written as:

$$FV = PV \times (1 + i)^n$$

> Suppose that Steadfast deposited $100,000 into an account that earns 5% interest, compounded annually, for 2 years. Because there are two interest periods in this calculation, the future value of Steadfast's initial investment is equal to
>
> $$FV = \$100{,}000 \times (1.05)^2$$
> $$= \$100{,}000 \times [(1.05)(1.05)]$$

The small "2" in this equation is an exponent—it indicates that the base value of 1.05 is raised to the second power, or multiplied once by itself.

Steadfast could manually calculate the future value of this investment fairly easily. The amount of interest earned for the first year is equal to the principal multiplied by the interest rate, or $5,000 ($100,000 × 0.05 = $5,000). The amount of interest earned for the second year is equal to the accumulated balance of $105,000 multiplied by the interest rate of 5%, or $5,250 ($105,000 × 0.05 = $5,250). The future value of Steadfast's investment at the end of two years, therefore, is equal to the principal (PV = $100,000) plus the total interest of $10,250, or $110,250.

Calculating future values manually for long investment periods is much more complicated. In practice, analysts use calculators or spreadsheets with built-in functions that calculate these values. For educational purposes, we will show you how to derive these values using tables that include future value interest factors for a wide range of interest rates (i) and interest periods (n). A *future value interest factor (FVIF)* is the future value of $1.00 at a given interest rate for a stated number of periods. For example, the *FVIF* for $1.00 invested for n periods at interest rate i appears as $FVIF(n, i)$. Figure 4.4 shows a portion of an *FVIF* table with three interest periods and four interest rates. According to this table, the future value of $100,000, earning 5% interest for 2 years, is equal to $100,000 × *FVIF* (2,5%) = $100,000 × 1.103 = $110,300. The $50 difference between the future value calculated manually and the future value taken from the *FVIF* table is due to rounding.

Figure 4.4. *FVIF* Table

Note that all of the numbers in an *FVIF* table are greater than 1.

Period (*n*)	Interest Rate (*i*)			
	1%	2%	5%	10%
1	1.010	1.020	1.050	1.100
2	1.020	1.040	1.103	1.210
3	1.030	1.061	1.158	1.331

It's also possible to calculate future values for interest rates that are compounded more than once each year, such as semiannually, quarterly, or monthly. In simple terms, the calculation involves

- Multiplying the number of years during which a sum is invested by the number of compounding periods per year to determine the number of compounding periods

> For example, an investment earning interest compounded quarterly over a period of five years would have 20 compounding periods (5 years × 4 periods per year = 20 periods).

- Dividing the stated annual interest rate by the number of compounding periods per year to determine the interest rate for each compounding period

> For example, a 10% interest rate compounded quarterly would result in an interest rate of 2.5% per quarter (10% ÷ 4 = 2.5%).

- Using the equation $FV = PV \times (1 + i)^n$ to calculate the future value of the investment

> For example, the future value of $100 invested at 10%, compounded quarterly for five years, is equal to $100 × $(1.025)^{20}$. Using values from an *FVIF* table, this amount becomes $100 × (1.639), or $163.90.

The Future Value of an Annuity

Insurance companies and other investors often need to calculate the future value of an investment that involves a series of payments. Financial analysts refer to any series of equal payments made at regular intervals over a specified period of time as an **annuity**. It's important to note three facts about an annuity as it is used to describe future values:

- An annuity is not the same as an annuity contract, and the formulas used to calculate the values of an annuity are valid without any reference to an actual annuity contract.

- An annuity can refer to any series of payments that are *equal* in amount and paid at *regular* intervals. However, an annuity does *not* include a series of unequal payments or payments made at irregular intervals.

- An annuity can refer to payments received by an insurer or other investor or to payments made by an investor. For example, premiums received by an insurer from policyowners and annuity income payments made by an insurer to contract owners are both examples of annuities.

Annuities can be classified according to when each periodic payment occurs.

- If periodic payments are made at the *end* of each payment period, the annuity is called an ***ordinary annuity***. A series of paychecks an employee receives at the end of each month or a series of interest payments on a bond are examples of an ordinary annuity.

- If periodic payments are made at the *beginning* of each payment period, the annuity is called an ***annuity due***. A series of rent payments made at the beginning of each month or a series of premiums for a whole life insurance policy paid at the first of each year are examples of an annuity due. Figure 4.5 summarizes the characteristics of ordinary annuities and annuities due.

Figure 4.6 shows timelines for payments made for an ordinary annuity and an annuity due over a three-year period. Because of the difference in the timing of the payments, the future value of an annuity due is equal to the future value of a corresponding ordinary annuity of one additional period, minus the amount of one payment.

Analysts have developed future value interest factors for annuities to simplify calculations, particularly for annuities with large numbers of payments and compounding periods. These compound interest factors, which are combined into tables, are called *future value interest factors for an annuity (FVIFAs)*. As with *FVIFs*, you can also use calculators and spreadsheets to calculate these values.

Figure 4.5. Ordinary Annuity and Annuity Due

	Ordinary Annuity	Annuity Due
Definition	A stream of periodic payments for which each payment occurs at the *end* of each payment period	A stream of periodic payments for which each payment occurs at the *beginning* of each payment period
Examples	A series of paychecks an employee receives after the work periods have been completed A series of bond interest payments in which the first interest payment occurs one period after the bond is issued	A series of rent payments A level series of whole life insurance premiums

Figure 4.6. Time Lines for the Future Value of an Ordinary Annuity and an Annuity Due

The following time line represents the future value of an ordinary annuity of $100 per year for three years. Note that, for an ordinary annuity, the first payment does not occur until the end of year 1. Therefore, the first payment earns interest for only two years. The second payment earns interest for only one year, and the third and final payment earns no interest.

Future Value—Ordinary Annuity

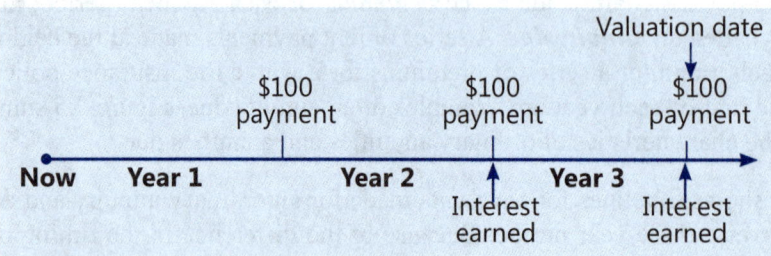

The following time line represents the future value of an annuity due of $100 per year for three years. For an annuity due, the first payment occurs at the beginning of the first year. Therefore, the first payment earns interest in each of the three periods. The second payment earns interest for two years, and the third payment earns interest for one year.

Future Value—Annuity Due

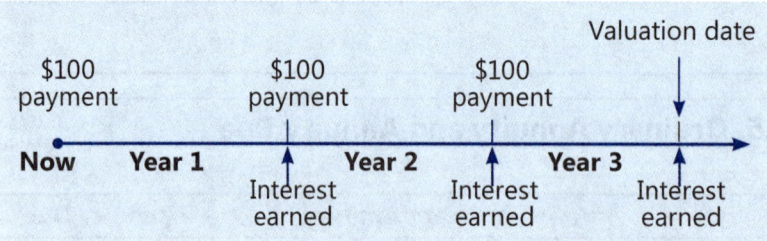

Calculating Present Values

In certain situations, investors have a specific investment goal and a specific investment period in mind and are interested in determining how much they will need to invest now in order to have the targeted amount at the end of the period. For example, a person might know that she wants to accumulate $1,000,000 by the time she retires at age 65. Similarly, an insurer might know that it will need $1,000,000 at the end of five years to repay a commercial loan. The question is, how much must be invested now to accumulate the expected amount in the future? Present value calculations provide a way to answer that question. As is the case with future values, present values can be calculated for a single amount over one or more interest periods or for an annuity.

Calculating the Present Value of a Single Amount for One Period

The basic formula for calculating the future value of a one-period investment at a given interest rate, i, when the present value is known, is:

$$FV = PV \times (1 + i)$$

We can determine the present value of a given future value by dividing both sides of the future value equation by the expression $(1 + i)$. The general formula for the present value of a single amount for a single period, therefore, is

$$PV = \frac{FV}{(1 + i)}$$

or

$$PV = FV \times \frac{1}{(1 + i)}$$

In effect, present value calculations reverse the compounding process. As a result, finding present values is often referred to as *discounting*.

Suppose Steadfast wants to know the amount of money it needs to invest today at 5% interest, compounded annually, in order to have $1,050,000 one year from today. Using $1,050,000 as *FV* and 1.05 for $(1 + i)$ in the *PV* equation, Steadfast determines that its initial investment should be $1,000,020:

$$PV = \$1,050,000 \times (1 \div 1.05)$$
$$= \$1,050,000 \times 0.9524$$
$$= \$1,000,020$$

Dividing 1 by 1.05 results in an answer of 0.95238. If this number had been used instead of rounding to 0.9524, the *PV* would have been exactly $1,000,000.

Calculating the Present Value of a Single Amount for Multiple Periods

In our discussion of future values, we showed how the formula for calculating the future value of a single amount for a single period can be modified for multiple compounding periods:

$$FV = PV \times (1 + i)^n$$

We can adapt our general present value formula in the same way. If the equation for the present value of a single amount for one period is equal to

$$PV = FV \times \frac{1}{(1 + i)}$$

Then the equation for two periods is equal to

$$PV = FV \times \frac{1}{(1 + i)^2}$$

The exponent "2" in this equation indicates that the base value of $(1 + i)$ is raised to the second power.

Suppose Steadfast wants to have $100,000 two years from today. At a 5% interest rate, the present value of this amount is equal to:

$$PV = \$100{,}000 \times [1 \div (1.05)(1.05)]$$
$$= \$100{,}000 \times 0.9070$$
$$= \$90{,}700$$

Extending this process over n periods produces the following general formula for calculating the present value of a single amount for multiple periods:

$$PV = FV \times \frac{1}{(1 + i)^n}$$

As with future values, analysts use calculators and spreadsheets to calculate present values. So that you can see how the process works, we will show the calculation of present values by using tables containing present value interest factors. A *present value interest factor (PVIF)* is the present value of $1.00 discounted at an interest rate of i percent per period for n periods. Figure 4.7 presents a portion of a *PVIF* table.

Figure 4.7. *PVIF* Table

Note that all of the numbers in a *PVIF* table are less than 1.

Period (n)	Interest Rate (i)			
	1%	2%	5%	10%
1	0.990	0.980	0.952	0.909
2	0.980	0.961	0.907	0.826
3	0.971	0.942	0.864	0.751

We can use the *PVIF* table to determine the present value of the $100,000 future amount from our earlier example, as follows:

$$PV = \$100,000 \times PVIF(2, 5\%)$$
$$= \$100,000 \times 0.907$$
$$= \$90,700$$

The present value of $90,700 calculated using the *PVIF* table is the same as the amount we calculated earlier.

As with future values, you can calculate present values for interest rates that are compounded more frequently than annually.

Steadfast needs to know how much money to invest now in order to have $1,000,000 three years from today. This investment will earn 6% interest, compounded semiannually. The formula for the present value of a single sum is:

$$PV = FV \times [1 \div (1 + i)^n]$$

Steadfast finds the value for *n* in this formula by multiplying the number of years—3—by the number of compounding periods per year—2.

$$n = 3 \times 2 = 6$$

The value for *i* is found by dividing the interest rate of 6% by the number of compounding periods per year—which is 2 in this case.

$$i = 6\% \div 2 = 3\%$$

Now all Steadfast has to do is plug the numbers into the formula:

$$PV = \$1,000,000 \times [1 \div (1 + 0.03)^6]$$
$$= \$1,000,000 \times [1 \div (1.03)^6]$$
$$= \$1,000,000 \times [1 \div (1.194)]$$
$$= \$1,000,000 \times 0.838$$
$$= \$838,000$$

So, Steadfast needs to invest $838,000 today, at 6% interest compounded semiannually, in order to have $1,000,000 three years from today.

The Present Value of an Annuity

Insurance companies often need to calculate the amount that must be invested now in order to provide for a specified, regularly spaced series of equal future payments, given a specified interest rate and a specified number of periods. In such cases, the value being calculated is the present value of an annuity. The present value of an annuity is equal to the sum of the present values of the separate periodic payments.

The present value of an annuity, like the future value of an annuity, can be calculated for both an ordinary annuity and an annuity due. Figure 4.8 shows the time lines for the present value of an ordinary annuity and an annuity due.

In addition, just as with future values, analysts have developed present value interest factors for annuities to simplify calculations, particularly for annuities with large numbers of payments and compounding periods. These compound factors, which are combined into tables, are called *present value interest factors for an annuity (PVIFAs)*. As with *PVIFs*, you can also use calculators and spreadsheets to calculate these values.

Figure 4.8. Time Lines for the Present Value of an Ordinary Annuity and an Annuity Due

The following time line represents the present value of an ordinary annuity of $100 per year for three years. Note that, for an ordinary annuity, the valuation date for the present value occurs at the beginning of the first period, which is one period before the first payment is made.

Present Value—Ordinary Annuity

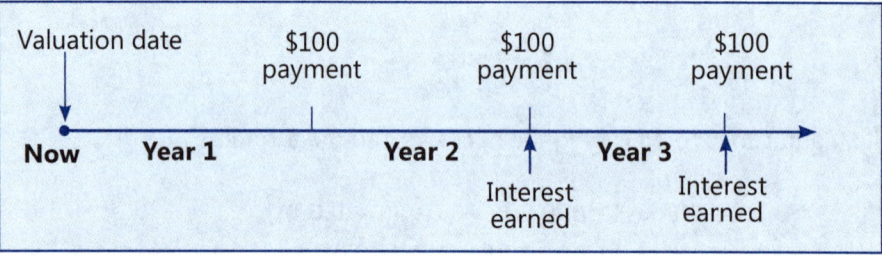

The following time line represents the present value of an annuity due of $100 per year for three years. Note that, for an annuity due, the valuation date for the present value occurs at the beginning of the first period, which is also the date on which the first payment is made.

Present Value—Annuity Due

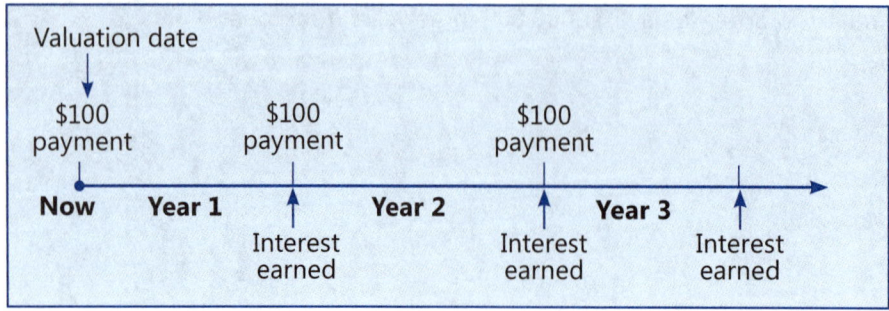

Important Insurer Applications of Present Values

Insurers use *PVIFs* and *PVIFAs* to determine the prices of one of their most important investments—bonds. You may recall that a bond provides periodic interest payments along with the payment of the bond's par value upon maturity. Therefore, in determining the price to pay for a bond, an insurer must calculate two present values:

- The present value of the bond's coupon payments, which represents the present value of an ordinary annuity

- The present value of the bond's par value, which is the present value of a single payment

Steadfast is considering purchasing a 20-year, 9.5% bond with a par value of $100,000. Current market interest rates are 10%, so Steadfast wants to calculate the price it should pay in order to earn a 10% return on the bond. The bond's annual coupon is $9,500 ($100,000 × 0.095). The bond's price is calculated as follows:

$$\text{Bond price} = (\$9{,}500 \times \textit{PVIFA for 10\% and 20 years}) +$$
$$(\$100{,}000 \times \textit{PVIF for 10\% and 20 years})$$

$$= (\$9{,}500 \times 8.514) + (\$100{,}000 \times 0.149)$$

$$= \$80{,}883 + \$14{,}900$$

$$= \$95{,}783$$

In this situation, Steadfast should be willing to pay $95,783 for this bond. At that price, Steadfast will earn a 10% return on the bond.

For simplicity, we assumed that the coupon payments on this bond were made on an annual basis. In practice, most bonds make coupon payments on a semiannual basis.

Insurers can also use present values to evaluate their stock investments. For example, an insurer can calculate the present value of a share of stock by calculating the present value of the stock's projected future dividend payments and then adding to this value the present value of the stock's projected future sales price. Note that this process is similar to the one used to evaluate a bond price.

General Rules Governing Future Values and Present Values

A number of general rules describe the effects of the interest rate, the type of interest, and the length of the interest period on the future and present value of a sum of money invested at interest.

- *RULE:* The future value of a sum of money invested at interest is always more than the present value of that sum.

As we stated earlier, the future value of a sum of money is equal to the principal invested plus accumulated interest earnings. Although interest rates can increase or decrease over time, interest earnings are always positive. Therefore, when a sum of money is invested at interest, the future value of the sum is always greater than its present value.

> Suppose a person invests $1,000 today for one year at a 4% interest rate. At the end of the year, the original sum will have earned $40 in interest:
>
> $$\$1,000 \times 0.04 = \$40$$
>
> The value of the investment at the end of the year, therefore, will be equal to $1,040:
>
> $$\$1,000 + \$40 = \$1,040$$

The reverse of the previous statement is also true: the present value of a sum of money invested at interest is always less than the future value of the sum. This relationship between present value and future value holds true regardless of the interest rate or the length of the interest period.

■   *RULE:* Changes in the interest rate or interest period will cause changes in the future value and the present value of a sum of money.

If the present value of a sum of money remains constant, then an increase in the interest rate will result in an increase in the future value of the sum. Conversely, a decrease in the interest rate will result in a decrease in the future value.

> At 4% interest, our $1,000 investment was worth $1,040 at the end of one year. If the sum had been invested at 5% interest, the value of the sum at the end of one year would be equal to $1,050:
>
> $$\$1,000 + (\$1,000 \times 0.05) = \$1,050$$
>
> If the sum had been invested at 3% interest, the future value at the end of the year would be equal to $1,030:
>
> $$\$1,000 + (\$1,000 \times 0.03) = \$1,030$$

Increasing the interest period also increases the future value, while decreasing the interest period will decrease the future value.

> At the end of one year, our original $1,000, invested at 4% interest, was equal to $1,040. If we leave our money invested for another year, it will earn an additional $41.60:
>
> $$\$1,040 \times 0.04 = \$41.60$$
>
> The amount of interest in the second year is greater than the amount of interest in the first year because of the effects of compounding. Our total investment at the end of year two, therefore, will be $1,081.60:
>
> $$\$1,000.00 + \$40.00 + \$41.60 = \$1,081.60$$

Changes in interest rates have the opposite effect on present values. That is, if the future value of a sum of money remains constant, then an increase in the interest rate will result in a decrease in the present value of the sum, while a decrease in the interest rate will cause an increase in the present value.

> Assume that $1,000 is the future value, one year from today, of an investment you must make today. At an interest rate of 4%, you would need to invest $961.54 now:
>
> $$\$1,000 \div 1.04 = \$961.54$$
>
> Now assume you can earn 5% on this investment. The present value will be less than it was for the 4% interest rate:
>
> $$\$1,000 \div 1.05 = \$952.38$$
>
> Finally, assume you can earn only 3% on this investment. The present value will be more than it was for both the 4% and the 5% interest rate:
>
> $$\$1,000 \div 1.03 = \$970.87$$

Similarly, an increase in the interest period will cause a decrease in the present value, while a decrease in the interest period will cause an increase in the present value.

> We saw in the above example that the present value of $1,000 at 5% interest for one year is equal to $952.38. If, instead of one year, the time period is increased to five years, the present value will be less than it was for one year:
>
> $$\$1,000 \div (1.05)^5 = \$783.53$$
>
> If, instead of five years, the time period is decreased to three years, the present value will be greater than it was for five years:
>
> $$\$1,000 \div (1.05)^3 = \$863.84$$

Figure 4.9 summarizes the effects on present values and future values of increases and decreases in interest rates and interest periods.

- **RULE:** A given present value can have any number of future values, and a given future value can have any number of present values.

Present values and future values are affected by the amount of the change in the interest rate or the interest period as well as by the direction of the change in these factors. Each incremental increase or decrease in the interest rate and the interest period produces a different future value for a given present value. Each incremental change in the interest rate or interest period also produces a different present value for a given future value.

- **RULE:** The timing of cash flows affects their present value and future value.

Not all investments involve a single principal payment. In addition, not all the money paid into an investment remains in the investment for the entire interest period. For example, life insurance policies often involve periodic premium payments over the life of the policy; or a contract owner may withdraw funds from

Figure 4.9. Rules for Understanding the Time Value of Money

Principal Sum

Because a principal sum invested at interest grows over time, the principal's

- *Present value* is less than its future value
- *Future value* is greater than its present value

Interest Rate

Because an interest rate is a rate of growth, for money earning a stated rate of interest for a specified period, an increase in the interest rate will result in

- A decrease in the *present value*
- An increase in the *future value*

Conversely, a decrease in the interest rate will result in

- An increase in the *present value*
- A decrease in the *future value*

Number of Periods

Because compound interest is paid periodically, for money earning a stated rate of interest for a specified period, an increase in the number of specified periods will result in

- A decrease in the *present value*
- An increase in the *future value*

Conversely, a decrease in the number of specified periods will result in

- An increase in the *present value*
- A decrease in the *future value*

a deferred annuity contract before the contract matures. The present value and future value of multiple cash flows depend on when cash is paid into an account and how long it remains in the account.

- **RULE:** Present value and future value are mathematically linked.

Any amount of money invested today has a future value that is equal to the present value of the investment plus accumulated interest. Similarly, any amount of money payable in the future has a present value that is equal to the future amount minus accumulated interest. Therefore, a person who knows the present value of a sum of money invested at a specified interest rate can calculate the future value of that sum, and a person who knows the future value of a sum of money invested at a specified interest rate can calculate the present value of the sum.

Key Terms

technical product design	compound interest
cost of benefits	nominal interest rate
mortality	effective interest rate
interest spread	time value of money
basis point (bp)	present value (PV)
model	future value (FV)
adverse deviation	future value interest factor ($FVIF$)
favorable deviation	annuity
interest rate	ordinary annuity
principal	annuity due
simple interest	present value interest factor ($PVIF$)

Chapter 5

Achieving Operating Efficiency

Objectives:

After studying this chapter, you should be able to

- Describe examples of insurance company expenses, such as investment expenses, expenses for contractual benefits, operating expenses, controllable and noncontrollable expenses, direct and indirect expenses, and fixed and variable expenses

- Describe how insurance companies use rightsizing, outsourcing, information technology, and remote work arrangements to eliminate or reduce general operating expenses

- Explain how insurers manage commission expenses for life insurance and annuity products

- Describe how insurers can use benchmarking, total quality management (TQM), Six Sigma, lean management, and business process reengineering (BPR) to improve operating efficiency

Outline

Overview of Insurer Expenses
- Investment Expenses
- General and Administrative Expenses

Managing General Operating Expenses
- Eliminating Expenses
- Reducing Expenses

Managing Marketing and Distribution Expenses
- Managing Commissions for Life Insurance Sales
- Managing Commissions for Annuity Sales

Methods for Improving Operating Efficiency
- Benchmarking
- Total Quality Management
- Six Sigma
- Lean Management
- Business Process Reengineering

The Employee's Role in Supporting Operating Efficiency

Y ou've probably heard the saying that "you need to spend money to make money." This statement is as true for insurance companies as it is for other businesses: insurers have to spend money—on commissions, salaries, advertising—in order to earn profits. A balancing act exists here, however—and that's where operating efficiency comes in. Basically, operating efficiency is a company's ability to generate revenue while keeping expenses at a reasonable level.

Overview of Insurer Expenses

Expenses are amounts that a company spends in the course of conducting business. To manage their expenses, insurers need a systematic way of recording and classifying those expenses. *Cost accumulation* is the process of capturing all of a company's costs and categorizing them in meaningful ways. For cost accumulation, insurance company expenses are divided into two main categories: (1) investment expenses and (2) general and administrative expenses. These categories are described in Figure 5.1.

Investment Expenses

For life insurance companies, *investment expenses* are the costs associated with investing the company's assets. Examples of investment expenses include the costs of analyzing investment opportunities, purchasing assets, selling assets, and servicing assets.

General and Administrative Expenses

An insurance company's noninvestment expenses are classified as *general and administrative expenses*—the expenses that result from undertaking normal business activities to generate sales of products and to support products. Insurance company general and administrative expenses can be subdivided into (1) expenses for contractual benefits and (2) operating expenses.

Figure 5.1. Classification of Insurance Company Expenses

Investment Expenses

Costs associated with investing the insurer's assets

General and Administrative Expenses

Costs incurred as a result of undertaking normal business activities to generate sales and to support products

- **Expenses for Contractual Benefits**
  Costs of paying contractual obligations to customers

- **Operating Expenses**
  Costs of operations other than expenses for contractual benefits; include development expenses, acquisition expenses, maintenance expenses, and overhead expenses

Expenses for contractual benefits are the total amount that an insurer must pay to fulfill the terms of its insurance and annuity contracts. *Operating expenses* are the costs of operations other than expenses for contractual benefits. Insurers typically track four important types of operating expenses:

- *Development expenses* for insurance and annuity products are the expenses an insurer incurs in designing, testing, and implementing a new product or product line.

Development expenses include costs associated with

- Designing and pricing new products
- Purchasing or designing new administrative software or systems
- Obtaining regulatory approval for new products
- Creating product brochures and sales information
- Developing customer and/or trade promotions

All development expenses are incurred before a new product or service is introduced to the market.

- *Acquisition expenses* for insurance and annuity products are the expenses an insurer incurs to obtain and issue new business. Pre-issue expenses are incurred before policies are issued and are not dependent on sales. Post-issue expenses are incurred at the time of or after a policy sale.

Pre-issue acquisition expenses include costs for	*Post-issue* acquisition expenses include costs for
■ Underwriting applications	■ Preparing new contracts and establishing customer records
■ Establishing investment accounts for variable products	■ Issuing contracts
■ Training sales producers and customer service representatives	■ Paying first-year commissions

Some companies combine pre-issue and post-issue expenses into a single acquisition expense category. Other companies classify only pre-issue expenses as acquisition expenses. For these companies, expenses incurred at the time of or after contract sale are classified as maintenance expenses.

■ *Maintenance expenses*, also known as *renewal expenses*, are the product-related expenses an insurer incurs while a contract is in force. For companies that classify all pre-issue and post-issue expenses as acquisition expenses, maintenance expenses include only those expenses incurred after the first year a contract is in force.

Maintenance expenses include costs for

- Renewal/trail commissions
- Premium taxes
- Changes to customer records
- Transaction processing
- Customer service activities
- Preparation and distribution of required communications, such as account statements, prospectuses, performance reports, proxies, and transaction processing

■ *Overhead expenses* are the costs an insurer incurs during normal business operations that are not directly connected to a specific product or service.

Overhead expenses include costs for

- Agency support
- Furniture and equipment
- Utilities
- Systems support
- General legal services
- General actuarial analyses
- Accounting services
- Taxes
- Licensing fees

For expense control purposes, operating expenses can be divided further into controllable and noncontrollable expenses, direct and indirect expenses, and variable and fixed expenses.

Controllable and Noncontrollable Expenses

Although an argument can be made that, in the long run, all expenses are controllable to some extent, an insurer can control some expenses more than others. A *controllable expense* is a cost over which a specified manager or organizational unit has power and influence.

> Advertising is essential for creating awareness and interest for new insurance products and services. The costs associated with advertising, however, vary widely according to the type of media used. For example, a 30-second advertisement on national TV can cost $500,000 or more. An advertisement with similar content can be placed in a magazine or newspaper for a fraction of that cost. An insurer can control advertising expenses by selecting the media that provide the greatest value at the lowest cost.

Other examples of controllable expenses are the costs of technology purchases, overtime compensation, accounting services, and various other administrative services.

A *noncontrollable expense* is a cost over which no specified manager or organizational unit has power or influence.

> Most jurisdictions require insurers to obtain a license in each jurisdiction in which they intend to conduct business. The cost of the license is set by the regulatory authority in the jurisdiction and is non-negotiable. The insurer has no choice but to pay the established fee.

Other noncontrollable expenses include depreciation on equipment and taxes.

The ability to differentiate controllable from noncontrollable expenses is important because an insurer can reduce controllable expenses to improve its operating efficiency.

Direct and Indirect Expenses

Direct expenses, also known as *traceable costs*, are product expenses incurred for or physically traceable to a specified life insurance or annuity product. Assigning direct expenses to a particular product is straightforward.

> A sales commission expense is a direct expense. When a sales producer sells a whole life insurance policy, the insurer's commission expense is assigned to that whole life insurance product.

Indirect expenses, also called *common costs*, are expenses that cannot be traced to or that aren't incurred for one specific product. Indirect expenses result from activities that relate to several or all of an insurer's products. An insurer incurs the same level of indirect expenses whether or not it offers a specific product.

> Insurance companies typically use the same accounting system to manage information for all the company's business units. The costs of establishing and maintaining the accounting system are not directly attributable to the operation of any one business unit or product. If an insurer stopped maintaining its group life insurance product line by transferring that business to another insurer, the costs associated with maintaining and operating the company's accounting system would remain essentially the same.

Figure 5.2 shows examples of direct and indirect expenses.

Variable and Fixed Expenses

An expense amount that varies in direct proportion to some variation in a specified level of operating activity is a *variable expense*. Some variable expenses vary according to the number of policies sold. Other variable expenses vary according to a particular contract feature, such as premium collected or unit of coverage. Policy issue expenses typically are expressed as a dollar amount per contract; commissions are expressed as a percentage of the premium; and medical examination costs are expressed as a dollar amount per unit of coverage.

Some variable expenses are *step functions* so that instead of increasing dollar for dollar with business volume, these expenses increase with every block of contracts sold. For example, a company might need to add a new employee salary for every 10,000 contracts sold.

A *fixed expense* is an expense that remains relatively constant regardless of the number of policies sold or some other measure of the level of operating activity. Figure 5.3 gives examples of variable and fixed expenses for insurance companies. In looking at these examples, you'll see that many fixed expenses are indirect expenses, and many variable expenses are direct expenses.

Figure 5.2. Direct and Indirect Expenses

	Direct Expenses	**Indirect Expenses**
Definitions	Product expenses incurred for or physically traceable to one specific product	Expenses that cannot be traced to or that are not incurred for one specific product
Examples	■ Producers' commissions ■ Issue expenses ■ Transaction processing expenses ■ Premium taxes, for most products ■ Product development expenses	■ Some information systems expenses ■ Accounting expenses ■ Executive compensation ■ Rent ■ Property taxes ■ Mailroom costs

Figure 5.3. Variable and Fixed Expenses

	Variable Expenses	Fixed Expenses
Definitions	Expenses that vary in direct proportion to some variation in a specified level of operating activity	Expenses that remain relatively constant regardless of the number of contracts sold or some other measure of the level of operating activity
Examples	■ Producers' commissions ■ Premium accounting ■ Policy issue costs ■ Premium taxes ■ Transaction processing costs	■ Executive salaries ■ Rent ■ Property taxes ■ Marketing research and advertising ■ Office equipment

Keep in mind that, even though fixed expenses don't vary with the number of policies sold, the amounts of these expenses can change, especially over a long period of time. For example, payments for salaries, rent, and services such as marketing research tend to increase from year to year along with increases in the cost of living. However, these changes generally aren't the result of the number of contracts sold or changes in operating activity.

Managing General Operating Expenses

Ongoing expenses that aren't properly controlled can have a negative effect on an insurance company's profitability. In fact, the higher an insurer's expenses are in relation to its revenues, the greater the risk that the insurer will fail to achieve its financial goals. In general, insurers can take one of two approaches to controlling operating expenses:

■ Eliminating expenses

■ Reducing expenses

Eliminating Expenses

An insurer can eliminate expenses by eliminating certain operations or functions. For example, a company that spins off or discontinues certain lines of business or closes selected field offices eliminates the expenses associated with maintaining those operations. Expenses can also be eliminated through rightsizing. *Rightsizing*, also known as *downsizing*, is the elimination of nonessential employees or jobs within an organization.

To be successful, rightsizing must be accompanied by careful redesign of work processes to determine the number and type of employee positions that are essential for effective business operations. Some rightsizing can be achieved through attrition, which occurs when a company purposefully elects to not replace employees who leave their jobs because of retirement, resignation, death, or disability. Additional methods that companies can use to eliminate employee positions include early retirement programs and layoffs.

Reducing Expenses

Companies can reduce expenses by finding more cost-effective ways to perform certain functions. For example, instead of having producers complete detailed applications in person, an insurer can have home office employees gather detailed underwriting information from proposed insureds by phone. Companies can also reduce operating expenses by outsourcing certain functions, using information technology to automate certain processes, or implementing remote work options such as telecommuting.

Outsourcing Operational Functions

Outsourcing is the practice of hiring an external vendor to perform specified operations. An outsourcing arrangement may cover all or only part of the functions for an operational area. For example, an insurance company might outsource its entire claim administration operation, or it might outsource only claim investigation and perform all other claim administration processes in-house. Operations that life insurance companies commonly outsource include

- Information technology functions

- Investment management functions

- Life insurance claim administration functions, such as claim investigation and claim processing

- Customer service functions, such as call center operations and premium billing and collection

- Human resource functions, such as payroll and benefits processing

Often, vendors can perform certain jobs at a lower cost to the insurer than can the insurer's employees. Before deciding whether to outsource a particular operation, an insurer evaluates the expected benefits and drawbacks associated with outsourcing that operation. The insurer generally considers the following factors:

- **The insurer's own ability to perform the operation efficiently, effectively, and cost-effectively**. External vendors tend to specialize in certain business functions, and their expertise often allows them to perform these functions faster, better, and/or less expensively than can the insurer.

- **The importance of immediate implementation**. If timing is critical, outsourcing the function to an external vendor that already has the necessary human resources, technology, and procedures in place can minimize delays and reduce costs.

- **The availability of start-up capital**. The start-up costs associated with new operations are often substantial. An insurer can relieve this strain by outsourcing capital-intensive functions to external vendors.

- **The importance of control over the operation**. When an insurer outsources a business function, it relinquishes some control over the day-to-day performance of that function. Before outsourcing the function, the insurer should weigh this loss of control against the savings in time and money offered by outsourcing.

Using Information Technology (IT)

An insurance company's information technology (IT) function develops and maintains the company's computer systems and oversees information management throughout the company. It also can support a company's efforts to improve operating efficiency. Although establishing IT systems can involve significant up-front costs, once implemented, they can eventually pay for themselves through ongoing reductions in expenses.

One important use of IT for insurers is electronic commerce (e-commerce), which is the use of the Internet and other computer networks to deliver commercial information and to facilitate business transactions, including the delivery of products and services. By performing certain functions electronically rather than by hand, companies can deliver service to customers wherever and whenever customers need it. In addition, IT systems can perform many functions faster and more accurately than humans can. In most cases, greater speed and accuracy translate into better service for customers and reduced costs for the insurer.

A more recent application of IT is *straight-through processing*, or *end-to-end processing*, which is designed to automate the steps in industry-specific transactions electronically, with little or no manual intervention. Insurance companies are currently investigating the use of straight-through processing as a way to automate the new business process, from application to policy issue. The primary advantages of straight-through processing are that it

- **Improves service turnaround time**. Manual new business processing methods are both paper- and time-intensive. Performing these functions electronically can significantly reduce the time required to perform them.

- **Reduces costs**. Electronic processing is generally cheaper than manual processing.

- **Enhances service quality**. Straight-through processing systems can be programmed to automatically flag missing or incorrect information, thereby reducing processing errors and improving processing time.

- **Increases customer satisfaction**. Insurance customers and producers have come to expect fast, accurate service. An insurer that can reduce the time needed to process and deliver policies and pay commissions can increase the satisfaction and retention of valuable customers and producers.

- **Facilitates regulatory compliance**. Because straight-through processing reduces the amount of data that must be re-keyed, it increases the likelihood that the data reported to regulators for compliance purposes is accurate.

Remote Work Arrangements

In recent years, U.S. life insurance companies have begun to experiment with remote-work arrangements as a means of cutting expenses. These arrangements include part-time and full-time telecommuting, hoteling, and virtual workplaces.

Telecommuting is a remote work arrangement that gives employees the flexibility to determine their working location and hours. Today, over 50 million Americans telecommute at least part of the time. Under a typical telecommuting arrangement, employees work at home using either their own computer and telephone equipment or equipment provided by their employer. Teleworkers also are given access to the information and tools they need to do their jobs, such as conference calling, video conferencing, specialized software programs, and private networks.

In recent years, an increasing number of U.S. life insurers have begun to offer telecommuting arrangements for certain employee groups. For example, insurers often offer telecommuting to their underwriting staff. Several companies are also allowing their customer service staff to have this option. In addition, many companies that don't offer telecommuting at the present time are considering it for the future as a cost-saving measure.

From an insurer's perspective, telecommuting has important advantages:

- The insurer can continue to operate, even under emergency conditions. For example, an insurer that gives its employees work-at-home privileges may be able to continue to operate during a catastrophic event such as a hurricane, terrorist attack, or pandemic.

- The insurer may be able to attract talented employees who need the work-at-home option.

- The insurer may be able to cut back on its workspace. With more employees working outside the company, companies need to maintain fewer dedicated workspaces and can therefore save on the overall cost of office space.

- If the insurer is also flexible about work hours, productivity could be enhanced, as employees can pick the hours to work when they are most productive.

- The insurer may receive tax benefits for offering work-at-home arrangements. Some states offer employers a tax credit for telecommuting arrangements.

Studies indicate that full-time telecommuting can save a company as much as $20,000 per employee. Telecommuting is also cost-effective for employees, who can save thousands of dollars in travel and work costs.

Telecommuting is not appropriate for all kinds of jobs, however. Allowing employees to work at home all the time can have disadvantages. For example, employees may feel cut off from their fellow employees if they never come in to the office. A company may decide to strike a balance by allowing telecommuting only part of the time.

As an alternative to having employees work at home on a full-time basis, some insurers are using *hoteling* to accommodate part-time telecommuters. Under this approach, a company provides personal workspaces only for those employees who work exclusively at company offices. It provides additional shared offices, or *hotels*, for those employees who come in to the office on an irregular basis. Each hotel is used by groups of people—who come in to the office at different times—

rather than by just one person. Companies often manage hotel usage by requiring employees to reserve space in advance.

Another option some companies are using is *virtual workplaces*, which are remote offices where employees can perform their jobs in an office setting rather than at home. For example, some companies have established offices, known as *telework centers*, located in places where large numbers of telecommuters live. Each center is equipped with a full range of office equipment and high-speed Internet connections. Another example of a virtual workplace is a *remote office center*. Such a center is similar to a telework center, except that a remote office center is available to employees from more than one company, usually through a leasing arrangement with the office center owner.

Managing Marketing and Distribution Expenses

For a typical insurance company, producer compensation is one of the company's biggest operating expenses. Although reducing compensation expenses might seem like a good way to improve operating efficiency, reducing commissions may cause independent producers to switch to other companies—and take policy sales and income with them. Compensation is one area in which insurers definitely need to "spend money to make money." Insurers, therefore, generally focus on managing rather than simply reducing compensation expenses.

Managing Commissions for Life Insurance Sales

Sales commissions for individual life insurance are generally divided into two categories:

- A *first-year commission* is equal to a stated percentage of the amount of the premium the insurer receives during the first policy year. Most insurers pay relatively large first-year commissions as a way to encourage sales.

- A *renewal commission* is a commission on policies that remain in force that is equal to a stated percentage of each premium paid for a specified number of years after the first policy year. Renewal commissions are designed to encourage persistency by providing producers with a continuing stream of income from existing policies. Persistency is extremely important for insurers because lapsed and surrendered policies reduce premium income and, in the case of surrenders, create cash outflows in the form of surrender values.

Most producer compensation schedules include both first-year and renewal commissions. The challenge for an insurer is to design a schedule that balances *quantity* of business with *quality* of business.

Most insurers use a heaped commission schedule for individual life insurance sales. A *heaped commission schedule* features relatively high first-year commissions and lower renewal commissions. Heaped commission schedules are attractive to producers because they offer considerable rewards for generating new business and minimal losses for low persistency. From a company perspective, heaped commission schedules are expensive because they stress generating new business over maintaining existing business. In fact, studies show that the cost of acquiring a new customer is about 10 times more than the cost of retaining an existing customer. However, because insurers face considerable competition for sales, and retaining top-notch producers is the key to generating sales, reducing first-year commissions generally isn't an option.

Insurers, however, have several options for managing renewal commissions and improving persistency.

■ An insurer can make persistency a requirement for earning vested renewal commissions. A *vested commission* is a commission that is guaranteed payable to a producer whether or not the producer represents the company when the commission becomes due.

■ An insurer can provide nonvested or conditionally vested commissions rather than renewal commissions that vest immediately. A *nonvested commission* is a commission that is payable to a producer only if the producer still represents the company when the commission becomes due. A *conditionally vested commission* is a commission that becomes vested only after a producer reaches a certain age or number of years of service with the company.

■ An insurer can link production bonuses to persistency. For example, some insurers vary the production bonus rate a producer is eligible to receive according to the persistency of the producer's sales. In these companies, bonuses increase when persistency is above average and decrease if persistency is below average. Other insurers count only commissions net of lapses when they establish production bonuses. As an alternative to production bonuses, insurers may offer producers a separate *persistency bonus*, which provides extra earnings for favorable persistency results.

■ An insurer can impose penalties for excessive policy lapses. For example, some companies charge back commissions for early lapses. A company may even cancel production bonuses if persistency is very low.

Managing Commissions for Annuity Sales

Annuity commission schedules are somewhat different from commission schedules for life insurance products. For example, annuities often feature large initial premiums with considerably smaller, if any, subsequent premiums. As a result, annuity commission schedules generally don't distinguish between first-year and renewal commissions and instead provide a relatively low commission rate on any premium—typically 4% to 7% of the premium. A commission schedule that pays commissions only on premium payments made by annuity owners is classified as a *deposit-based commission schedule*.

> Suppose a producer sold a $250,000 deferred annuity purchased with 5 equal payments of $50,000. If the insurer used a 5% deposit-based commission schedule, the producer would receive 5 payments of $2,500 each for a total of $12,500 in commissions [($50,000 x 0.05) x 5 = $12,500].

Many deposit-based commission schedules also stipulate that a producer must return part or all of the commissions received on an annuity that is surrendered within the first year after issue.

In addition to deposit-based commissions, some insurers use asset-based commission schedules for deferred annuities. An ***asset-based commission schedule*** is a commission schedule in which commissions are calculated as a percentage of the accumulated value of a deferred annuity contract's funds. Under an asset-based schedule, commissions earned after premium payments stop are referred to as *trail commissions*. Asset-based commission schedules are designed to improve persistency, conserve annuity assets, and persuade producers to provide better service to annuity contract owners.

Suppose a producer sold a $250,000 deferred annuity purchased with 5 equal payments of $50,000. The insurer used a 1% asset-based commission schedule. The accumulated values shown in the following table reflect both the premiums and accumulated interest. The commission amounts are based on the accumulated values at the beginning of each year.

Accumulated Value		Commission
Year 1	$50,000	$500 (50,000 x 0.01)
Year 2	$101,500	$1,015 (101,500 x 0.01)
Year 3	$154,545	$1,545 (154,545 x 0.01)
Year 4	$209,181	$2,092 (209,181 x 0.01)
Year 5	$265,456	$2,655 (265,456 x 0.01)
Total commissions		**$7,807**

Note that some of these values are rounded to the nearest dollar.

Although the commissions for the first five years are lower under an asset-based schedule than under a deposit-based schedule, the producer is likely to make up the difference because of trail commissions earned in subsequent years.

Most insurers today use a combination of deposit-based and asset-based commission schedules for annuity sales. Figure 5.4 describes possible combination commission schedules. Deposit-based commissions in these schedules encourage producers to generate new business, while asset-based commissions improve persistency by encouraging producers to keep policies in force.

Methods for Improving Operating Efficiency

Expense reduction is a key goal for all insurance companies. But simply cutting costs is a limited way of operating over the long run. An insurer that simply cuts costs to save money is losing sight of the revenue component of operating efficiency—controlling costs *must* be combined with making new sales *and* ensuring that current customers stay with the company. When we talk about customers here, we don't just mean owners of life insurance and annuity contracts. The producers who sell an insurer's products are also valuable customers. An insurance company needs to make sure that *both* of these groups of customers continue to do business with the company.

To keep its customers satisfied, an insurer must have effective and efficient processes. In this context, a ***process*** is a series of ongoing activities directed toward achieving a goal. At an insurance company, important processes are carried out

Figure 5.4. Sample Combination Commission Schedules

The following combination commission schedules are commonly used for the sale of individual deferred annuities.

Schedule 1:

4% deposit-based commission on new premium plus 0.5% asset-based commission on accumulated contract value, starting one year following the end of the surrender penalty

Schedule 2:

2% deposit-based commission during the first contract year plus 1% asset-based commission on accumulated contract value, starting in the second contract year

in every department. However, the processes that have the greatest impact on customers are

- Developing new products that meet customer needs

- Evaluating applications for life insurance policies and annuity contracts and issuing policies and contracts when they're approved

- Offering service and support to current policyowners and contract owners, as well as to producers

- Determining whether claim payments for life insurance policies or benefit payments for annuity contracts need to be paid

Insurers can use many methods to ensure that their business processes are the very best they can be. In the following sections, we will look at five of these methods: benchmarking, total quality management, Six Sigma, lean management, and business process reengineering.

Benchmarking

One of the most popular ways to manage operating costs and improve operating efficiency is to benchmark company operations. ***Benchmarking*** consists of

- Identifying the best outcomes that other companies have achieved for a specific activity or process and the practices that produced those outcomes

- Implementing the best practices to equal or surpass the best outcomes

In effect, benchmarking allows companies to improve operations without "reinventing the wheel."

The Steadfast Life Insurance Company used benchmarking to improve the efficiency of its customer service processes. As a first step, Steadfast enlisted the help of its business intelligence unit to identify organizations with extremely high customer satisfaction in the area of service. Management then analyzed the practices those companies used to achieve such good results. This analysis pointed to three practices that lowered customer service expenses and increased customer satisfaction: (1) implementing self-service options such as Web-based service or automated response options in telephone systems, (2) outsourcing, and (3) relying more on dedicated call centers. Steadfast decided that outsourcing its customer service function would not be a viable option. However, adding Web-based service options and increasing the services provided through its call center were possible. Although implementing these changes required spending money up front, Steadfast was able to improve customer satisfaction and reduce its customer service expenses over time.

Insurers also frequently use benchmarking to improve the efficiency of their

- Employee training and development programs

- Document management processes

- Accounting processes

- Compensation and incentive programs

- Distribution systems

Figure 5.5 illustrates how an insurer can use benchmarking to manage distribution costs.

Total Quality Management

Total quality management (TQM) can be defined as the process of creating an organizational culture committed to continuous improvement. An insurer using TQM can pursue continuous improvement in areas such as job skills, teamwork, product and service quality, and customer satisfaction.

TQM consists of four principles:

- Do it right the first time

- Be customer-centered

- Make continuous improvement a way of life

- Build teamwork and empowerment

Do It Right the First Time

This principle rests on the assumption that it is cheaper to design a quality product that meets customer needs than to try to fix a faulty product after the fact. As you recall, in our discussion of product design, we emphasized the time and effort that go into developing a new life insurance or annuity product. If an insurer doesn't make sure that a new product is of the highest quality—and that it meets the needs

Figure 5.5. Benchmarking Distribution Costs

To find ways to reduce its distribution costs, Steadfast gathered information about the costs it incurred for marketing and distributing its life insurance products. Steadfast supplemented this information with industry data from a benchmarking study of several comparable companies with similar products and markets. Steadfast collected the following cost information.

	Steadfast's Data (per policy)	Benchmark Data (per policy)	Gap
Agency Costs			
First-year producer commissions	$50	$55	- $5
Agency manager commissions	$25	$25	$0
Agency benefits	$15	$10	+$5
Agency operating expenses	$40	$20	+$20
Total Agency Costs	$130	$110	+$20
Home office costs	$25	$10	+$15
Total Marketing and Distribution Costs	$155	$120	+$35

These results indicate that Steadfast is exceeding the expense benchmark by $35 per policy. In addition, results show that the areas that most need improvement are agency operating expenses (+$20) and home office costs (+$15). By modifying its current practices in these key areas to match the practices that produced the benchmarked amounts, Steadfast should be able to reduce costs in these areas.

of a group of customers—the product isn't likely to succeed. If the product fails, it could end up costing the insurer a lot of money. The insurer may decide to abandon the product entirely—although it could still have policies out there that it must support—or it could decide to redesign the product in order to fix its defects. In either case, the impact on the insurer's financial situation could be negative.

"Do it right the first time" also applies *after* a product has been introduced. The product's customers could need support from the insurer in a number of areas. For example, a customer who calls the insurer with a question about her variable annuity should have her question answered right away—and answered correctly. Similarly, insurers need to respond in a timely and appropriate fashion to customers who file claims.

Be Customer-Centered

Being *customer-centered* means (1) anticipating the customer's needs, (2) listening to the customer, (3) learning how to satisfy the customer, and (4) responding appropriately to the customer. As we said earlier, insurers need to satisfy two groups of customers: the customers for their products and the producers who sell those products.

Make Continuous Improvement a Way of Life

Improvement isn't something a company achieves once and never considers again. To be successful, a company needs to make constant improvement part of the way it does business. *Kaizen*, the Japanese word for "continuous improvement," means improving a system by constantly improving the little details. An insurer that follows kaizen focuses on small, incremental improvements in the way it does business rather than on radical changes or innovation. For example, an employee in the customer service department might suggest updates to a checklist that employees use in answering frequently asked questions; or an employee in the underwriting department could recommend clarifying a confusing section in an application.

Build Teamwork and Empowerment

TQM is an employee-driven process. As such, it can succeed only when employees are empowered to carry out its principles. Empowerment occurs when employees are adequately trained, provided with all relevant information and the best possible tools, fully involved in key decisions, and fairly rewarded for results.

In TQM, teamwork goes along with employee empowerment. One of the most effective applications of teamwork and empowerment is the quality control circle. A *quality control circle*, also known as a *QC circle* or simply a *quality circle*, is a voluntary problem-solving group of 5 to 10 employees from the same work area who meet regularly to discuss quality improvement and ways to reduce costs. A QC circle typically meets for an hour each week during company time. The advantage of voluntary participation is that anyone who wants to contribute has the opportunity to do so. Figure 5.6 shows how Steadfast recently resolved a problem by applying the principles of TQM.

In this situation, Steadfast was able to resolve its problem by making minor changes. Not all problems are that simple, however. Sometimes, radical changes are necessary to resolve problems.

Six Sigma

One popular application of TQM is Six Sigma. *Six Sigma* is a disciplined approach for improving quality by reducing process defects or correcting problems so that results fall within customer specifications. A *defect* is simply anything outside of customer specifications, and *Sigma* is a measure of how close performance is to specifications. Sigma levels range from one to six, with one representing significant defects and six representing minimal defects.

> Companies often use Six Sigma to evaluate transaction defects. At Three Sigma, a company might have 500 incorrect transactions recorded each minute. At Six Sigma, the number of incorrect transactions might drop to 0.6 per minute.

In general, the higher the Sigma status a company attains, the more effective its processes are. For most applications, fewer than 3.4 defects per million opportunities are necessary to achieve Six Sigma status.

Figure 5.6. TQM at Steadfast

Some of Steadfast's best producers were unhappy with how long the company took to approve new applications for life insurance policies. They told the company that prospective customers were complaining about the delays, and they were concerned that these individuals would simply take their business elsewhere.

Do it right the first time.

Steadfast knew it needed to resolve this problem right away—after all, these were some of its best producers, and it knew that its relationship with them was on the line. But the company also knew that it couldn't just tell underwriters to work faster. It needed to improve the approval process so that the problem wouldn't come up again.

Be customer-centered.

Steadfast listened carefully to its producers and asked them how the system could be improved. The company talked to underwriters, too. Steadfast used producers' and underwriters' recommendations to clarify and, in some cases, redesign its application approval process.

Make continuous improvement a way of life.

Although the new system was a big improvement, as employees became familiar with it, they noticed small things that could make the approval process run more smoothly. By making minor adjustments, Steadfast was able to reduce delays even more.

Build teamwork and empowerment.

Steadfast's underwriting department formed a quality control circle that met weekly to discuss problems like the one above. At their next meeting, the QC circle discussed additional ways that they could speed up their response time to applications.

From a process improvement standpoint, Six Sigma provides a way to identify and reduce the variables that cause defects or inefficiencies in a given business process before they cause serious damage.

The Six Sigma Team

Six Sigma uses some colorful terms—derived from the martial arts—to describe team members. Different roles range from champions to master black belts to yellow belts. In this hierarchy, some individuals spend more time than others on the Six Sigma initiative. For example, *master black belts* and *black belts* generally devote 100% of their time to Six Sigma, whereas *green belts* spend only a portion of their time on Six Sigma.

An insurer can choose to train its own employees to be Six Sigma team members or it can seek out vendors who specialize in providing help with Six Sigma programs.

Five-Step Improvement Process

For existing processes that need improvement, Six Sigma deploys a five-step improvement process known as DMAIC. The five steps of DMAIC are:

- **Define** the process that needs improvement

- **Measure** the existing performance

- **Analyze** the performance and other data to determine where the problems are

- **Improve** the process and eliminate the errors

- Establish **controls** to prevent future problems

During the analysis step of DMAIC, a company attempts to identify the problems with a given process. Here, an approach known as root-cause analysis (RCA) can be helpful. ***Root-cause analysis (RCA)*** is a set of problem-solving methods and tools that attempts to determine the actual causal factors that led to an incident so that these factors can be corrected or removed. In the insurance industry, RCA has been effective in identifying and correcting service issues.

Unlike most statistical analysis tools, RCA goes beyond asking "What?" and "How?" RCA focuses on "Why?" and the company continues to ask questions until the root cause of the problem is exposed.

Steadfast received a number of complaints from customers about being put on hold and having to wait a long time when they called the company with questions about their variable annuity contracts. To identify the root cause of this problem, Steadfast began asking *Why?* questions and did not stop until the root cause was identified.

- The first question that Steadfast asked was, *Why* are customers having to wait so long to get their questions answered?

  The customer service representatives (CSRs) said they were doing the best that they could, but the information sheet they were given on the particular product customers were asking about was inadequate in helping them answer customers' questions.

- Why was the information sheet inadequate?

  The information sheet that the CSRs were using was out of date.

- Why was the information sheet out of date?

  The marketing department was supposed to get an updated information sheet to the CSRs last month but did not do so.

- Why didn't the marketing department get the updated sheet to the CSRs last month?

  The individual in charge of getting the sheet to the CSRs was out on vacation. *This was the root cause of the problem.*

Steadfast first made sure that the CSRs received the new information sheets. Then it instituted a new policy to ensure that this kind of problem would not happen again.

Implementing Six Sigma

Although Six Sigma began in the manufacturing sector, it has been successfully applied to the service sector of the economy. For example, financial services companies have successfully applied Six Sigma to reduce errors and correct problems in a number of functional areas. In the insurance industry, Six Sigma has been used to improve call center efficiency and quality and to reduce the length of time it takes a claim department to make benefit payments. Insurers also use Six Sigma to improve the following types of defects or problems in their processes:

■ Insurance claims are improperly denied

■ A proposed insured who should have been issued coverage is denied coverage

■ A proposed insured who should have been denied coverage is issued coverage

■ Client transactions are not processed or are processed incorrectly

■ A company Web site is difficult for customers to access or navigate through

■ Regulatory requirements, such as requirements related to product advertisements and claim investigation, are not met

■ Applications that contain incomplete or incorrect information are submitted to underwriting

The following issues must be addressed in order to have a successful Six Sigma program:

■ In selecting projects, pick only those that are core to the business and the customer.

■ In assessing the costs of the program, be aware that up-front training and implementation costs can be high, outweighing any savings in the first few months of a project.

■ Six Sigma may not work for every functional area or project. In particular, if a process has not been standardized, it is generally not a good candidate for Six Sigma.

■ Data collection can be difficult and time consuming.

■ Management support is critical.

Overall, Six Sigma works well in situations where the goal is to eliminate errors or reduce the expenses associated with a particular operational process.

Lean Management

Lean management is a quality improvement method that emphasizes teams or "cells" that process work with fewer hand-offs, greater speed, and better communication. According to lean management, a lean process is one that relies on continuous-flow processing, a "just-in-time" approach that minimizes wait time and eliminates waste. In this context, "waste" refers to duplication of work, delays, unclear communication, and reworking items that fail to meet quality or service standards. At an insurance company, processes that lend themselves to the lean management approach are (1) new business processing; (2) the product development process, especially where "speed to market" is an issue; and (3) claim processing.

The lean management approach is based on five principles:

- **Specifying value**. Companies should focus on finding out what customers want from a particular process.

- **Identifying the value stream**. Each step in a process should be identified and analyzed to ensure that necessary steps are included and unnecessary steps are eliminated.

- **Creating a continuous flow**. Steps that survive the value-stream identification should be organized into a flow designed to eliminate wait time and reduce unnecessary hand-offs and delays.

- **Using pull strategies**. Processes should encourage customers to "pull," or extract, value from the process rather than forcing the organization to "push" a process towards them.

- **Pursuing perfection**. An organization should continuously examine its processes to look for ways of improving.[1]

Some insurers have combined lean management principles with those of Six Sigma to create a hybrid quality improvement method known as Lean Six Sigma.

Business Process Reengineering

Most of the methods we've discussed so far involve making incremental improvements to work processes over time. In contrast, business process reengineering is a radical approach to improving business processes. ***Business process reengineering (BPR)***, sometimes called *reengineering*, is a comprehensive and systematic analysis and redesign of an organization's work processes. A company applying BPR often starts from the beginning to design a given process. In deciding which of its processes need reengineering, an insurer should first ask three questions. Which of the company's processes are

- The most critical in terms of customer satisfaction?

- Causing the most problems for customers?

- Likely to be successfully reengineered?

For insurance companies, the processes generally targeted for BPR are claims processing, customer service support, and new business processing. The main reason that insurers turn to reengineering is to improve customer satisfaction while cutting costs. Reengineering goals tend to be very ambitious. For example, a company might decide to reengineer a given process so that it can achieve a 35% improvement in customer satisfaction while cutting costs by 35%.

Most reengineering projects go through certain standard phases. Although the terminology for these phases can vary from company to company, most projects include

- A *research phase*, in which people gather information about the existing process and determine customers' needs. The purpose of this phase is to determine how the current process is falling short of customer expectations. For example, a process may include activities that add no value for the customer—in reengineering the process, these activities should be eliminated. This phase is built around the assumption that the existing process—and all the problems associated with it—must first be understood before it is reengineered.

- A *design phase*, in which a company develops alternatives to the existing process. Benchmarking is often used in this phase, as companies seek out the best practices of their competitors.

- An *implementation phase*, in which a new process is first tested on a limited scale. If the results from this testing are favorable, the company can adopt the process on a larger scale.

- An *evaluation phase*, in which the company monitors the results of the new process. Does the new process meet the goals set at the beginning of the project? For example, has customer satisfaction improved dramatically? Have costs been cut drastically? If the answers to these questions are no, the company needs to determine why the reengineered process has failed.

Although BPR can be effective, it also has weaknesses. For example, BPR assumes that ineffective processes are the primary cause of poor performance. In some cases, poor performance may be caused by factors outside the process. Another weakness of BPR is that it generally assumes that starting over is the only way to improve processes. As a result, BPR tends to ignore the parts of existing systems that work well. Finally, BPR doesn't always acknowledge the existence of constraints—that is, factors that limit a company's ability to make process changes. Constraints can come from a variety of sources, including equipment, people, policies, and outside environmental conditions.

The Employee's Role in Supporting Operating Efficiency

Ultimately, the most powerful expense-reduction tool that insurers have is the employees who handle the insurer's business. Company employees in various functional areas can make positive contributions to the company's operational efficiency by understanding how the company makes money and how each function contributes to achieving the company's goals.

Knowledgeable employees have the expertise to spot opportunities for cost reductions, which improve profitability. For example, employees can

- Analyze work processes and suggest improvements to increase productivity and reduce duplicated or wasted efforts

- Detect irregularities in records related to dealings with customers or vendors, and report incidents that suggest fraud or unnecessary expenditures

- Use the lowest-cost, most effective way of working and buying services and supplies

- Apply a team-oriented, cooperative attitude to improve work processes and procedures

Regardless of specific job duties, a company's employees can work together across functional lines, with the guidance of the company's policies and procedures, to increase the company's operating efficiencies.

Key Terms

expense
cost accumulation
investment expenses
general and administrative expenses
expenses for contractual benefits
operating expenses
development expense
acquisition expense
maintenance expense
overhead expense
controllable expense
noncontrollable expense
direct expense
indirect expense
variable expense
fixed expense
rightsizing
outsourcing
straight-through processing

telecommuting
first-year commission
renewal commission
heaped commission schedule
vested commission
nonvested commission
conditionally vested commission
persistency bonus
deposit-based commission schedule
asset-based commission schedule
process
benchmarking
total quality management (TQM)
kaizen
quality control circle
Six Sigma
root-cause analysis (RCA)
lean management
business process reengineering (BPR)

EndNote

1. Womack, James P., and Daniel T. Jones. "Preface." *Lean Solutions.* Free Press, October 2005.

Chapter 6
How the Economy Affects Insurance Companies

Objectives:

After studying this chapter, you should be able to

- Define gross domestic product (GDP) and explain how it is used to measure an economy's performance

- Define the unemployment rate and be able to calculate the unemployment rate for a country

- List the phases of the business cycle and describe what occurs during each phase

- Recognize the effects of trends and seasonal, cyclical, and random variations

- Describe the purpose of the leading, coincident, and lagging economic indicators and be able to give examples of each

- Define inflation, deflation, and related terms, and explain how changes in price levels can affect insurance companies

- Explain the effects on insurers of increasing market interest rates and decreasing market interest rates

- Differentiate between fiscal policy and monetary policy and explain how each is used to stabilize an economy

Outline

Usually, there's a lot of talk in the news about the economy, especially in tough economic times. Is the economy improving or getting worse? How can we know?

To address these concerns, the commentators bring up measures like the unemployment rate and changes in real GDP. They also talk about actions the government is taking to help the economy, such as increasing the money supply and decreasing taxes. Will these actions help? Only time will tell.

Businesses typically measure their performance in terms of profits, but how do we measure the performance of an entire economy?

Measuring the Economy

Economists use a variety of measures to evaluate an economy. Two of the most widely reported measures are gross domestic product and the unemployment rate.

Gross Domestic Product

Gross domestic product (*GDP*) is the market value of all final goods and services produced within a country in a given time period, usually a year. In this context, *market value* is the price that people would be willing to pay for a good or service, rather than the cost of producing it. *Final goods* are those goods that are consumed rather than those used to produce another product. GDP is the basic measure of how much a country produced in a year. GDP that has not been adjusted for changes in price levels is known as *nominal* GDP, or simply GDP. When GDP is adjusted for changes in price levels, it's called *real GDP*. By tracking annual and quarterly data for real GDP in a given country, we can assess the performance of that country's economy over time.

> The real GDP for Country A has been steadily growing for the past decade, indicating that the country's economy is expanding.
>
> Conversely, Country B's real GDP has been declining in recent years, indicating that the country's economy is shrinking.

Figure 6.1 shows GDP for 2008 for a number of countries. Although the United States has the highest GDP, it does not have the highest per capita GDP. ***Per capita GDP*** refers to GDP divided by a country's population ("per capita" means "per person"). Per capita GDP is considered to be a broad indicator of a country's economic well-being. Figure 6.2 presents per capita GDP for 2008 for a selection of countries.

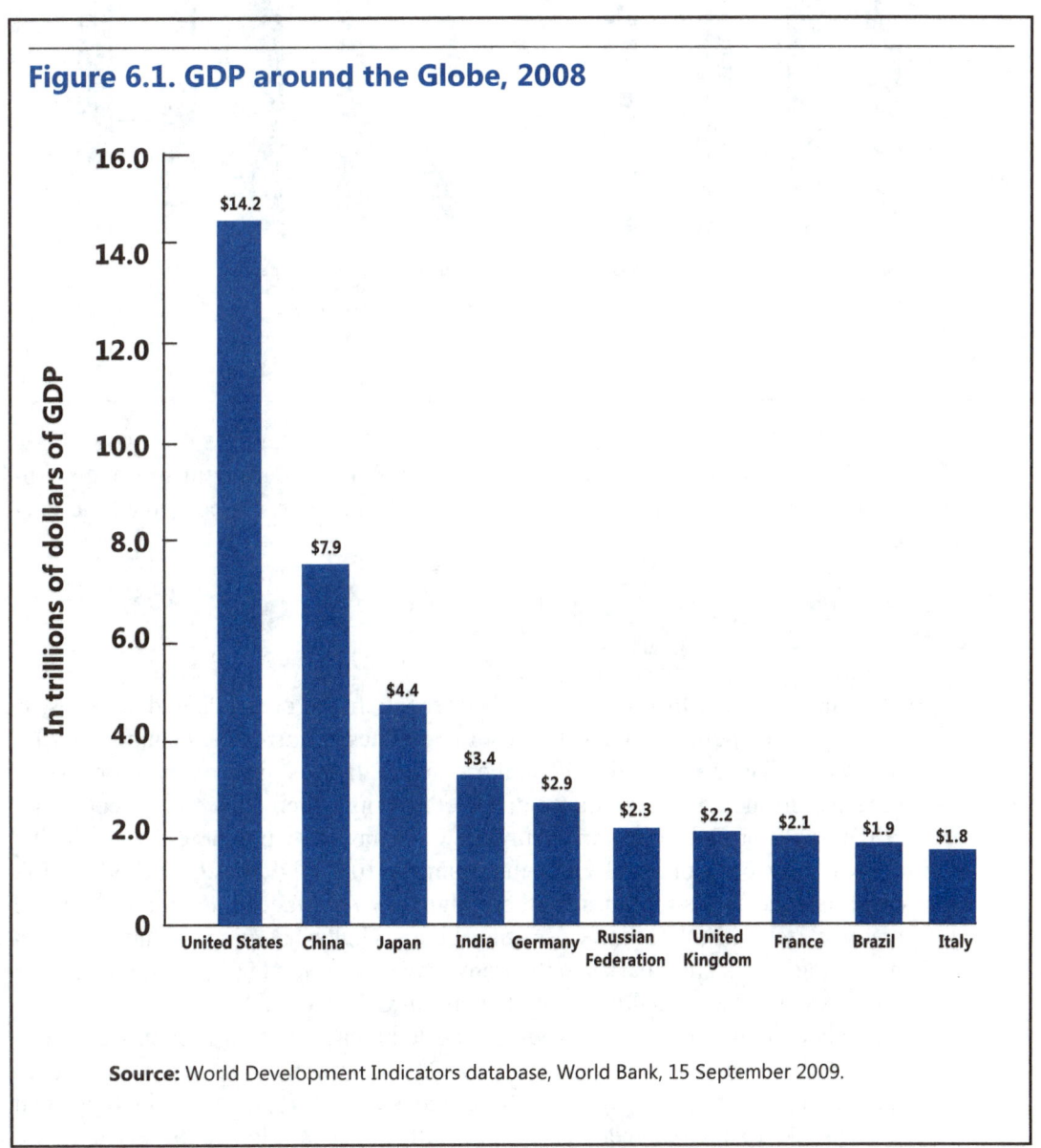

Figure 6.1. GDP around the Globe, 2008

Source: World Development Indicators database, World Bank, 15 September 2009.

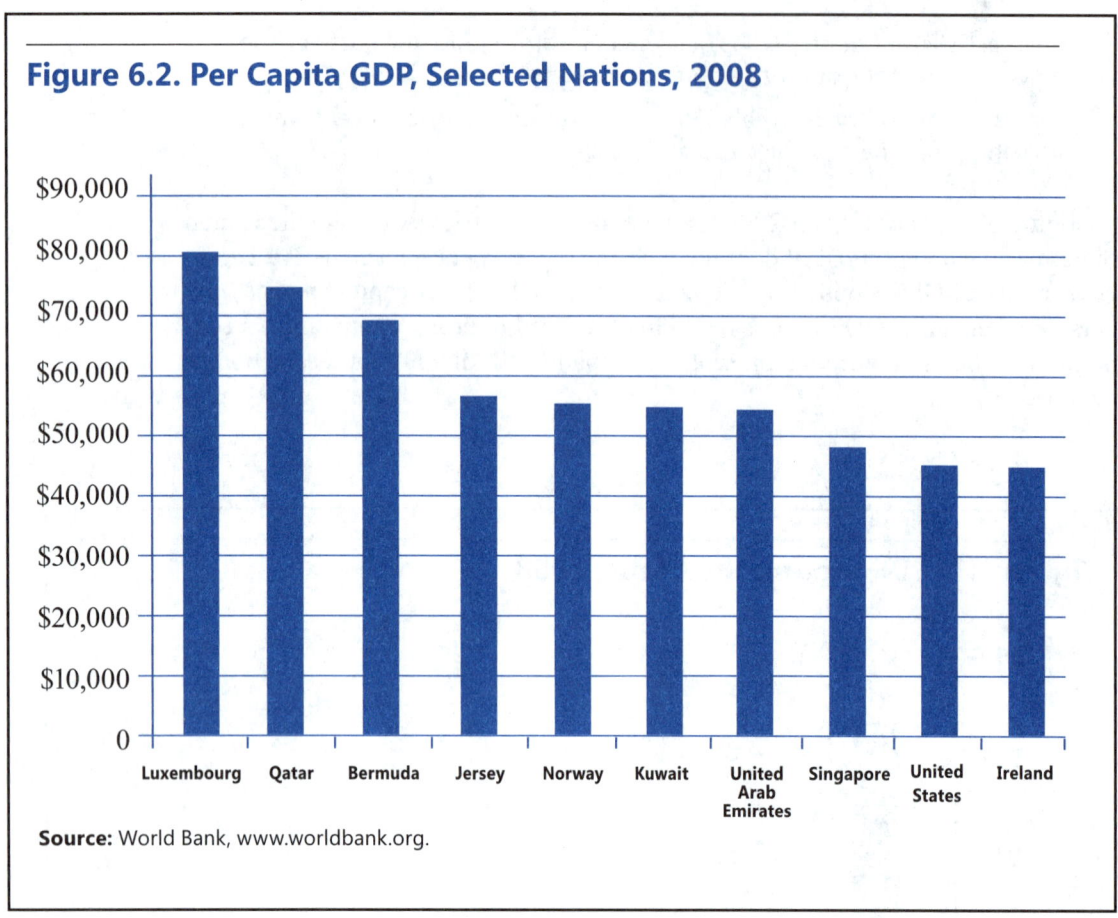

Figure 6.2. Per Capita GDP, Selected Nations, 2008

Source: World Bank, www.worldbank.org.

GDP consists of four components—consumption (C), investment (I), government purchases (G), and net exports (X_n)—and can be expressed in the following equation:

$$GDP = C + I + G + X_n$$

Here, we will focus on consumption.

Consumption, which refers to consumer purchases of goods and services, is the largest component of GDP. In the United States, it currently accounts for 70% of every dollar spent. Of this 70%, more than half goes towards the purchase of services, including life insurance and medical insurance. Any time a consumer purchases a product from an insurance company, that purchase goes into the consumption component of GDP, increasing overall GDP. In 2007, the U.S. life insurance industry's revenues from premium payments accounted for 4.4% of the country's total GDP.[1] Insurers also contribute to GDP by serving as employers and by paying wages and salaries to their employees, who then use that money to buy goods and services, resulting in an increase in GDP.

Although GDP is the most widely reported measure of an economy's performance, there are drawbacks to using it as the central measure of a nation's economic well-being. For example, GDP excludes certain types of production, such as housework and volunteer work. It also fails to account for improvement in the quality of goods and services over time. Another problem with GDP is that what is *included* isn't always an indicator of economic well-being. For example, GDP includes the cost of natural resource depletion. Because of these limitations, GDP is typically used in conjunction with other measures to attain a more balanced view of an economy's condition.

Several alternative measures for GDP are currently in use. One such measure is the Genuine Progress Index (GPI). The GPI is derived by starting with personal consumption expenditures, which is also the first step in the determination of GDP. However, GPI then adds to this number the various services that GDP ignores—such as housework and volunteer work—and then subtracts the cost of harmful activities such as crime, natural resource depletion, and pollution. Tracking GPI figures over the past three decades presents a more realistic picture of economic conditions than does tracking GDP figures.[2]

The Unemployment Rate

The unemployment rate is also considered a key indicator of conditions in an economy. The ***unemployment rate*** is the percentage of people in the labor force who are without jobs but who are actively seeking jobs. Note that this rate does not include individuals who have given up on finding work or those who have dropped out of the labor force altogether. The unemployment rate is calculated as:

> Unemployment rate = Unemployed ÷ Civilian labor force

> In Country A, the number of unemployed individuals who are actively seeking jobs is 500,000. Country A also has 200,000 individuals who are unemployed but who are not currently seeking work. The civilian labor force in this country is 10 million people.

> Country A's unemployment rate can be calculated as follows: 500,000 ÷ 10 million, or 0.05. Therefore, Country A's unemployment rate is 5%. (Note that the 200,000 individuals who are without work but who are not currently seeking work are not counted as part of Country A's unemployed population.)

Contrary to what you might think, full employment does *not* refer to a 0% unemployment rate. Even in a healthy economy, a certain rate of unemployment—known as the natural rate of unemployment—still exists. Some people are currently unemployed because they are in the process of moving from one job to another, while others are unemployed because their skills are no longer needed. The concept of full employment does not include either of these groups—it only counts those who are unemployed as the result of a recession or other drop in economic activity. Therefore, most experts believe that, rather than being 0%, the natural rate of unemployment is closer to 5%.

The unemployment rate in Country A is currently 5%, while that of Country B is 12%.

Country A most likely has full employment, even though 5% of its labor force is currently unemployed. This 5% matches the natural rate of unemployment. Country B, with its 12% rate of unemployment, is exceeding the natural rate by 7%.

The Business Cycle

Changes in real GDP and the rate of unemployment are used to identify the expansions and contractions of the business cycle. The **business cycle** is a recurring pattern of fluctuations in the economic activity of a nation over a specified period of time, generally a year or more. We should state right away that the term "business cycle" is a bit misleading. A "cycle" suggests regularity, and the business cycle is anything but regular. Business cycles vary in terms of

- How long they last

- How many businesses they affect

- The degree to which they affect those businesses

Despite these variations, studying the business cycle offers value. A company can form a clearer picture of the general trend of the economy if it knows (1) which phase of the business cycle an economy is currently in and (2) how long that phase is expected to last.

The different phases of the business cycle are called expansion, contraction, recession, and recovery. Let's look at each of these phases.

Expansion

An **expansion**, also known as a *boom*, is the phase in the business cycle in which unemployment is low and real GDP rises for two or more consecutive quarters. During an expansion, business profits rise, overall spending increases, and production increases. Housing prices also tend to increase during an expansion. When business is booming, insurers have a lot of options. They are more likely to develop new products or offer existing products to new markets, and their investment opportunities widen as well. They may also need to hire more employees if their operations are growing.

Contraction

During a **contraction**, also known as a *downturn*, unemployment begins to rise and real GDP decreases from an earlier quarter. Overall spending, including spending on insurance and financial services products, also tends to decrease. Construction on new homes tends to stabilize and might even stagnate. Insurers are less likely to develop new products when the economy is contracting. However, downturns may offer opportunities for some companies. For example, life insurance sales may increase during a downturn because people are less optimistic and want to protect, as much as possible, their existing assets. They also want products that will secure their financial futures.

Recession

A *recession*, also known as a *slump*, is a significant decline in economic activity spread across the economy, lasting more than a few months. During a recession, unemployment is generally high and real GDP usually falls for two or more quarters. Most businesses, including insurance companies, stop growing, and housing prices and interest rates typically decrease. Figure 6.3 discusses the impact of the recent recession on the insurance industry.

Figure 6.3. The Great Recession

The most recent worldwide recession began in December 2007. This recession forced many insurers to lay off employees or institute salary cuts simply to survive.

Losses on Investments

The primary cause of the recent recession was an unsustainable rise in housing prices—a phenomenon known as a housing bubble. When the bubble burst, many insurers incurred serious losses on their mortgage investments. The initial losses occurred mainly in the residential mortgage market, but losses also occurred in the commercial mortgage market. Although insurers' mortgage investments were the most severely affected, many other types of fixed income investments—such as corporate bonds—also declined in value.

Variable Annuities with Guaranteed Benefits

Most insurers offering variable annuities with guaranteed benefits suffered losses on those products. These guaranteed benefits were intended to protect customers from market losses, and they did. Many insurers discovered, however, that they had not taken adequate steps to mitigate the risks associated with these guarantees. After re-evaluating their variable annuity products, some insurers decided they could no longer afford to offer them; others began charging higher prices for these products and/or reducing the benefits provided.

Back to Basics?

The recession changed customers' product demands. Many customers want simpler and safer products, and guarantees are high on their list. A prime example of this demand is the renewed popularity of whole life insurance in the United States. Insurers are reconsidering their product offerings and weighing the risk of selling products with guarantees against the risk of losing customers to competitors.

Despite the many challenges posed by the recession, insurers who adapt to the changing business environment could find themselves well-positioned to thrive in a new landscape—one where customers desire products that can offer them financial security, even in challenging times.

A recession can worsen and turn into a depression. Economists differ over the conditions that are required for this rare economic condition to occur. However, in general, a *depression* is an economic condition in which real GDP declines drastically and, for a period of at least two years, unemployment is unusually high, prices for most goods and services are unusually low, and there is a general inability to purchase goods and services relative to the amount that could be produced using current resources and technology.

Recovery

A *recovery* is the phase of the business cycle in which real GDP increases for two or more quarters after a recession or depression. Typically, a recovery begins in the last quarter or two of a recession or depression. During the recovery phase, business profits generally improve, and employment moves toward full employment. Overall spending begins to increase as well.

Trends and Variations

Trends and variations affect the business cycle. A *trend* is a movement in a specific direction, either upward or downward. For insurers, one important long-term trend is the increase in life expectancy for the population as a whole. *Life expectancy* is the average number of years of life remaining for a group of people. This trend affects insurers in the following ways:

- Increased life expectancies tend to result in a decrease in benefit costs for issuers of life insurance—as insureds live longer, insurers are able to invest premiums for longer periods before they have to pay benefits.

- Increased life expectancies tend to cause an increase in benefit costs for issuers of life annuities—longer life spans mean that insurers may pay benefits on life annuities for longer periods than they had anticipated.

A *variation* is a change or fluctuation in a trend. For example, during an upward trend in the prices of goods, a variation might appear during a specific period, in which the prices of specific goods are actually decreasing. Three common types of variations are

- *Seasonal variations*, which result from routine patterns that typically occur in the course of one year. For insurance companies, weather changes and flu season are examples of seasonal variations: property/casualty insurers face more claims on homeowners insurance during hurricane season, while health insurance companies are likely to see more medical claims during flu season.

- *Cyclical variations*, which result from changes that affect more than one phase in the business cycle over a period of several years. Cyclical variations occur as an economy changes from recession to recovery or from expansion to contraction. One example of a cyclical variation is a change in interest rates, which typically increase as the economy expands and decrease as the economy contracts.

■ *Random variations*, which result from changes that are either unexpected or are one-time occurrences. These variations are difficult to predict and include the economic impact of wars and natural disasters, such as hurricanes and floods. Natural disasters can affect insurance companies if they have to pay claims on a large number of life insurance policies at the same time.

Forecasting Business Cycles

Specific tools such as economic indicators are used to forecast and monitor changes in the business cycle. *Economic indicators* are statistical variables that demonstrate the direction of an economy. Three key types of economic indicators are leading indicators, coincident indicators, and lagging indicators.

Leading Indicators

Leading indicators are statistical variables that tend to change *before* GDP changes. Therefore, leading indicators typically predict what the economy will be like in the near future. Examples of leading indicators are presented in Figure 6.4.

Coincident Indicators

Coincident indicators are statistical variables that tend to change about the same time that GDP changes. Examples of coincident indicators include figures on industrial production and personal consumption. *Industrial production* measures the raw volume of goods produced by industrial firms, such as factories, mines, and electrical utilities. It also includes newspaper businesses and the publishing industry. One drawback to using industrial production as an economic indicator is that it excludes the services sector of the economy, which represents the majority of the output in many economies. In the United States, a report, called the *Non-Manufacturing Report*, or *Service Report*, contains figures on economic activity in the services sector. The report is published monthly and indicates whether economic activity contracted or expanded in various service industries, including the life insurance industry.

The Bureau of Economic Analysis publishes a monthly report called the *Personal Consumption Report*. This report contains figures on *personal consumption expenditures (PCE)*, which indicate how much money people are spending on goods and services. PCE is another name for the "consumption" component of GDP. As the largest component of GDP, PCE is a coincident indicator: any time GDP rises, PCE rises with it, and any time GDP declines, PCE declines with it.

Lagging Indicators

Lagging indicators are statistical variables that tend to change *after* GDP changes. Common examples of lagging indicators include the prime rate and the unemployment rate. The *prime rate* is the interest rate that commercial banks charge their best corporate customers. During an economic recovery, the prime rate generally doesn't begin to increase until after GDP has increased. Similarly, during a recovery, the unemployment rate, which we discussed earlier, typically remains high and doesn't begin to decrease until after GDP increases.

Figure 6.4. Examples of Leading Indicators

Unemployment benefits claims

Signs that employment may be falling—in other words, the unemployment rate may be on the rise—occur when first-time claims for unemployment insurance benefits rise. An increase in claims for unemployment benefits in two non-consecutive quarters can be used to forecast that the economy is moving into a recession.

New building permits issued

New construction of buildings is a sign of growth in the economy. For example, an increase in new building permits can be used to forecast that the economy is moving out of a recession and into a recovery.

New orders for goods and materials

Manufacturers adjust their output, depending on the size of the orders that they receive for goods and materials. For example, when manufacturers receive smaller orders, they are likely to cut back on their output. These smaller orders may indicate that the economy is contracting.

Stock prices

An overall change in stock prices typically predicts changes in a nation's economy: stock prices tend to decline before the economy declines, and they tend to rise before the economy begins to come out of a recession.

Consumer expectations

When consumers are confident about the future, they tend to spend more money, which leads to an increase in economic growth. Conversely, when consumers begin to lose confidence in the future, they tend to make fewer purchases.

How Changes in Price Levels Affect Insurance Companies

Insurance companies, like all businesses, are affected by changes in the prices of goods and services. For example, most people are familiar with the effects of inflation, but deflation can be a problem as well. Other related conditions include hyperinflation, disinflation, and stagflation.

Inflation

In economics, ***inflation*** is a rise in the general level of prices in an economy over a period of time. When the general level of prices rises, each monetary unit—whether it be the dollar, peso, yen, euro, or rupee—buys fewer goods and services, resulting in a loss in the purchasing power of money.

In the United States and Canada, the most important measure of inflation is the Consumer Price Index (CPI). The ***Consumer Price Index (CPI)*** is a measurement that compares the average price of a market basket of goods and services at a stated point in time to the average price of the same market basket at a different point in time. The market basket consists of 80,000 goods and services that a typical urban family buys. In the U.S., the Bureau of Labor Statistics reports CPI monthly. Many other countries throughout the world publish their own consumer price indexes, and some indexes are published for several countries combined. For example, the European Central Bank publishes the Harmonised Index of Consumer Prices (HICP), which shows money spent by households in the European Union member states.[3]

To discover how price levels have changed, you can look at CPI values for different time periods. For example, assume that the CPI was 200 one year ago but has risen to 206 this year. What is the rate of inflation for this one-year period? The equation to use is as follows:

$$\text{Rate of inflation in \%} = \frac{(\text{Current CPI} - \text{Previous CPI})}{\text{Previous CPI}} \times 100$$

Putting the numbers into this equation,

$$\text{Rate of inflation} = \frac{(206 - 200)}{200} \times 100$$
$$= (6 \div 200) \times 100$$
$$= 0.030 \times 100 = 3\%$$

In this situation, $1.00 now will buy what $0.97 bought one year ago.

Another concept related to the CPI is the ***real rate of interest***, which is defined as the difference between the *nominal*, or *stated*, *rate of interest* and the *expected inflation rate*.

$$\text{Real rate of interest} = \text{Nominal rate of interest} - \text{Expected inflation rate}$$

The real rate of interest acknowledges inflation—whereas the nominal rate does not. For example, suppose a friend of yours wants to borrow money from you but can't pay you back for a year. Your friend also insists on paying interest on the amount borrowed. How much interest should you charge? If you charge your friend a nominal interest rate of 5%, and the expected inflation rate over the one-year period is 3%, then the real rate of interest on this loan is only 2%. That's a pretty good deal for your friend, but is it enough for you? Your decision of how much nominal interest to charge could be affected by the expected inflation rate. For example, you might decide to charge 8% because you want to get 5% back on this loan. This example is fairly informal—a loan between two friends—but it illustrates the necessity of factoring inflation into any investment decision.

So how are insurance companies affected by inflation? One typical effect of inflation is an increase in salary expenses. As a result, an insurer's actual expenses may exceed the expenses that it assumed in pricing its products. In addition, an increase in the rate of inflation can lead to an increase in market interest rates. When market interest rates increase, an insurer may experience a reduction in the value of its fixed-income investments, such as bonds.

During periods of inflation, insurers can also face problems with their fixed-rate products. Before we discuss these problems, we need to go over some important terms used with fixed deferred annuity products. First of all, a fixed deferred annuity's ***accumulated value*** is the net amount paid for the annuity, plus interest earned, less the amount of any withdrawals or fees. The interest rate that an insurer applies to annuity contract values to determine the annuity's accumulated value is an *interest-crediting rate*. Fixed deferred annuity contracts provide for at least two interest-crediting rates:

- A ***guaranteed minimum interest-crediting rate***, which is the minimum rate that the insurer must credit to the contract's accumulated value. In most jurisdictions, this rate must be either 2% or 3%.

- Most contracts also allow the insurer to pay contract owners a higher interest rate known as the ***current interest-crediting rate***, which is the rate the insurer declares and pays. The amount of current interest is based on the owner's election to keep the contract in force for a chosen minimum interest-crediting period. The insurer typically sets a new current interest rate at the end of the interest-crediting period, and this new rate is based on current market conditions. The current rate may be higher or lower than the previous current rate, but it can *never* be lower than the guaranteed minimum interest-crediting rate.

> The Nutmeg Life Insurance Company issued a fixed deferred annuity product that had a guaranteed minimum interest-crediting rate of 2.5%. The current interest-crediting rate on this product was 3.5%. If Nutmeg chose to change the current interest-crediting rate on this product, it could set a value higher or lower than 3.5%, but it could *never* go below the guaranteed minimum interest-crediting rate of 2.5%.

When inflation is a factor, owners of fixed deferred annuities may decide to sell or give up these products in exchange for products that offer higher current rates or products whose value varies by market performance to try to earn better returns.

> June Ernst owned one of Nutmeg's fixed deferred annuities. Prices were on the rise, and June was concerned that the return on her annuity wasn't keeping up with inflation. She decided to surrender her annuity and use the surrender value to invest in a Treasury note that offered a higher interest rate.

Occasionally, changes in inflation are big enough to cause large numbers of customers to remove money from an insurance product to earn higher returns on other investments. When large numbers of customers withdraw funds from financial intermediaries, such as banks, savings and loan associations, and insurance companies, in order to directly invest in instruments yielding higher returns, this process is known as ***disintermediation***.

> June Ernst wasn't the only Nutmeg customer who was unhappy with the fixed return on Nutmeg's deferred annuity. A high number of these customers surrendered their contracts so that they could invest in higher-yielding instruments, such as Treasury notes or stock. Because these customers surrendered their contracts with Nutmeg in order to pursue direct investments with higher yields, their surrenders illustrate the process of disintermediation.

For insurers, any widespread withdrawal of funds by customers can reduce premium income, prevent recovery of expenses, and possibly disrupt cash flows because of payments (surrender values) to customers who abandon the company or some of its products.

An opportunity exists for insurers in the previous situation, however. The unhappy customers at Nutmeg might be willing to replace their fixed annuities with variable annuities. A variable annuity would give these customers the ability to participate in financial markets without giving up the advantages of owning an annuity.

Deflation

Deflation, which is a fall in the general price level, is the opposite of inflation. With deflation, the purchasing power of money rises. Historically, deflation tends to occur during recessions or depressions—any time that aggregate demand in an economy drops sharply or stagnates, deflation is a possibility. Deflation is of concern to insurers because of their corporate debt investments: bond issuers are far more likely to default on their principal and interest payments when deflation is a factor. Other investment values, such as those for stocks, plummet as well. In fact, the only truly safe investment during a deflationary period is cash.

During periods of deflation, customers with fixed-rate products are likely to keep these products in force. Customers with products whose value varies by market performance are likely to sell these products and buy fixed-rate products that offer guaranteed returns. Insurers that offer fixed deferred annuity products must be careful during periods of deflation. During a period of deflation, an insurer could find itself earning less on its investments than it credits to these contracts.

> Let's continue to look at Nutmeg's fixed deferred annuity contracts with the guaranteed minimum interest-crediting rate of 2.5%. When the economy began to experience deflation, Nutmeg still had to credit these contracts with at least 2.5%. Unfortunately, Nutmeg was earning less than 2.5% on the investments backing these products. Therefore, the company suffered losses on these products.

Figure 6.5 presents terms related to inflation and deflation.

How Changes in Market Interest Rates Affect Insurance Companies

Market interest rates represent a nondiversifiable risk to life insurance companies. Recall that a nondiversifiable risk is one that affects all assets in an economy and

Figure 6.5. Disinflation, Hyperinflation, and Stagflation

Disinflation is a decrease in the rate of inflation. For example, if the inflation rate has been 8% for several years, and then it falls to 4%, that's disinflation. Inflation still exists, but its rate of growth has fallen.

Hyperinflation is an out-of-control inflationary spiral. Most analysts agree that an economy is facing hyperinflation once the inflation rate reaches double-digit levels, say 10% or 12%. One of the most famous instances of hyperinflation occurred in Germany after World War I. At that time, prices in Germany were rising 10% *per hour.* More recent cases of hyperinflation occurred in 1989 in several South American countries: in Argentina, the inflation rate was 3,500%; in Peru, it was 2,500%; and in Brazil, it was 1,200%.

Stagflation is a term that refers to a combination of inflation, slow economic growth, and high unemployment. This term was created to describe the U.S. recession of the 1970s, when declining output and inflation occurred at the same time.

is therefore not specific to an individual asset or issuer. As the name suggests, a nondiversifiable risk cannot be controlled by diversification. Therefore, changes in market interest rates are beyond the control of insurers.

Life insurance companies face interest-rate risk in a variety of financial contexts. Market interest rates influence the interest-crediting rates that life insurance companies pay to customers who own interest-sensitive products, such as fixed cash value life insurance and fixed deferred annuity products. Market interest rates also influence the market values of bonds, mortgages, and other interest-bearing securities.

To further appreciate how changes in market interest rates affect a life insurance company, we will examine the usual effects of increases and decreases in interest rates.

Effects of an Increase in Market Interest Rates

An inverse relationship exists between the market values of most bonds and market interest rates. This relationship means that, when market interest rates increase, the market values of bonds (bond prices) tend to decrease. In an environment of increasing interest rates, bond purchasers typically demand a lower bond price—that is, one that will yield a return equal to the new, higher market interest rate. Under these circumstances, if a life insurance company sells a bond, that bond will sell at a depressed market price, and the company will realize a loss on the sale if the market interest rate exceeds the interest rate that prevailed when the bond was purchased.

> The Malabar Corporation issued bonds with a $10,000 par value and a stated interest rate of 5%. The Peaberry Life Insurance Company purchased 100 of these bonds at their $10,000 par value. One year later, market interest rates rose to 7%. Therefore, comparable new bonds were providing $700 a year in interest income (0.07 x $10,000) rather than the $500 a year (0.05 x $10,000) that the Malabar bonds provided. If Peaberry decided to sell its Malabar bonds, it would receive less than the $10,000 par value it paid for each bond.

When interest rates are increasing, an insurer may decide to keep its bonds instead of selling them at the prevailing lower market prices. If the insurer then waits until the bonds mature, it will collect the par value of the bonds. In this situation, the insurer has avoided incurring a loss by holding the bonds until maturity.

> Peaberry decided to hold on to the Malabar bonds until they matured. At maturity, Peaberry will receive $10,000 for each bond. However, by continuing to hold on to the bonds, Peaberry will earn a rate that is lower than the rate available on new investments.

Increasing market interest rates are likely to have the following additional effects on insurers:

- Insurers may experience the phenomenon of spread compression. Here, *spread* refers to the difference between the interest rate the insurer is earning on its invested assets and the interest rate the insurer must pay to customers. Recall that the formula for the interest spread, or interest margin, is:

> Interest spread = Interest rate earned – Interest-crediting rate

Spread compression refers to the narrowing of an insurer's interest spread. Spread compression occurs in an increasing interest-rate environment when customers immediately demand that they receive the higher market interest rate on their investments. At the same time, the average rate of return on the insurer's existing invested assets rises only slowly, because these assets continue to earn the lower interest rates that were available in the financial markets when the assets were purchased. Spread compression does not occur automatically when market rates are increasing, because an insurer can choose to keep its spread constant. However, when choosing to keep an interest spread constant, the insurer must be prepared to face increased lapse rates and a decrease in sales.

When it priced its fixed deferred annuity product, Peaberry determined that it needed a 1.5% interest spread in order to achieve its profit goals. When Peaberry issued the contracts, it was earning 7% on the investments supporting this product. Therefore, Peaberry set the initial interest-crediting rate at 5.5% (equal to the 7% earned rate minus the 1.5% interest spread).

Two years later, market interest rates had increased by 1%. Some of Peaberry's competitors were now crediting 6.5% on their fixed deferred annuities. Peaberry had to decide whether to increase its rates to match its competitors. Peaberry was still earning 7% on the investments supporting this product. If it raised its interest-crediting rate to 6.5%, it would face a reduced interest spread of 0.5% (7% earned rate minus 6.5% credited rate). This reduced spread would be lower than the spread Peaberry needed in order to meet its profit target.

■ Insurers could have to choose between (1) increasing their current interest-crediting rates and accepting a lower spread in an effort to retain customers' funds or (2) leaving current interest-crediting rates at the lower levels so as to avoid incurring a negative interest spread, a situation that is likely to cause a decline in the volume of new and existing interest-sensitive business. Another option is to choose a course of action somewhere between these two.

Peaberry decided to pick the middle ground: it raised the current interest-crediting rate on its fixed deferred annuities from 5.5% to 6%. Peaberry realized that it could lose some customers, but it hoped that these losses would be offset by the interest spread of 1% (7% earned rate – 6% credited rate) that it would earn on its investments.

Figure 6.6 summarizes the expected effects of market interest-rate increases on an insurer's investments and its products.

Figure 6.6. Market Interest-Rate Increases

Effects on bonds and other interest-bearing assets

When market interest rates increase, the market value of interest-bearing assets tends to decrease.

Effects on interest-sensitive products

When market interest rates increase, an insurer is likely to experience increases in withdrawal rates, lapse rates, and surrender rates on interest-sensitive products.

Effects of a Decrease in Market Interest Rates

The inverse relationship between bond prices and market interest rates also holds when interest rates are decreasing. When market interest rates decrease, bond prices typically increase. Let's go back to see what happens to Peaberry's bonds when interest rates fall.

> Two years after Peaberry purchased the Malabar bonds, interest rates fell to 3%. Thus, comparable new bonds were providing $300 a year in interest income (0.03 x $10,000) rather than the $500 a year (0.05 x $10,000) that the Malabar bonds provided. If Peaberry chose to sell its bonds, it would receive more than the $10,000 par value it paid for each bond.

When market interest rates are decreasing, one negative outcome for life insurance companies is that their liabilities could lengthen. Liabilities lengthen when fixed-rate products, such as fixed deferred annuities, remain in force for longer than the insurer assumed, because the company's guaranteed rate is higher than market interest rates.

> Peaberry's fixed deferred annuity products provide a guaranteed minimum interest-crediting rate of 4%. When market interest rates fell to 3%, customers held on to these annuity products because they were guaranteed to receive a return greater than the market was currently yielding.

In an environment of decreasing interest rates, companies can experience spread expansion or spread compression, depending on whether products are supported by existing invested assets or new invested assets:

Spread expansion	Spread compression
The rate of return on the company's existing assets declines only slowly. For products supported by these assets, insurers may enjoy the effects of spread expansion. *Spread expansion* is the widening of an insurer's interest spread. Spread expansion occurs when market interest rates fall and the insurer reduces interest-crediting rates to the new market level while continuing to earn a higher overall rate of return on its existing invested assets. Spread expansion does not occur automatically, because an insurer can choose to keep its spread constant.	The company's new invested assets will earn only the new lower market interest rate. If market interest rates drop so as to approach an insurer's current interest-crediting rates, the insurer could experience spread compression on products supported by new invested assets. Spread compression tends to emerge slowly over time as principal payments on bonds are reinvested at lower rates.

In times of decreasing interest rates, borrowers who are paying higher interest rates on older debt may choose to repay the debt before repayment is due. Those same borrowers can usually *refinance*—that is, make new borrowing arrangements at the new lower prevailing interest rates. In such a situation, the insurer would lose the higher-yielding older assets. This circumstance would cause spread compression on insurance and annuity products with long-term guarantees. Thus, insurers typically match their products having long-term guarantees with assets that are unlikely to be refinanced.

Figure 6.7 summarizes the effects that decreasing market interest rates have on an insurer's investments and its products.

Government Policy Options

As far as the economy is concerned, consumers are number one—with their spending, they tend to have the greatest influence on the economy. But governments also influence the direction of the economy through fiscal policy and monetary policy. Fiscal policy and monetary policy have the same goals: price stability, relatively full employment, and a satisfactory rate of economic growth. The two types of policies differ in how they pursue these goals, however.

Fiscal Policy

In economics, a country's *fiscal policy* is its use of government spending and taxation to change aggregate demand—indicated by the level of spending—in the economy. Legislative and/or executive parts of each country's government typically develop fiscal policy. In the United States, the President and Congress are in charge of fiscal policy.

As a general rule, a government's fiscal policy is either expansionary or contractionary. An *expansionary fiscal policy* is used to increase aggregate demand in order to increase the pace of the economy. This type of policy is typically used to fight a recession. In this situation, government spending generally exceeds government revenues, resulting in a budget deficit. A *budget deficit* is a budget in which government expenditures exceed government revenues in a given time period. Expansionary fiscal policy calls for an increase in government spending, a decrease in taxes, or some combination of the two.

Figure 6.7. Market Interest-Rate Decreases

Effects on bonds and other interest-bearing assets

When market interest rates decrease, the market value of interest-bearing assets tends to increase.

Effects on interest-sensitive products

When market interest rates decrease, an insurer is likely to experience decreases in withdrawal rates, lapse rates, and surrender rates on interest-sensitive products.

Fiscal policy is also used to fight inflation. In this case, the policy is called a **contractionary fiscal policy**, or a *restrictive fiscal policy*, and it decreases aggregate demand to slow down the economy. The remedies are the reverse of those used for a recession: decrease government spending, increase taxes, or do some combination of the two. If a budget deficit is present, a contractionary fiscal policy tends to cause the size of the budget deficit to decrease; if a budget surplus is present, its size tends to increase. A **budget surplus** is a budget in which government revenues exceed government expenditures in a given time period. Figure 6.8 summarizes the two main kinds of fiscal policy.

Monetary Policy

Most countries have a monetary authority and/or central banking system, which is charged with developing and overseeing the country's monetary policy. By **monetary policy**, we mean the strategy a country's monetary authority uses to increase or decrease the money supply in an effort to stabilize the economy. The **Federal Reserve System**, often called *the Fed*, is the central banking system and monetary authority in the United States. Figure 6.9 lists the names of the central banks of several other countries and of Europe.

To pursue the goals of economic growth, relatively full employment, and price stability, a country's central bank can adopt a loose or a tight monetary policy. When the central bank adopts a loose monetary policy, its actions cause the money supply to increase. A loose monetary policy can have a positive effect on employment and economic growth, but can result in inflation. A tight monetary policy, in which the central bank's actions cause the money supply to decrease, can reduce the negative impact of inflation. However, a tight monetary policy tends to increase unemployment and decrease economic growth, all other factors remaining the same.

Figure 6.8. Expansionary and Contractionary Fiscal Policy

	Expansionary Fiscal Policy	Contractionary Fiscal Policy
Purpose	To fight a recession	To fight inflation
Examples of Typical Actions Taken	Increase government spending	Decrease government spending
	Decrease taxes	Increase taxes
Effects on Budget	Tends to cause the size of a budget deficit to increase	Tends to cause the size of a budget deficit to decrease or the size of a budget surplus to increase

---

Figure 6.9. Central Banks around the World

Bank of Canada

The People's Bank of China

Hong Kong Monetary Authority

European Central Bank (ECB)

Bank of Mexico

Bank of Thailand

Bank of Brazil

Reserve Bank of India

Swiss National Bank

Bank Indonesia

Monetary Authority of Singapore

Bank of Korea

Key Terms

gross domestic product (GDP)

market value

final good

real GDP

per capita GDP

unemployment rate

business cycle

expansion

contraction

recession

depression

recovery

trend

life expectancy

variation

seasonal variation

cyclical variation

random variation

economic indicator

leading indicator

coincident indicator

industrial production

personal consumption expenditures (PCE)

lagging indicator

prime rate

inflation

Consumer Price Index (CPI)

real rate of interest

accumulated value

guaranteed minimum interest-crediting rate

current interest-crediting rate

disintermediation

deflation

disinflation

hyperinflation

stagflation

spread compression

spread expansion

refinance

fiscal policy

expansionary fiscal policy

budget deficit

contractionary fiscal policy

budget surplus

monetary policy

Federal Reserve System

Endnotes

1. The American Council of Life Insurers (ACLI), "The Systematic Importance of the Life Insurance Industry" (March 2009).
2. *The Genuine Progress Indicator 2006: A Tool for Sustainable Development*. www.rprogress.org.
3. European Central Bank, "Harmonised Index of Consumer Prices (HICP) and Prices," http://www.ecb.int/stats/prices/hicp/html/index.en.html (25 March 2010).

Chapter 7

Financial Reports and Plans

Objectives:

After studying this chapter, you should be able to

- Recognize essential information contained in the income statement and the balance sheet and explain how these financial statements relate to one another

- Describe the purpose of a cash flow statement and a statement of owners' equity

- Explain the purpose, content, and intended audience of the annual report and the Annual Statement

- Describe the benefits and disadvantages of budgeting

- Distinguish between various approaches to budgeting and describe examples of budgets that insurers use

Outline

Financial Statements
- The Income Statement
- The Balance Sheet
- Linking the Income Statement and the Balance Sheet
- Other Financial Statements

Reports for Stakeholders and Regulators
- The Annual Report
- The Annual Statement

Budgets
- Why Budget?
- Budgeting Approaches
- Types of Budgets

> Winnie Tanner has just started a new job as a claim analyst at the Paradigm Life Insurance Company. On her second day of work, Winnie was getting coffee in the break room, when she overheard a conversation between two of Paradigm's accountants. They were talking about the company's financial situation, and their conversation was filled with terms like "net income," "capital," "balance sheet," and "annual report." She even thought she heard them say, "zero-based budgeting," but wondered, how could a budget be based on nothing?
>
> Winnie was baffled by this conversation. Shaking her head, she thought, "I'm *so* glad I'm not an accountant! I don't need to know *any* of that stuff."

The terms that baffled Winnie may not be familiar to you either—but they are all a part of financial reporting and planning. And even if you, like Winnie, don't work in the accounting area—the area primarily responsible for compiling financial reports and plans in most insurance companies—you still need to have a basic understanding of this area of insurer operations.

For insurers, ***financial reporting*** is the process of presenting financial data about a company's financial position, its operating performance, and its flow of funds during a specified period of time. For a typical life insurance company, the most important financial reports are its financial statements, annual report, and Annual Statement. In addition to financial reports, insurers also rely on financial plans. Unlike financial reports, which record a company's past performance, an insurer's financial plans contain estimates of future activities. The most important financial plans for insurers are budgets.

Financial Statements

Like most businesses, insurance companies use financial statements to measure their financial performance and financial condition. A ***financial statement*** is a report that summarizes a company's financial situation or major monetary events and transactions. Both internal users and external users rely on the information contained in a company's financial statements. For example, company managers use financial statements to assess the company's performance and to plan for its future. In addition, investors examine a company's financial statements to decide whether to invest in the company. The two primary financial statements of any business are the income statement and the balance sheet.

The Income Statement

An *income statement*, also called a *statement of operations* or a *profit and loss statement (P&L)*, is a financial document that lists an insurer's revenue and expenses over a specific period, such as a year, and shows whether the insurer experienced a profit or a loss during that period.

■ *Revenues* are amounts that a company earns from its business operations. For insurers, money coming in from product sales—premium income and annuity considerations—typically is the most important source of revenue. The second most important source is earnings on insurers' investments, such as interest on bonds and dividends on stocks. Insurers also earn fee income, which results from providing services such as third-party administration services.

■ *Expenses* are amounts that a company spends in the course of conducting business. Expenses are a necessary part of doing business because a company cannot generate revenue without also incurring expenses. People buy insurance products for the benefit payments, so it makes sense that an insurer's greatest expense is its contractual benefit payments to policyowners and beneficiaries. Operating expenses are the next biggest expense. For insurers, examples of operating expenses include producer commissions, employee salaries and benefits, product development costs, and taxes.

An insurer subtracts its expenses from its revenue to arrive at its *net income*. When people talk about a company's "bottom line," or whether the company is "in the red" or "in the black," they are referring to the company's net income. Although it may seem a bit confusing, income statements for insurers don't use the term *profit*. On an income statement, the difference between revenue and expenses is referred to as either a *net gain* or a *net loss*.

> If net income is positive—meaning, revenue is greater than expenses—the result is called a *net gain*.
>
> If net income is negative—meaning, expenses are greater than revenue—the result is called a *net loss*.

Figure 7.1 shows an example of a simplified income statement.

According to Figure 7.1, Paradigm earned $6,072,000 in revenue in 201X and incurred $5,880,000 in expenses. Therefore, Paradigm's net income for the year was $192,000.

> **Revenue – Expenses = Net income**
> $6,072,000 – $5,880,000 = $192,000 (net gain)

Companies can increase their profits by increasing revenues, decreasing expenses, or both. For example, assume that Paradigm earned an additional $2,000,000 in revenue—through an increase in product sales or investment earnings—while incurring the same $5,880,000 in expenses.

Figure 7.1 Simplified Income Statement

Paradigm Life Insurance Company
Income Statement
December 31, 201X

Revenues

Premiums	$3,600,000	
Investment income	2,392,000	
Fee income	80,000	
Total Revenues		$6,072,000

Expenses

Benefits and claims	$4,000,000	
Operating expenses	1,600,000	
Investment expenses	10,000	
Taxes	270,000	
Total Expenses		$5,880,000
Net Income		$192,000

Note: This income statement lists investment income and investment expenses separately so that you can see the major types of revenues and expenses that insurers report on the income statement. Most insurers subtract investment expenses from investment income to show net investment income under Revenues.

Revenue – Expenses = Net income
$8,072,000 – $5,880,000 = $2,192,000 (net gain)

Now let's see what happens if Paradigm's revenues stayed the same at $6,072,000, but the company reduced its expenses by $1,000,000—through a reduction in operating expenses.

Revenue – Expenses = Net income
$6,072,000 – $4,880,000 = $1,192,000 (net gain)

If Paradigm is able to increase its revenue to $8,000,000 and reduce its expenses to $4,000,000, its net income will increase even more.

Revenue – Expenses = Net income
$8,000,000 – $4,000,000 = $4,000,000 (net gain)

Of course, revenue could go down and expenses could go up instead. However, as long as revenues are greater than expenses, the company will make a profit.

So what happens when expenses are greater than revenues? Assume that, for 201X, Paradigm earned revenue of $5,000,000 and incurred expenses of $6,000,000. In this situation, Paradigm experienced negative net income—in other words, a net loss.

Revenue – Expenses = Net income

$5,000,000 – $6,000,000 = -$1,000,000 (net loss)

The income statement measures the financial success (or failure) of a company during a relatively short period of time—at most, over a one-year period. It is a type of *dynamic report* because it presents the movement or flow of a company's financial transactions during a specified accounting period. However, the income statement does not reflect the company's profitability over the long term. For this information, insurers rely on the financial statement known as a balance sheet.

The Balance Sheet

A *balance sheet*, also known as a *statement of financial position* or *statement of financial condition*, is a financial document that lists the values of a company's assets, liabilities, and capital and surplus as of a specific date. Typically that date is the last day of the accounting period, such as March 31, June 30, September 30, or December 31. Unlike the income statement, the balance sheet is considered to be a *static report* because it is a snapshot of a company's financial condition at a specific moment.

A balance sheet takes its form from the *basic accounting equation*, which states that a company's assets equal the sum of the company's liabilities and its capital and surplus.

Assets = Liabilities + Capital and surplus

The amount of an insurer's assets must equal the sum of its liabilities and its capital and surplus at all times. To help remember this concept, imagine a balance sheet as having two sides, with assets on the left side and liabilities and capital and surplus on the right side. The total of the left side *always* equals the total of the right side.

A shorthand way of remembering the items on a company's balance sheet is to ask: What does the company *own*? What does it *owe*? And what is it *worth*? In terms of the basic accounting equation,

- *Assets* are the "own" part of the balance sheet—they are all things of value owned by a company. For insurers, assets include such items as investments, cash, buildings, furniture, and land. Investments in securities, such as stocks and bonds, are the most important asset category for insurers.

- *Liabilities* are the "owe" part of the balance sheet—they are a company's debts and future obligations. For insurers, the major liability item on the balance sheet is *contractual reserves*, which identifies the amount that, together with future premiums and investment income, an insurer estimates it will need in order to pay contractual benefits as they come due. Another significant liability for insurers consists of commissions that are owed to producers.

- *Capital and surplus* is the "worth" part of the balance sheet—the amount remaining after liabilities are subtracted from assets. *Capital* represents the amount of money invested in a company by its owners, usually through the purchase of the company's stock. *Surplus* is the cumulative amount of money—calculated as an insurance company's assets minus its liabilities and capital—that remains in the company over time. Mutual insurers and fraternal insurers do not have stockholders, so, for these insurers, capital and surplus is known simply as *surplus*. Capital and surplus is also known as *owners' equity* because it represents the owners' financial interest in the company. If a company goes out of business, the company's owners—the stockholders of a stock insurer and the policyowners of a mutual insurer or fraternal insurer—are entitled to whatever remains of the company's assets after all creditor claims and policyowner claims have been paid.

Figure 7.2 shows a simplified balance sheet.

Linking the Income Statement and the Balance Sheet

Insurers prepare income statements on a regular basis, such as quarterly or monthly. Each time an insurer prepares an income statement, it transfers the resulting net

Figure 7.2 Simplified Balance Sheet

Paradigm Life Insurance Company
Simplified Balance Sheet
December 31, 201X

Assets		=	Liabilities + Capital and Surplus	
Assets			**Liabilities**	
Investments	$16,000,000		Contractual reserves	$14,000,000
Cash	$500,000		Long-term debt	$400,000
Other assets	$100,000		Other liabilities	$600,000
Total Assets	**$16,600,000**		Total Liabilities	**$15,000,000**
			Capital and Surplus	
			Capital	$600,000
			Surplus	$1,000,000
			Total Capital and Surplus	**$1,600,000**
			Total Liabilities + Total Capital and Surplus =	**$16,600,000**

income to the capital and surplus account on the balance sheet. If the net income amount on the income statement is a net gain, then this amount is added to the amount of capital and surplus on the balance sheet. If the income statement shows a net loss, then the amount of the net loss is subtracted from the capital and surplus account on the balance sheet.

As a result, over a period of time, the capital and surplus account on a company's balance sheet reflects the cumulative effects of the company's operations. If the company's operations have been profitable, the capital and surplus account shows continuing growth, unless all net income has been paid out as stockholder or policyowner dividends.

For example, at the end of the previous accounting period, Paradigm's balance sheet showed assets of $16,408,000, liabilities of $15,000,000, and capital and surplus of $1,408,000. At the end of the current period, Paradigm's income statement showed net income in the form of a net gain of $192,000. As a result, Paradigm's balance sheet at the end of the current accounting period showed an increase in capital and surplus of $192,000, for a total of $1,600,000 in the capital and surplus account. Paradigm's assets also increased by $192,000, for a total of $16,600,000 in assets. Figure 7.3 illustrates this result.

Other Financial Statements

Two other financial statements that insurers, and other businesses, prepare are the cash flow statement and the statement of owners' equity. The **cash flow statement**, also called a *statement of cash flows*, provides information about a company's cash receipts (inflows), cash disbursements (outflows), and net change in cash during a specific accounting period. The primary purpose of a cash flow statement is to show how a company manages its cash over time. The cash flow statement is also linked to the balance sheet because it provides information about the change in cash between the company's current balance sheet and previous balance sheet.

The **statement of owners' equity** is a financial statement that provides information about changes in owners' equity between two sequential balance sheets. Stock insurers refer to this financial statement as the *statement of stockholders' equity*.

Figure 7.3 Linking the Income Statement to the Balance Sheet

Balance Sheet (End of Previous Period)		Income Statement (Current Period)		Balance Sheet (End of Current Period)	
Assets	$16,408,000	Revenues	$6,072,000	Assets	$16,600,000
		less			
Liabilities	$15,000,000	Expenses	$5,880,000	Liabilities	$15,000,000
Capital & Surplus	$1,408,000			Capital & Surplus	$1,600,000
Total Liabilities and Capital & Surplus	$16,408,000	*Plus* Net Income	$192,000	*Equals* Total Liabilities and Capital & Surplus	$16,600,000

Mutual insurers and fraternal insurers, which do not issue stock, often prepare a *statement of policyowners' equity* or *statement of policyholders' equity* for their customers.

Like the income statement, the cash flow statement and the statement of owners' equity are examples of *dynamic reports*, illustrating the movement or flow of a company's financial transactions during a specified accounting period. Figure 7.4 brings us up to date on Winnie's experiences at Paradigm.

Reports for Stakeholders and Regulators

A company includes its financial statements in a variety of financial reports, including an annual report, and, for insurance companies that conduct business in the United States, an Annual Statement. Although both of these reports are intended for external parties, the audience for each is different. While the annual report contains general-purpose financial information for public use, regulators and rating agencies are the primary audience for the Annual Statement.

Figure 7.4 Winnie Learns about Financial Statements

During her second week at Paradigm, Winnie attended a training session for new employees that focused on financial basics. To her surprise, she found that items like income statements and balance sheets weren't as puzzling as she had thought. In fact, she was able to come up with some ways of keeping the different kinds of financial statements straight.

When she needs to know the "bottom line," she thinks of "net income"—when you're looking at something on a "net" basis, you're looking at a final result. Net *income* is found on the *income* statement. The income statement is also where she can find information on Paradigm's revenue and expenses.

When it's a question of "own," "owe," or "worth," that's the balance sheet—with its assets, liabilities, and capital and surplus (owners' equity). As the name implies, the balance sheet must always balance—that is, Paradigm's assets must always be equal to the sum of its liabilities and capital and surplus.

A cash flow statement is just what it sounds like—it shows the flow of, or change in, Paradigm's cash for a given period.

The statement of owners' equity sounds a bit intimidating, but not if you recall that owners' equity is another name for capital and surplus. Paradigm is a stock insurer, so changes in its capital would include any changes in the amount of its stock outstanding. Any change in the amount that Paradigm was accumulating over time would be a change in surplus.

The Annual Report

All stock insurers and most mutual insurers and fraternal insurers develop an annual report to provide financial information to stockholders and investors (if a stock company), policyowners, and others. The *annual report* is a document that a company's management sends to interested parties to report on the company's financial performance during the past year. In certain circumstances, a U.S. insurer must file an annual report with the Securities and Exchange Commission. The *Securities and Exchange Commission (SEC)* is a federal government agency that regulates the investment industry in the United States. A U.S. insurer must file an annual report with the SEC if either of the following is true:

- The insurer is a publicly traded stock insurer, in which case its stock is a security and subject to securities regulation

- The insurer offers variable products, such as variable annuities or variable universal life insurance, which are securities subject to securities regulation

Consider whether the following three insurers, all with operations in the United States, must file an annual report with the SEC:

- The Melody Mutual Life Insurance Company sells term and whole life insurance products and variable products.

- The Stellar Life Insurance Company, a publicly traded stock insurer, sells term and whole life insurance products.

- The Friendly Fraternal Life Insurance Company sells term and whole life insurance products and fixed immediate annuities.

Of these insurers,

- Melody Mutual must file an annual report because it sells variable products.

- Although Stellar Life does not sell any variable products, it must file an annual report because it is a publicly traded stock insurer.

- Friendly Fraternal is not required to file an annual report because, as a fraternal insurer, it does not issue stock; in addition, it does not sell any variable products. Friendly Fraternal may choose to submit an annual report, but it is not required to do so.

The annual report is a broad assessment of a company's financial performance. It assumes that the company will be in business going forward and helps users assess a company's profitability—its success in generating returns for its owners—as well as its financial strength. Most companies regard the annual report as an important document, not only from an accounting point of view, but from a promotional point of view. An annual report is an opportunity for a company to promote itself to its current owners and to potential investors and customers.

The heart of the annual report consists of the four financial statements—the income statement, the balance sheet, the cash flow statement, and the statement of owners' equity—and their accompanying notes and supplementary information. In addition to the company's financial statements, an annual report typically includes

- A letter from the company's president to its stockholders or policyowners, describing the company's performance during the past year

- A table of financial highlights that presents summaries of the company's financial achievements during the previous 5 or 10 years

- A list of the company's officers and directors

- Notes to the financial statements, which are factual in nature and disclose the details behind some of the amounts presented in the financial statements

- Management's Discussion and Analysis of Financial Condition and Results of Operations (MD&A), which is a narrative explanation of the company's financial performance written by the company's management

- An independent auditor's report, which is a statement by independent public accountants who have audited the annual report and attest that the information in it fairly represents the operations of the company

In the United States, the SEC requires that a company's annual report include the current and previous year's balance sheet and the current and previous two years' income statements, cash flow statements, and statements of owners' equity so that stockholders and other interested parties can evaluate the company's performance over time.

Figure 7.5 contains some online sources for annual reports.

Figure 7.5 Annual Reports Online

You can find plenty of examples of annual reports on the Internet. The following Web sites contain annual reports for life insurance companies:

- http://www.annualreports.com
- http://www.annualreportservice.com
- http://nasdaq.ar.wilink.com

Please take a look at a few examples. You will notice that they contain a great deal of information and are quite lengthy. You might also see if you can get a copy of your company's latest annual report.

The Annual Statement

Unlike the other statements and reports that have been discussed in this chapter, the Annual Statement is unique to insurance companies. The *Annual Statement* is a document that presents information about an insurer's operations and financial performance, with an emphasis on demonstrating the insurer's solvency. The information presented in the Annual Statement is designed to show that an insurer can meet its obligations to customers, even if it stops doing business tomorrow.

The Annual Statement is the primary basis for solvency monitoring by government regulators in the United States. Every life insurer operating in the United States must file, on both an annual and a quarterly basis, an Annual Statement with the National Association of Insurance Commissioners and the insurance department of every state in which the insurer conducts business. The *National Association of Insurance Commissioners (NAIC)* is an association of state insurance commissioners designed to promote consistent insurance regulation.

The general form of the Annual Statement was developed by the NAIC, although each state's insurance commissioner specifies the exact format and contents of that state's Annual Statement. The Annual Statement typically includes the company's financial statements, along with exhibits, schedules, and supplemental reports that support the totals shown in the primary financial statements. Although the Annual Statement applies specifically to U.S. life insurance companies, insurers in other countries typically must comply with similar reporting requirements.

Figure 7.6 summarizes the differences between the annual report and the Annual Statement.

Budgets

You may recall that a *budget* is a financial plan of action, expressed in monetary terms, that covers a specified period, such as one year. *Budgeting* is an accounting process that includes creating a financial plan of action designed to help an organization achieve its goals. Unlike the financial reports discussed in this chapter, budgets are generally reserved for internal company use. In addition, while financial reports focus on the past performance of a company, budgets are plans that contain estimates, or projections, of a company's future activities.

An insurer can use budgets to plan for something as minor as office supplies that the underwriting department will use in one month or as major as the premium income and investment income the company expects for the entire year. Once a budget is in place, the company uses it to monitor performance. This dual role of budgeting—to first establish performance levels and then evaluate whether these levels are being achieved—is central to the control function in a company.

Why Budget?

All companies budget, however informally. Budgets outline a company's plans for its financial resources. A primary objective of a budget is to project systematically—for a given department, division, or line of business—the anticipated revenues and expenses during a specified accounting period. The budgeting process enables a company to

■ Allocate scarce resources effectively

Figure 7.6 The Annual Report versus the Annual Statement

Annual Report	Annual Statement
Its purpose is to...	
Help users assess the company's profitability	Demonstrate a company's solvency
The audience is...	
Primarily investors and the general public	Primarily regulators and rating agencies
Are a company's financial statements included?	
Yes	Yes
It assumes that the company...	
Will be in business going forward	Can fulfill its obligations to customers, even if it stops doing business tomorrow
Who must file it?	
All publicly traded companies Companies that sell variable products, such as variable life insurance or variable annuity contracts	All insurance companies operating in the United States

- Control and reduce expenses

- Monitor and evaluate ongoing operations

- Evaluate managerial performance

- Communicate information throughout the company

- Motivate employees

Although budgeting has many benefits, it also has some disadvantages, including the potential for those involved in budgeting to

- Consume time that might otherwise be spent performing their primary job duties

- Spend the entire budgeted amount, even when unnecessary

- Overestimate costs so that they will not be blamed if they overspend

- Become discouraged from experimenting with innovative solutions to changing market conditions

- Disregard quality and customer service because of budgetary constraints

A budget committee comprising various executives and senior managers usually oversees the budgeting process, and each department or business unit is usually responsible for drafting its own budget within the guidelines set by the budget committee.

Budgeting Approaches

Three distinct approaches to budgeting are (1) top-down budgeting, (2) bottom-up budgeting, and (3) zero-based budgeting. In practice, most companies use a combination of these approaches.

Top-Down Budgeting and Bottom-Up Budgeting

As their names imply, *top-down budgeting* begins at the "top" of a company—with the company's senior management—and is passed "down" to lower-level management, while *bottom-up budgeting* starts at the "bottom" of a company, with lower-level managers generating budgets for their areas, which are then presented in the form of recommendations to senior management.

Bottom-up budgeting typically includes a larger number of employees and takes considerably more time than does top-down budgeting. Bottom-up budgets reflect the input and participation of the employees who will be responsible for achieving the company's operational goals. Thus, bottom-up budgeting is more likely to reflect the realities of the company's core business operations. Moreover, bottom-up budgeting tends to have more grassroots support among company employees than does top-down budgeting. Although a bottom-up budget begins at a lower level of the company and expresses the objectives of that operational area, it must adhere to overall corporate objectives.

Despite the differences between top-down budgeting and bottom-up budgeting, both of these approaches typically use the current year's budget as a starting point for making adjustments to the next year's budget.

Zero-Based Budgeting

Zero-based budgeting differs from other budgeting approaches because it does not allow planners to use the current year's budget as a starting point—instead, planners are forced to justify their continued existence and operation every budgeting period. In other words, planners must begin each budgeting period at "zero." In addition, although companies can apply top-down and bottom-up budgeting approaches to both revenue and expense budgets, zero-based budgeting generally applies only to expense budgets.

With *zero-based budgeting (ZBB)*, the company begins with the premise that no resources will be allocated for the next accounting period unless and until each expense is shown to be in accord with the company's strategic and operational goals. In effect, ZBB treats each activity and function as though it were a new project under consideration.

Lower-level employees play a key role in ZBB because they are often called on to provide details that help a company assess the importance and financial requirements of each activity. Benefits of using ZBB include the breadth and quality of financial information contained in the budgets and the training and education employees receive as part of their contribution to the ZBB process. The main disadvantages of using ZBB are that it is both costly and time consuming. Much work associated with ZBB involves (1) collecting and analyzing data to justify each item and (2) preparing contingency budgets in case unanticipated expenses arise. Because of these disadvantages, many companies use a modified ZBB process, such as applying ZBB to specified activities or functions only or performing ZBB every other year.

Figure 7.7 compares the three budgeting approaches.

Figure 7.7 Comparing the Budgeting Approaches

Two months into her job at Paradigm, Winnie was asked to participate on a task force designed to evaluate Paradigm's current budgeting approaches. Paradigm has mostly been using top-down budgeting, but it would like to try bottom-up budgeting and possibly zero-based budgeting. Why might Paradigm want to change its budgeting approach? In order to answer this question, Winnie drew up the following chart summarizing the benefits and disadvantages of each approach.

Budgeting Approach	Benefits	Disadvantages
Top-Down	Tends to be less time consuming and less costly than other approaches Reflects upper management's intentions	Can result in a lack of commitment from lower-level employees Is less reflective of operational realities than other methods
Bottom-Up	Increases the likelihood of employee support and co-operation More likely to reflect the realities of day-to-day operations	Can be time consuming
Zero-Based	Requires planners to justify all expenses by relating them to strategic and operational goals Requires extensive employee participation Produces high-quality information	Tends to be more time consuming and more costly than other approaches May not include sufficient input from upper management Applies only to expense budgets

After drawing up her chart, Winnie could see some advantages to moving away from the top-down approach. Although this approach is the least time consuming of the three, the other two approaches would involve more employees who are lower down in the company—and employees would be more likely to accept a budget created with their input. On the other hand, upper management tends to have the greatest control with the top-down budgeting approach. With the other approaches, upper management may have to relinquish some control over the process.

Types of Budgets

At a typical life insurance company, the individual budgets for each department or area are combined into the company's *master budget*, which shows the overall operating and financing plans for the company during a specified accounting period. Companies refer to the master budget by different names, such as *comprehensive budget*, *corporate budget*, or *performance plan*. A company's master budget can also be thought of as a *profit plan*, because achieving the company's goals should result in profit for the company. Developing the master budget begins with a forecast of the company's revenues, expenses, cash flows, and capital investment activities. Most companies compile the master budget annually and update it semiannually. The master budget generally consists of several key types of budgets, including (1) operational budgets, (2) cash budgets, and (3) capital budgets.

Operational Budgets

A budget that includes part or all of a company's core business operations is called an *operational budget*. All operational budgets begin with a forecast of sales revenue and investment income. Although the format and content of operational budgets vary widely among companies, operational budgets generally include a revenue budget and an expense budget.

A *revenue budget* indicates the amount of income from operations—policy sales, investments, and fees—that the company expects in the coming budget period. The revenue budget determines the limits of the other budgets, so it must be prepared before them.

After developing its revenue budget, a company then prepares its expense budget. An *expense budget* is a schedule of expenses expected during an accounting period. An expense budget is useful in controlling expenses, measuring management performance, and assigning responsibility for expenses.

Figure 7.8 shows an example of a revenue budget and an expense budget.

Cash Budgets

Remember the cash flow statement described earlier in this chapter? The budgeting counterpart to the cash flow statement is the cash budget. A *cash budget* projects a company's beginning cash balance, cash inflows, cash outflows, and ending cash balance for a specified accounting period, typically by quarter. Unlike the cash flow statement, which presents the actual flow of cash experienced by a company in a reporting period, a cash budget contains estimates of future cash activity. By examining the cash budget, an insurer can estimate the timing and amount of cash shortages that will require short-term borrowing or the amount of excess cash that the insurer can invest in assets. Many companies divide the annual cash budget into quarterly, monthly, weekly, and sometimes daily budgets to monitor cash flow more closely.

Figure 7.8 A Revenue Budget and an Expense Budget

Paradigm sells individual life insurance, group life insurance, and individual annuities. Paradigm's annual revenue and expense budgets are itemized by quarter. Quarter 1 is shown.

Revenue Budget
Quarter 1

Premium Income

Individual life insurance	$400,000
Group life insurance	200,000
Individual annuities	400,000
Total Premium Income	$1,000,000

Investment Income

From securities	$350,000
Mortgage income	150,000
Total Investment Income	500,000
Total Revenues	**$1,500,000**

Expense Budget
Quarter 1

Contractual Benefits

Individual life insurance	$500,000
Group life insurance	100,000
Individual annuities	200,000
Total Contractual Benefits	$800,000

Operating Expenses

Commissions	$170,000
Leases	20,000
Payroll	150,000
General	250,000
Depreciation	10,000
Total Operating Expenses	$600,000
Total Expenses	**$1,400,000**

To develop a cash budget, an insurer must first create a cash receipts budget and a cash disbursements budget. A *cash receipts budget* is a schedule of cash receipts (cash inflows) expected during an accounting period. An insurer estimates the timing and amount of all of its cash disbursements (cash outflows) in the *cash disbursements budget*. The insurer uses data in its sales forecast and investment forecast to obtain projections for its cash receipts and cash disbursements.

After these two budgets have been developed, the next step is to combine them into the cash budget. This process is quite detailed and will not be discussed here. Figure 7.9 illustrates examples of typical cash receipts and cash disbursements used to develop an insurer's cash budget.

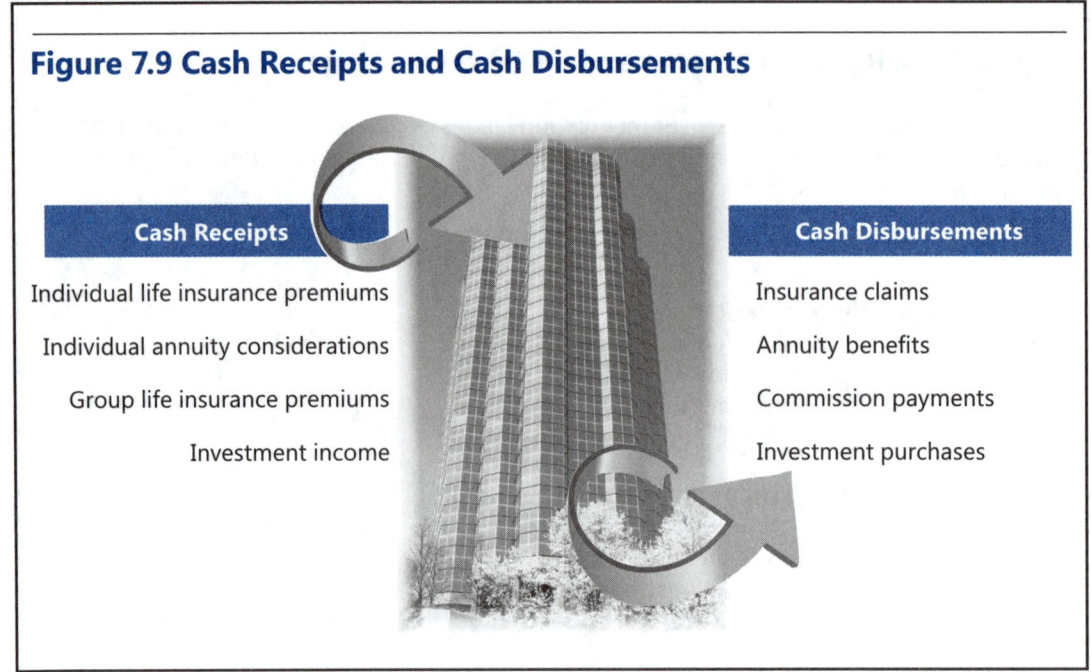

Figure 7.9 Cash Receipts and Cash Disbursements

Cash Receipts	Cash Disbursements
Individual life insurance premiums	Insurance claims
Individual annuity considerations	Annuity benefits
Group life insurance premiums	Commission payments
Investment income	Investment purchases

Capital Budgets

Capital budgeting is the process companies undertake to analyze decisions about investing in long-term projects or assets. Therefore, a *capital budget* shows a company's plans for the financial management of its long-term, high-cost investment proposals. Such investment proposals include

- New investments in equipment or real estate

- Major repairs to or remodeling of existing investments

- Acquisitions of other companies or lines of business

- Mandated safety and environmental improvements

- Expense reduction projects

- Purchases of new computer systems and equipment

A common trait of capital budgeting is that these investments are expected to produce income or other benefits for more than one year.

We have now reviewed all of the major pieces of a company's master budget—its operational budgets, its cash budget, and its capital budgets. Keep in mind that a company doesn't view its budgets in isolation from its financial statements and other reports. For example, an insurer routinely compares its budgeted results with the actual results recorded in its financial statements. By comparing its actual results to its budgeted expectations, a company can evaluate and control its overall performance, as well as the performance of individual departments and employees. Through such comparisons, a company can gain insights that help it plan new courses of action.

Figure 7.10 summarizes the various financial reports and plans discussed in this chapter.

Figure 7.10 Summary of Financial Reports and Plans

Name of Report or Plan	Time Frame: Past or Future?	Intended for Internal and/or External Users?	Examples of Typical Users
Income Statement	Past	Both internal and external users	Managers and investors
Balance Sheet	Past	Both internal and external users	Managers and investors
Cash Flow Statement	Past	Both internal and external users	Managers and investors
Statement of Owners' Equity	Past	Both internal and external users	Managers and investors
Annual Report	Past	External users	Investors and prospective customers
Annual Statement	Past	External users	Regulatory authorities and rating agencies
Budgets	Future	Internal users	Managers

Key Terms

financial reporting
financial statement
income statement
revenue
net income
net gain
net loss
balance sheet
basic accounting equation
capital and surplus
capital
surplus
owners' equity
cash flow statement
statement of owners' equity
annual report
Securities and Exchange Commission (SEC)

Annual Statement
National Association of Insurance Commissioners (NAIC)
budgeting
top-down budgeting
bottom-up budgeting
zero-based budgeting (ZBB)
master budget
operational budget
revenue budget
expense budget
cash budget
cash receipts budget
cash disbursements budget
capital budgeting
capital budget

Chapter 8

Understanding Financial Ratios

Objectives:

After studying this chapter, you should be able to

- Describe what a ratio is and explain the role ratios play in analyzing an insurance company's performance

- Describe and calculate the types of financial ratios that insurers use and be able to interpret what the numbers mean

- Describe the ratio-based systems used by regulators and rating agencies to monitor and evaluate insurance company solvency and profitability

Outline

Ratio Basics
- Ratio Calculations
- Ratio Analysis

Financial Ratios Used by Insurance Companies
- Activity Ratios
- Profitability Ratios
- Solvency Ratios
- Leverage Ratios
- Interpreting the Numbers

Ratios Used for Formal Insurance Reporting
- Regulatory Reporting
- Investor Reporting

> Now that Winnie, our insurance company employee, has studied the company's financial statements, she has a better understanding of what her co-workers are talking about. But she still doesn't understand how all the pieces fit together or what kind of information they provide.

You might be confused, too. Unless a person can put the figures on an insurer's financial statements into a context, the numbers are just numbers. No need to worry, though. Insurers have a fairly simple tool they can use to turn the numbers from various financial statements into usable information about the company's financial and operational performance: it's called a ratio.

Ratio Basics

In simple terms, a *ratio* is a comparison of two numeric values expressed in the form of a fraction or percentage. Fractions and percentages are parts of a whole expressed in numbers rather than words. For example, if you have 50 pennies, you have ½ of a dollar. This is a fraction. You could also say that you have 50% of a dollar. This is a percentage.

All ratios consist of two parts: a numerator and a denominator. The numerator is the numeric value being studied. It appears in the top part of the ratio. The denominator is the value the numerator is compared to. It appears in the bottom part of the ratio. The structure of a ratio is

$$\text{Ratio} = \frac{\text{Numerator}}{\text{Denominator}}$$

Ratio Calculations

To see how a ratio works, consider the following example:

> Winnie is one of 10 analysts who work in the Paradigm Life Insurance Company's claim processing department. Of these 10 analysts, 4 are senior analysts.

It's possible to compare the number of senior analysts to the total number of analysts in the department by putting the values into the form of a ratio. In this ratio, the number of senior analysts is used as the numerator because that's the value we want to study. The total number of analysts in the department, which is the value the numerator is compared to, is used in the denominator. When we plug the numbers from our example into the formula, we get a ratio of $^4/_{10}$. In this example, the result is expressed as a fraction. It says that four-tenths of the analysts in the department are senior analysts. In decimal form, $^4/_{10} = 0.4$ ($4 \div 10 = 0.4$). The result also can be expressed as a percentage instead of a fraction by completing the calculation; that is, by determining the value of $^4/_{10}$ of 100%. The result is 40% ($0.4 \times 100 = 40$).

If we change either the numerator or the denominator in a ratio, but not both, then the value of the ratio will change. The table below summarizes what always happens to a ratio if either the numerator or the denominator, but not both, changes:

If the *numerator* is...	The value of the ratio will...
Increased	Increase
Decreased	Decrease
If the *denominator* is ...	**The value of the ratio will...**
Increased	Decrease
Decreased	Increase

The value of the ratio also changes if both the numerator and the denominator change in the same direction, but the percentage change in the numerator is either greater than or less than the percentage change in the denominator. If both the numerator and the denominator in a ratio *increase*, then

If the percentage change in the numerator is ...	The value of the ratio will ...
Greater than the percentage change in the denominator	Increase
Less than the percentage change in the denominator	Decrease

If both the numerator and denominator *decrease*, then

If the percentage change in the numerator is ...	The value of the ratio will ...
Greater than the percentage change in the denominator	Decrease
Less than the percentage change in the denominator	Increase

The value of the ratio will remain the same if the percentage change in the numerator is the same as the percentage change in the denominator.

Ratio Analysis

Although a company's financial statements can provide companies and investors with valuable information, it's important to recognize that these statements

- **Offer a limited view of company performance.** An insurance company's financial statements describe the company's financial performance at a specific point in time or over a specified period of time. They don't explain whether that performance is good or bad or whether it meets, exceeds, or is below company expectations. That's because the numbers in the statements aren't compared to anything.

- **Shouldn't be analyzed in isolation.** Financial statements are an important source of company-specific information, but they aren't the only source. Financial periodicals, analysts' reports, and outside studies also contain valuable information. To get an accurate picture of company performance, analysts should also examine data about economic and industry conditions. Adding outside information to company-specific information helps put the company's performance in perspective.

- **Don't tell the whole story.** Although financial statements are useful in determining whether a company is profitable, they generally don't report on all the factors that affect profitability. For example, financial statements don't describe the risks involved in achieving profitability.

- **Don't forecast the future.** A company's financial statements provide a picture of the company's financial condition at the end of the reporting period. They generally don't include projections about the company's future performance. Companies usually describe what they expect their financial results will be in budgets prepared at the beginning of a reporting period.

One way to make a company's numbers more meaningful is to translate them into financial relationships. The study of the relationships between various financial statement amounts is called *ratio analysis*. Ratio analysis can be used to identify relationships between one element on an insurance company's balance sheet (or income statement) and another element on the balance sheet (or income statement). It can also be used to identify relationships between balance sheet elements and income statement elements.

The first step in ratio analysis is to extract information from a company's financial statements and turn it into one or more ratios. The next step is to compare the company's current financial ratios to company or industry standards to evaluate the company's performance.

The value of ratio analysis is that it

- **Evaluates company performance over time.** Ratio analysis can compare the company's current performance to its past performance to produce a picture of the company's performance over several years. This long-term comparison allows analysts to identify trends in company performance. Ratio analysis can also be used to identify the amount and direction of any change.

■ **Provides input for the control process.** Ratio analysis can be used to compare a company's actual financial and operational performance levels with the company's planned performance levels. It also can compare company performance to external standards and benchmarks. Because it identifies variances between actual and expected performance, ratio analysis functions as a feedback control during the control cycle.

■ **Identifies possible causes for performance variance.** In addition to measuring company performance, ratios can be used to measure other factors that affect a company's financial performance, such as interest rates, taxation rates, employee turnover rates, persistency rates, and mortality rates. Information provided by these ratios can pinpoint the causes of changes in company performance. For example, a company's net income is affected by product persistency, mortality experience, sales, net investment income, expenses, changes in reserves, reinsurance, and taxes. Changes in any of these factors can cause changes in net income. Analyzing these factors can help a company identify which factors are responsible for changes in net income from one period to the next.

■ **Helps estimate future performance.** Comparing current ratios to similar ratios over successive periods can help identify emerging trends in a company's external and internal environments. By extending these trends into the future, companies may be able to make projections about their future performance. For example, an insurer can use ratios to monitor expenses by product to determine which products are more profitable. Companies can use the information to determine where resources should be allocated and to determine if unprofitable products should be discontinued.

Financial Ratios Used by Insurance Companies

The financial ratios that insurance companies use most often can be divided into the following categories: activity ratios, profitability ratios, solvency ratios, and leverage ratios. The information needed to create ratios comes from a company's financial statements. Figure 8.1 shows the information included in the Paradigm Life Insurance Company's end-of-year income statement. Figure 8.2 shows the company's corresponding balance sheet.

Activity Ratios

Activity ratios, which are sometimes called *operating efficiency ratios* or *turnover ratios*, measure the rate at which a company's various assets are converted (turned over) into sales or cash. Activity ratios thus indicate how efficiently a company is using its assets to produce income. In general terms, activity ratios are expressed as revenues divided by assets, or

$$\frac{\text{Revenues}}{\text{Assets}}$$

8.1. Simplified Income Statement

Paradigm Life Insurance Company
Income Statement
December 31, 201X

Revenues

Premiums	$3,600,000	
Investment income	2,392,000	
Fee income	80,000	
Total Revenues		$6,072,000

Expenses

Benefits and claims	$4,000,000	
Operating expenses	1,600,000	
Investment expenses	10,000	
Taxes	270,000	
Total Expenses		$5,880,000
Net Income		$192,000

The most common activity ratio for insurance companies is the ***total asset turnover ratio***, which indicates how efficiently a company is using its cash, investments, and other assets to support income-producing activities. The total asset turnover ratio is expressed as:

$$\textbf{Total asset turnover} = \frac{\text{Total Revenues}}{\text{Total Assets}}$$

Insurance company revenues come from two primary sources—premium income and investment income. Insurers also earn revenue from various fees and charges. Insurers, therefore, typically use the total revenue amount on the income statement as the numerator in the ratio. An insurer's total assets, taken from the company's balance sheet, are used in the denominator.

Paradigm's year-end income statement shows $3,600,000 in premium income, $2,392,000 in investment income, and $80,000 in fee income, for a total of $6,072,000 in annual revenues. The company's balance sheet shows $16,600,000 in total assets. Paradigm's total asset turnover ratio, using the numbers from its financial statements, is

$$\textbf{Total asset turnover} = \frac{\$\,6,072,000}{\$\,16,600,000}$$

Doing the math shows that the value of the ratio is 0.37 (6,072,000 ÷ 16,600,000 = 0.37).

Figure 8.2. Simplified Balance Sheet

Paradigm Life Insurance Company
Simplified Balance Sheet
December 31, 201X

Assets		=	Liabilities + Capital and Surplus	
			Liabilities	
Investments	$16,000,000			
Cash	$500,000		Contractual reserves	$14,000,000
Other assets	$100,000		Long-term debt	$400,000
Total Assets	**$16,600,000**		Other liabilities	$600,000
			Total Liabilities	**$15,000,000**
			Capital and Surplus	
			Capital	$600,000
			Surplus	$1,000,000
			Total Capital and Surplus	**$1,600,000**
			Total Liabilities + Total Capital and Surplus =	**$16,600,000**

Generally, the higher a company's total asset turnover ratio, the more efficiently it has used its assets. At first glance, Paradigm's total asset turnover ratio might seem a little low, because the company is generating only $0.37 in revenue for every $1.00 invested. However, 0.37 is neither a good result nor a bad result unless it's compared to something else. For example, if Paradigm had generated $6,072,000 in revenue from $15,000,000 in total assets during the previous year, its total asset turnover ratio for that year would have been 0.40. Comparing this year's performance to last year's performance would indicate that Paradigm is not managing its assets as efficiently as it did in the past. In fact, insurers typically aim for a total asset turnover ratio of at least 0.25. Paradigm's total asset turnover ratio of 0.37, therefore, is fairly solid and indicates that the company's assets are well managed and contributing to company profits.

Profitability Ratios

Profitability is the degree of a company's success in generating returns to its owners and increasing the value of the company. *Profitability ratios* provide insurers with a relative measure of their overall success by comparing the company's profits, or gains from operations, to the resources used to generate those profits. For most insurers, resources are usually measured in terms of total assets, investments, or capital. Insurers can use either profit before taxes or profit after taxes as a measure of gains from operations. Profit *before* taxes allows the company to focus on total earnings. Profit *after* taxes shows the net earnings that are available to the company and its owners.

Insurers use four ratios to measure profitability: net profit margin, return on assets, return on invested assets, and return on equity. The net profit margin ratio provides information about a company's overall profitability. Return on assets, return on invested assets, and return on equity ratios provide companies with a picture of how effectively resources are being used to generate income. Figure 8.3 summarizes these ratios and the information they provide.

Net Profit Margin

The **net profit margin**, or *return on revenue ratio*, shows how much after-tax profit is generated by each dollar of total revenue. The net profit margin is calculated as

$$\text{Net profit margin} = \frac{\text{Net income}}{\text{Total revenues}}$$

For most companies, the net profit margin provides a picture of the "bottom line" of company operations. According to Paradigm's financial statements, the company had net income of $192,000 and total revenues of $6,072,000. This means that Paradigm's net profit margin for the reporting period was 3.2% ($192,000 ÷ $6,072,000 = 0.032). Company owners generally like to see high net profit margins. However, because of the trade-off between risk and return, insurance companies need to ensure that they are not jeopardizing company solvency by taking excessive risks in order to generate profits.

Figure 8.3. Profitability Ratios

Ratio	Measures	Description
Net Profit Margin	Net income as a percentage of total revenues	Provides companies with information about the overall profitability of their operations
Return on Assets (ROA)	Relationship between net income and total assets	Provides information about management's effectiveness in using assets to generate profits
Return on Invested Assets (ROIA)	Net income as a percentage of average invested assets	Provides information about how efficiently an insurance company uses its investment portfolio to generate profits
Return on Equity (ROE)	Net income as a percentage of owners' equity	Indicates the return a company is generating on the owners' investment

Return on Assets Ratios

The *return on assets ratio (ROA)* provides companies with information about a company's success in using assets to earn a profit. Because ROA indicates how productively management uses business resources, it is among the most important measures of company success. It is widely used to rank companies within the same industry.

The return on assets ratio compares the company's net income, shown on the income statement, to its total assets, shown on the balance sheet. The formula for calculating ROA is

$$\text{ROA} = \frac{\text{Net income}}{\text{Total assets}}$$

The ROA for insurance companies varies depending on the type of business they sell.

According to the information in Paradigm's financial statements, the company had net income of $192,000 and $16,600,000 in total assets. This means that Paradigm's ROA was equal to 1.2% ($192,000 ÷ $16,600,000 = 0.012). As a rule, companies want to maintain as high an ROA as possible because the higher the ROA, the more profitable the company is. The industry average for ROA is generally between 0.5% and 1.0%.

Insurers also use a variation of the general ROA ratio—the return on invested assets ratio—to evaluate profitability. The *return on invested assets ratio (ROIA)* compares the company's net income to its average invested assets. The equation for ROIA is expressed as

$$\text{ROIA} = \frac{\text{Net income}}{\text{Average invested assets}}$$

The value of the company's average invested assets is determined by adding the total invested assets at the beginning of the reporting period (from the previous year's balance sheet) and the total invested assets at the end of the reporting period (from the current year's balance sheet) and then dividing the total by 2. Invested assets include assets in the insurer's investment portfolio and exclude the company's cash, property, equipment, and other noninvested assets.

> Suppose Paradigm's balance sheet for the previous year showed a total of $13,000,000 in investments. The company's average invested assets, therefore, would be equal to $14,500,000 [($13,000,000 + $16,000,000) ÷ 2 = $14,500,000]. Because net income for the period was $192,000, Paradigm's ROIA is equal to 1.3% ($192,000 ÷ $14,500,000 = 0.013).

By focusing on invested assets rather than total assets, an insurer can see how efficiently the company is using its investment portfolio to earn a return. The higher the return, the more efficiently the company is managing its investments. To evaluate long-term profitability, however, the company needs to assess the impact of returns over several years rather than a single year.

Return on Equity Ratio

The ***return on equity ratio (ROE)*** measures the return to a company's owners by relating profits to owners' equity. Owners' equity represents all owner investments in the company. For a stock insurance company, owners' equity is the total of capital and surplus. For mutual companies and fraternal benefit societies, which do not have stockholders, owners' equity is equal to the company's surplus. The equation for the return on equity ratio is

$$\text{ROE} = \frac{\text{Net income}}{\text{Owners' equity}}$$

Insurers usually aim for a ROE of between 10% and 15%. However, the ROE target depends, in part, on how risky the business is. The higher the risk, the higher the ROE company owners expect.

According to Paradigm's income statement, the company's net income was $192,000. The total capital and surplus amount on the company's balance sheet was $1,600,000. Putting these numbers into ratio form produces a return on equity of 12% ($192,000 ÷ $1,600,000 = 0.12).

However, to determine its actual level of efficiency, a company needs to compare current results against a standard, such as the company's performance in earlier years, its objectives for the year, or an industry-based benchmark.

Solvency Ratios

One of the major financial concerns for insurance companies is whether they have enough assets to cover their financial obligations, over both the short term and the long term. In general, insurance companies use the current ratio to measure short-term solvency and the capital and surplus ratio to measure long-term solvency. Figure 8.4 describes these ratios and the information they provide.

Figure 8.4. Solvency Ratios

Ratio	Measures	Description
Current Ratio	Relationship between current assets and current liabilities	Shows the amount of resources a company has available to cover each dollar of current debt
Capital and Surplus Ratio	Relationship between a company's capital and surplus and its liabilities	Provides a measure of a company's financial strength

Current Ratio

The *current ratio* compares a company's current assets to its current liabilities. As such, it provides a measure of the company's ability to meet its maturing short-term obligations without borrowing or selling long-term investments. The current ratio is expressed as

$$\text{Current ratio} = \frac{\text{Current assets}}{\text{Current liabilities}}$$

Current assets usually include cash and readily marketable assets—such as securities available for sale—that can be converted into cash within one year. Current assets don't include fixed assets, such as property and equipment, or a company's long-term investments. Current liabilities include commissions, dividends and claims payable, accrued expenses, and short-term debt. The current ratio shows the amount of resources a company has available to cover each dollar of current debt.

In general, a current ratio of 100% (1.00) or better indicates that a company has adequate liquidity. A current ratio of less than 100% (which means the company's current liabilities are greater than its current assets) is generally a sign that an insurer may not have enough cash and other current assets on hand to pay its contractual benefits and general operating expenses.

Suppose that $12,000,000 of Paradigm's $16,600,000 in total assets for the reporting period represented current assets and that $12,500,000 of the company's $14,000,000 in total liabilities were current liabilities. Using these amounts in the current ratio equation shows that Paradigm's current ratio is equal to 96% ($12,000,000 ÷ $12,500,000 = 0.96).

$$\text{Current ratio} = \frac{\$12,000,000}{\$12,500,000}$$

According to the current ratio, Paradigm may not have sufficient current assets to cover its financial obligations and may need to borrow money or sell some of its assets to cover the difference.

A very high ratio can also be a problem because current assets generally produce low returns, and low returns can damage profits. The goal for most insurers, therefore, is to maintain a moderate level of liquidity.

Insurers can evaluate liquidity levels by comparing ratios for two consecutive periods and determining the cause of any changes. For example, if Paradigm's current ratio this year is lower than its ratio for the previous year, it means that the company's overall liquidity is lower now than it was during the previous reporting period. Such a decrease can be the result of (1) a decrease in the amount of current assets the insurer holds or (2) an increase in the company's contractual reserves.

Capital and Surplus Ratio

The *capital and surplus ratio* describes the relationship between a company's capital and surplus and its liabilities. For insurance companies, the capital and surplus ratio provides a measure of an insurer's long-term solvency. Ratios can also evaluate capital and surplus separately. The amounts for capital and surplus and total liabilities used in the ratio are taken from the balance sheet. The formula for calculating the capital and surplus ratio is

$$\text{Capital and surplus ratio} = \frac{\text{Capital and surplus}}{\text{Total liabilities}}$$

If we use the information from Paradigm's balance sheet, the company's capital and surplus ratio would equal 10.7% ($1,600,000 ÷ $15,000,000 = 0.107).

In general, the greater the capital and surplus ratio, the stronger the company's financial position. If a company's ratio is low, it may mean that the company's solvency is in jeopardy and the company needs to take action. An insurer can increase its ratio results in two ways: (1) by increasing the amount of capital or surplus it holds or (2) by decreasing its total liabilities. However, if a company's capital and surplus ratio is too high, the company may have trouble earning an adequate return on equity. Therefore, insurers must carefully weigh the trade-offs between solvency and profitability.

The main drawback of basic capital and surplus ratios is that they don't take a company's level of risk into account. An insurer's capital position is subject to risk from a number of sources, and not all insurance companies are exposed to the same levels of risk. Not all insurance companies follow the same reserving practices, either. As a result, when calculating a company's capital and surplus ratio, it's necessary to consider the company's reserving practices and the risks to which the company is exposed. To account for risk, insurers often use weighted values to calculate capital ratios. A *weighted value* is a value that has been multiplied by a percentage. Regulators and rating agencies often require insurers to use weight-adjusted, or risk-based, capital ratios in their financial reports.

Leverage Ratios

In general terms, the *leverage effect*, or *leverage*, is a measure of the impact of fixed costs—either operating costs or financing costs—on a company's potential risks and returns to company owners. Figure 8.5 describes how leverage works.

Leverage ratios measure the amount of debt a company is using to support its resources and operations. In general, as leverage increases, a company's exposure to risk of loss increases, because its debt is larger (or increasing more quickly) than its capital and surplus. However, because of the risk-return trade-off, potential earnings also increase. Company owners are often willing to accept relatively high levels of leverage, and the accompanying high levels of risk, because higher risks are usually associated with higher potential returns. Policyowners and regulators usually prefer companies to maintain lower levels of leverage because increasing risks can have a negative effect on company solvency.

Insurance companies use two primary leverage ratios to evaluate leverage: the debt-to-equity ratio and the insurance leverage ratio. The *debt-to-equity ratio* compares long-term debt to owners' equity.

Figure 8.5. Financial Leverage

When an insurance company borrows funds from a bank or other financial intermediary, it usually reinvests those funds. While the funds are invested, the insurer earns returns and pays interest to the lender.

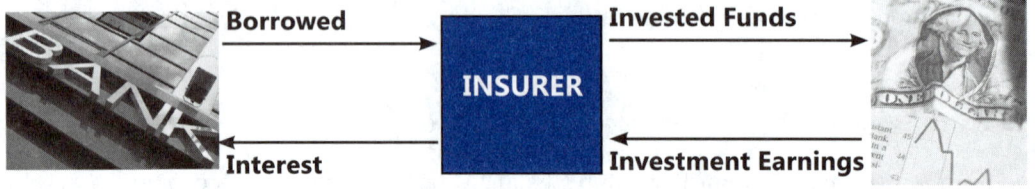

If the rate of return the insurer earns on its investments is greater than the rate the insurer owes on the borrowed funds, the excess returns become part of the company's profits. In this case, leverage has a positive effect on profit. Leverage will have a negative effect on profit if the rate of return the insurer earns on its investments is less than the rate the insurer owes on the borrowed funds.

$$\text{Debt-to-equity ratio} = \frac{\text{Long-term debt}}{\text{Owners' equity}}$$

According to Paradigm's balance sheet, the company had $400,000 in long-term debt. Comparing this amount to the company's $1,600,000 in capital and surplus produces a debt-to-equity ratio of 0.25 ($400,000 ÷ $1,600,000 = 0.25).

In general, the lower the value of the ratio, the stronger the insurer's financial position. High ratio results are generally an indication that a company relies heavily on borrowed funds to cover its financial obligations. High ratio results also indicate relatively high risk, and high levels of risk can have a negative effect on company solvency.

Another ratio insurance companies use to evaluate leverage is the ***insurance leverage ratio***, which compares a company's contractual reserves to its capital and surplus.

$$\text{Insurance leverage ratio} = \frac{\text{Contractual reserves}}{\text{Capital and surplus}}$$

The insurance leverage ratio focuses on the insurer's ability to cover its contractual obligations with existing resources. Insurers usually have high insurance leverage ratios because contractual reserves make up a large portion of total liabilities. Most insurers, however, try to maintain ratio values of 4.0 to 6.5. Using information from Paradigm's balance sheet in the equation above shows that Paradigm's insurance leverage ratio is equal to 8.75 ($14,000,000 ÷ $1,600,000 = 8.75).

Interpreting the Numbers

The final step in evaluating a company's financial performance is comparing ratio results with established performance standards. Insurance companies can use internal or external standards for this evaluation. Internal standards consist of the company's own historical performance data over a period of three to five years or longer. Figure 8.6 includes hypothetical financial ratio information for Paradigm over the past five years and for the industry as a whole.

The information in Figure 8.6 shows that Paradigm's

■ **Asset turnover is solid.** Paradigm's performance over the last four years shows a steady decline in asset turnover, which indicates that the company is not using its assets to generate revenues as effectively as it has in the past. Clearly, the company can do better. However, other companies in the industry are not doing nearly as well in this area of performance. Compared to the industry average, Paradigm's performance is solid.

■ **Profitability picture is attractive.** The company's net profit margin, return on assets, and return on invested assets are all above industry averages. Paradigm's return on equity is equal to the industry average. The company is doing a good job of managing its profits and getting as much as it can from its assets, investments, and capital.

■ **Solvency needs improving, especially over the short-term.** The current ratio has been decreasing each year, and this year's ratio indicates that the company's current assets may not be sufficient to cover all of its current liabilities. Paradigm may need to sell some of its assets to improve its short-term liquidity position. However, Paradigm has been doing better than most companies. According to Paradigm's capital and surplus ratio results, the company's long-term solvency outlook is lower than the industry average, but the company has demonstrated consistent improvement in its use of capital.

Figure 8.6. Comparative Historical Performance Data

	Historical Ratio Results for the Paradigm Life Insurance Company					Industry Average
	Year 1	Year 2	Year 3	Year 4	Year 5 (Current)	
Activity Ratios						
Total Asset Turnover	0.50	0.55	0.45	0.40	**0.37**	**0.25**
Profitability Ratios						
Net Profit Margin	3.40%	3.50%	4.00%	3.75%	**3.20%**	**3.15%**
ROA	1.50%	1.60%	1.00%	0.95%	**1.20%**	**0.75%**
ROIA	1.40%	1.50%	1.55%	1.42%	**1.30%**	**0.95%**
ROE	11.45%	11.25%	11.55%	11.60%	**12.0%**	**12.00%**
Solvency Ratios						
Current	140%	137%	125%	100%	**96%**	**63%**
Capital and Surplus	8.30%	8.90%	9.30%	9.80%	**10.70%**	**12%**
Leverage Ratios						
Debt-to-Equity	0.45	0.59	0.40	0.30	**0.25**	**0.25**
Insurance Leverage	8.50	7.75	9.00	8.65	**8.75**	**6.00**

■ **Leverage position needs attention.** At 0.25, the company's debt-to-equity ratio is at the industry average. Its insurance leverage ratio, which shows the company's leverage on its contractual reserves, is higher than the industry average. This higher ratio may indicate that the company is over-financing its operations. Another possible explanation for the high insurance leverage ratio is that Paradigm's surplus has been decreasing because of high first-year costs and reserve requirements associated with new products. If Paradigm is accepting too much risk, reinsurance—which would allow Paradigm to transfer some of its risk and reserve burden to another insurer—could be an option.

Ratios Used for Formal Insurance Reporting

Most of the information presented so far focuses on the use of ratio analysis by insurance company management. However, ratio analysis is also an integral part of efforts by regulators and investors to monitor the financial stability of insurance companies.

Regulatory Reporting

Regulatory monitoring typically relies heavily on ratio analysis. For example, insurance regulators in the United States use two ratio-based systems to evaluate the solvency of life insurers operating within the jurisdiction. The ***Insurance Regulatory Information System (IRIS)*** uses 12 standardized financial ratios to identify insurance companies that are most likely to experience financial difficulty. Eight of the 12 ratios test insurance company solvency and profitability; the remaining 4 ratios test financial stability. The information needed to calculate IRIS ratios is taken from the Annual Statement each insurer must submit. Companies whose results on 4 or more ratios fall outside the usual range undergo additional analysis. Canadian regulators use a similar set of ratios, known as ***early-warning financial ratio tests***, to analyze insurers' financial statements. The information for these ratio tests is taken from the Annual Return filed by all Canadian insurers.

Another system for evaluating the solvency of U.S. insurers is the ***Financial Analysis and Solvency Tracking (FAST) system***. The FAST system evaluation is based on (1) ratio analysis of an insurer's most recent financial statements and (2) analysis of a five-year history of specific aspects of the insurer's financial statements. Regulators select the specific factors that will be analyzed on a case-by-case basis. Insurers whose financial statements produce unusual ratio results may be subject to corrective action by the state insurance department. Figure 8.7 describes international agencies that study insurance company solvency.

Investor Reporting

In some jurisdictions, rating agencies play an important role in providing policyowners and investors with information about insurance company solvency and profitability. A ***rating agency*** is an independently owned, private organization that evaluates the financial condition of insurers and provides information to potential customers of and investors in insurance companies. Most rating agencies provide information in the form of credit ratings. A credit rating is an indication of a company's ability to repay its financial debts, including its ability to meet its

Figure 8.7. International Studies of Insurer Solvency

Organization for Economic Co-operation and Development (OECD)

Provides an overview of the structures for monitoring solvency in the OECD's 30 member companies and in various non-member companies.

European Union (EU)

Reports on solvency and risk management practices in the 25 countries that make up the European economic union.

International Association of Insurance Supervisors (IAIS)

Research focuses on risk-based approaches to insurer solvency in 130 countries around the world.

International Actuarial Association (IAA)

Monitors insurance solvency assessment globally through the efforts of an established working party.

obligations to policyowners. Figure 8.8 lists some of the major rating agencies for insurance companies.

Most rating agencies rate insurers on two key factors:

- **Financial strength.** Rating agencies define a company's financial strength in terms of its solvency. Financial strength ratings are designed specifically for current policyowners and potential buyers of insurance products. Ratings are based on an examination of a company's balance sheet entries (assets, liabilities, owners' equity), its operating performance, and its business (risk) profile. In most cases, ratings are expressed in the form of a letter grade. To receive a high rating, an insurer is expected to maintain at least a minimum standard of capital, known as rating agency capital. Rating agency capital requirements are generally higher than regulatory capital requirements.

- **Investment potential.** All investors require their investments, including their investments in insurance companies, to provide a sufficient return. To provide that return, an insurance company needs to demonstrate at least a minimum level of profitability. Investors are also concerned about a company's ability and willingness to pay financial guarantees to investors on a timely basis. Agency ratings, which are based on a company's investment performance and its risk profile, are often used as a source of investment information. Rating agencies usually divide insurance companies into two groups: investment grade (companies with recognized potential) and non-investment grade/speculative (companies with little or no potential). They also describe various levels within each of these categories.

Much of the information needed to calculate ratings comes from evaluating a company's financial ratios.

Figure 8.8. Major Insurance Rating Agencies

A. M. Best	Provides ratings of over 10,000 insurers in 95 countries. Ratings of financial strength are based on balance sheet strength, operating performance, and business profile. Ratings range from A++ (superior) to F (in liquidation). Ratings on investment potential divide companies into investment grade and non-investment grade categories, with A++ assigned to companies with exceptional potential and F assigned to companies considered to be extremely speculative.
Standard & Poor's	Provides market intelligence to potential investors in the form of credit ratings, indices (e.g., S&P 500), investment research, and risk evaluation. Credit ratings, which describe a company's relative level of credit risk, range from AAA (extremely strong capacity to meet financial obligations) to D (payment default).
Moody's	Provides credit ratings, research and risk analysis of more than 12,000 corporate issuers in 100 countries.
Fitch	Provides credit ratings and reports on financial and operational strength of companies in 150 countries. Ratings are based on public information and non-public information provided by issuers. Ratings range from AAA (investment grade) to D (speculative grade).

Key Terms

ratio

ratio analysis

activity ratio

total asset turnover ratio

profitability ratio

net profit margin

return on assets ratio (ROA)

return on invested assets ratio (ROIA)

return on equity ratio (ROE)

current ratio

capital and surplus ratio

weighted value

leverage effect

debt-to-equity ratio

insurance leverage ratio

Insurance Regulatory Information System (IRIS)

early-warning financial ratio tests

Financial Analysis and Solvency Tracking (FAST) system

rating agency

Chapter 9

Presenting Data Visually

Objectives:

After studying this chapter, you should be able to

- Explain the primary benefits of using tables to present data and describe the different ways tables can be organized

- Describe the three primary types of charts insurance companies use to display data and the benefits they offer

- Explain how insurers use flow charts, Gantt charts, and PERT networks to manage projects

- Describe how insurance companies can use dashboards and balanced scorecards to manage business performance

- Describe situations in which tables, charts, and graphs can present deceptive information and identify ways to avoid these problems

Outline

Tables

Charts
- Bar Charts
- Pie Charts
- Line Diagrams

Other Ways to Present Data Visually
- Flow Charts
- Project Scheduling Charts
- Performance Management Charts

Avoiding Deceptive Uses of Visual Presentations

Anyone who works in an insurance company knows that insurers and other financial services companies are in the numbers business. For example, an insurance company uses numbers to

- Create financial statements that describe company performance
- Predict gross sales revenue for each of the company's products
- Show how many policies a company and its producers have sold in a specified period
- Evaluate the risks and costs of developing a new product
- Calculate the average earnings per share of the company's outstanding common stock
- Make investment decisions
- Track the time it takes company employees to process claims and answer customer questions
- Determine the policy reserves needed to support product liabilities
- Calculate the mortality rates for certain groups of people
- Develop project schedules and track progress on those projects
- Describe company goals and objectives
- Track changes in interest rates and other economic factors
- Determine the premium rate to charge for a life insurance policy
- Analyze customer satisfaction with the company's products and services

People even use numbers to verify hunches. For example, suppose an insurance sales manager thinks that producers in one territory are earning higher monthly incomes than producers in another territory. The manager can use numbers to support or disprove his theory.

Sometimes, numbers represent financial amounts. For example, policy reserves, stock prices, and profits and losses are expressed in terms of money. Other numbers, such as interest rates, mortality rates, the number of products a company sells, the number of employees in the company's home office, and the time needed to process claims or answer telephone calls, are not monetary amounts. When numbers are used to represent specific quantities, they're called data. It's important to note that not all data are numbers. For example, characteristics such as gender (male or female) and address (city and state) are also data. When data are analyzed so that they are useful for users, they become information.

Managers and other insurance company employees generally don't have trouble finding the data they need. Most company-specific data are stored in the company's records and databases, and users can generally find noncompany data in external databases and reports. The problem is in finding a way to arrange, sort, and condense large amounts of data into a form that makes sense. Using tables, charts, and graphs to present collected data is a way to solve that problem.

Tables

Putting data into a table is one of the easiest ways to condense large amounts of data and to arrange the data so that they provide meaningful information. A *table* is an orderly listing of data. In fact, order is one of the primary benefits of using tables to present data.

Amy Cranston is an administrative assistant in the Orion Insurance Company's marketing division. Recently, her manager gave her an alphabetized list of the six producers working in a particular regional office and asked her to prepare a report on the sales generated by those producers during the past month. Amy looked up the monthly sales report for the office and found the following sales figures for each producer:

Chan	15 policies
Draper	7 policies
Epstein	2 policies
Greyson	8 policies
Maynard	3 policies
Portman	6 policies

Amy has all the information she needs to prepare a report, but it doesn't really convey much in this format because the data aren't presented in any meaningful order. Now suppose that Amy put the data into a table that lists sales in descending order—that is, from highest to lowest.

Producer	Number of Policies Sold
Chan	15
Greyson	8
Draper	7
Portman	6
Maynard	3
Epstein	2

By organizing the data in descending order, Amy can provide her boss with useful information. For example, her boss can

- Determine the range of sales generated by producers in the field office—from a high of 15 to a low of 2

■ Identify the top producers in the field office—Chan is clearly outstanding, with nearly twice as many sales as the next producer

■ Identify the producers who are not meeting standards and may need additional training or supervision—the sales figures for Maynard and Epstein are not only far below Chan's, but also are less than half as high as the rest of the other producers

Data can also be presented in *ascending* order—that is, from lowest to highest—or arranged in order of time, age, or importance. Figure 9.1 shows how insurers use an ascending order table to show the growth of a $100,000 whole life insurance policy's cash value over time. Looking at the table in Figure 9.1, a customer can easily identify when the insurance policy will begin to generate a cash value and what the expected amount of that value will be at the end of any given policy year.

Figure 9.1. Growth of Cash Value in a $100,000 Whole Life Insurance Policy

End of Policy Year	Cash Value
1	---------
2	---------
3	$ 400
4	1,400
5	2,400
6	3,500
7	4,500
8	5,600
9	6,800
10	8,000
11	9,300
12	11,000
13	12.900
14	14,800
15	16,700
16	18,700
17	20,700
18	22,700
19	24,800
20	26,900
Age 60	32,300
Age 65	41,700

Mortality tables also are important for insurance companies. A mortality table shows, for each age of a given group of people, the mortality rate, number of people surviving, number of people dying, and remaining life expectancy. Mortality tables do not indicate when a given individual in the group is expected to die. Figure 9.2 shows a portion of a mortality table that includes basic mortality data for men, arranged by age.

In this table, column 1 (age) shows the ages of the men included in the table. Most mortality tables start at age 0 and extend to 99 or 100. Some tables show rates for ages as high as 120. Column 2 (mortality rate) shows the number of men per thousand who are expected to die at each age. Column 3 shows the total number of men living at the beginning of the year for each age. Column 4 shows the total number expected to die at each age. Column 5 shows the remaining life expectancy at each age.

Mortality rates are generally expressed as the number of deaths per thousand. According to the information in the sample mortality table, 11 out of every 1,000 men age 65—or a total of 1,100 of the original 100,000—will die before they reach age 66. We can convert this number into a percentage by dividing the number of men dying at age 65 (Column 4) by the number of men age 65 alive at the beginning of the year (Column 3). In this case, the mortality rate is 0.011, or 1.1%.

$$1,100 \div 100,000 = 0.011$$

Extracting this same information from unorganized data would be far more difficult.

Knowing how many people in a given age group are expected to die each year helps insurers determine the number and timing of future benefit payments. Actuaries also use mortality information to establish the premium rates for life insurance and annuity products during product design and to calculate the amount of the reserve needed to support a product.

Tables can be organized to show grouped or ungrouped data. Ungrouped data record each number individually. The sales figures in the table that Amy constructed are ungrouped data. The individual sales figures were listed in order, but they weren't grouped. Grouped data divide values into classes, or categories, and then show the number of times the observed data fall within the range for each class. A table that displays the number of times observed grouped data fall within specified classes is called a **grouped frequency distribution**. For example, Amy could have arranged the sales figures into ranges, such as "1–4," "5–10," and "11 and over."

Figure 9.2. Sample Mortality Table—Men

Age	Mortality rate (deaths per 1,000)	Total Number living	Total Number dying	Remaining Life Expectancy
65	11	100,000	1,100	18.4
66	12	98,900	1,187	17.7

Range	Number of Producers
1–4 policies	2
5–10 policies	3
11 and over	1

Ungrouped data generally provide greater precision and accuracy than grouped data, because ungrouped data allow users to see individual values. However, grouped data are often a more effective way to show trends and may be the only way to manage extremely large sets of data.

Charts

Although tables are a valuable tool for condensing and ordering data, they aren't very effective for showing relationships among the data. Charts allow users not only to compare data, but also to see the relationships graphically. Identifying relationships can be especially important if data amounts or sizes are important. Insurance companies use three primary types of charts to compare data: bar charts, pie charts, and line diagrams.

Bar Charts

Bar charts use bars to display the relative size or quantity of various units of data. The bars in the chart can be presented vertically or horizontally along a specified scale. In addition, bars can be presented as plain solid lines, three-dimensional bars, or even symbols, called pictographs, that represent the items being described. Figure 9.3 shows an example of a simple bar chart displaying the number of different types of life insurance policies sold by an insurance company's sales office during a specified time period. In this example, the scale on the side shows a range of 0 to 90 policies sold.

Bar charts can also compare multiple sets of data. For example, the insurer in our example could show data from the Southern field office and the Eastern field office in the same chart, as shown in Figure 9.4. In this figure, policy sales for the two field offices are shown side by side for each category. The manager can tell at a glance the best (and worst) selling products for the two offices. In addition, the manager can see that, in all but two categories—variable life and universal life—sales from the Southern office were higher than those from the Eastern office.

As an alternative to comparing data sets side by side, companies can combine data from two or more data sets into a component bar chart such as the one shown in Figure 9.5. A *component bar chart* is a bar chart that combines the component values from two or more data sets into a single set of bars and indicates the percentage of the total attributable to each set. Each of the bars in this chart represents 100% of sales in each product category, and the colored segments show the percentage of total sales that come from each of the two field offices.

The bar charts shown in Figure 9.3, Figure 9.4, and Figure 9.5 display ungrouped data. Bar charts can also be used to display grouped data. When grouped data are displayed in a bar chart, the bars represent the number of times observed data fall within specified ranges. Bar charts showing grouped data are known as *histograms*. For example, suppose our insurer wants to see how the amounts of

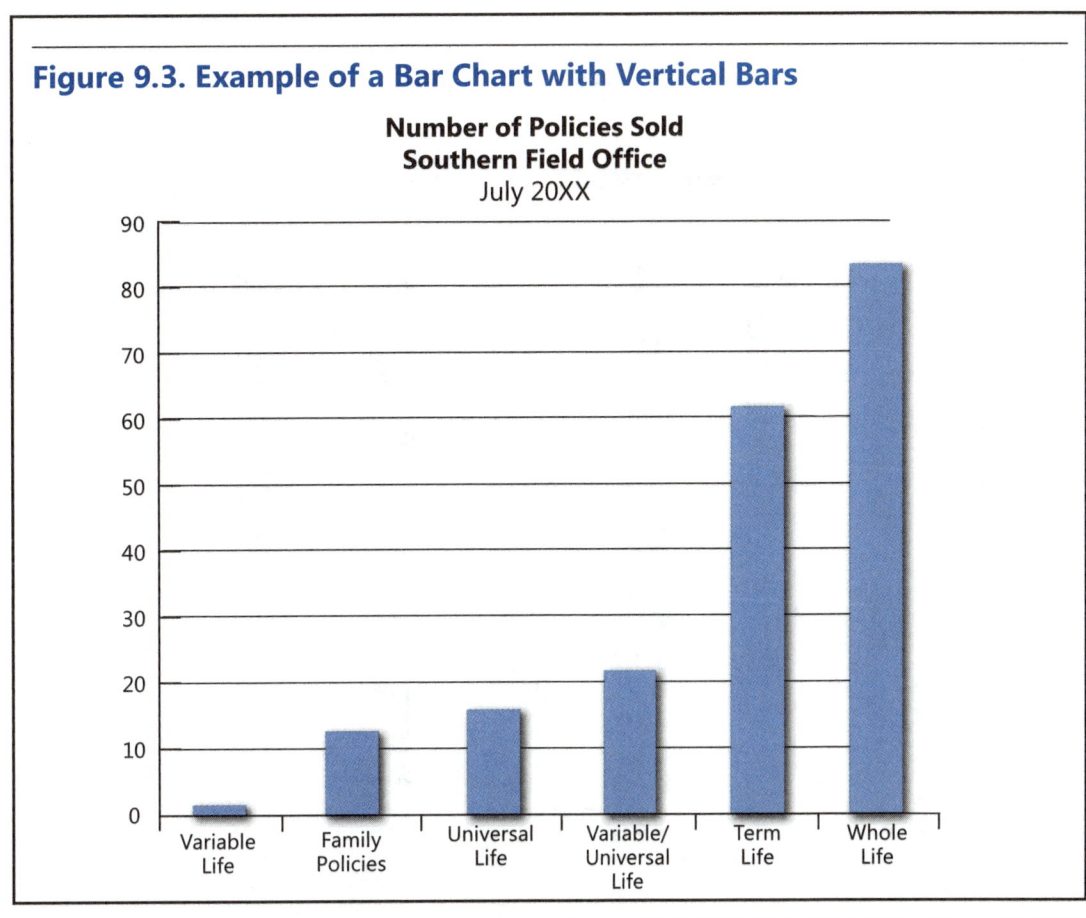

Figure 9.3. Example of a Bar Chart with Vertical Bars

Number of Policies Sold
Southern Field Office
July 20XX

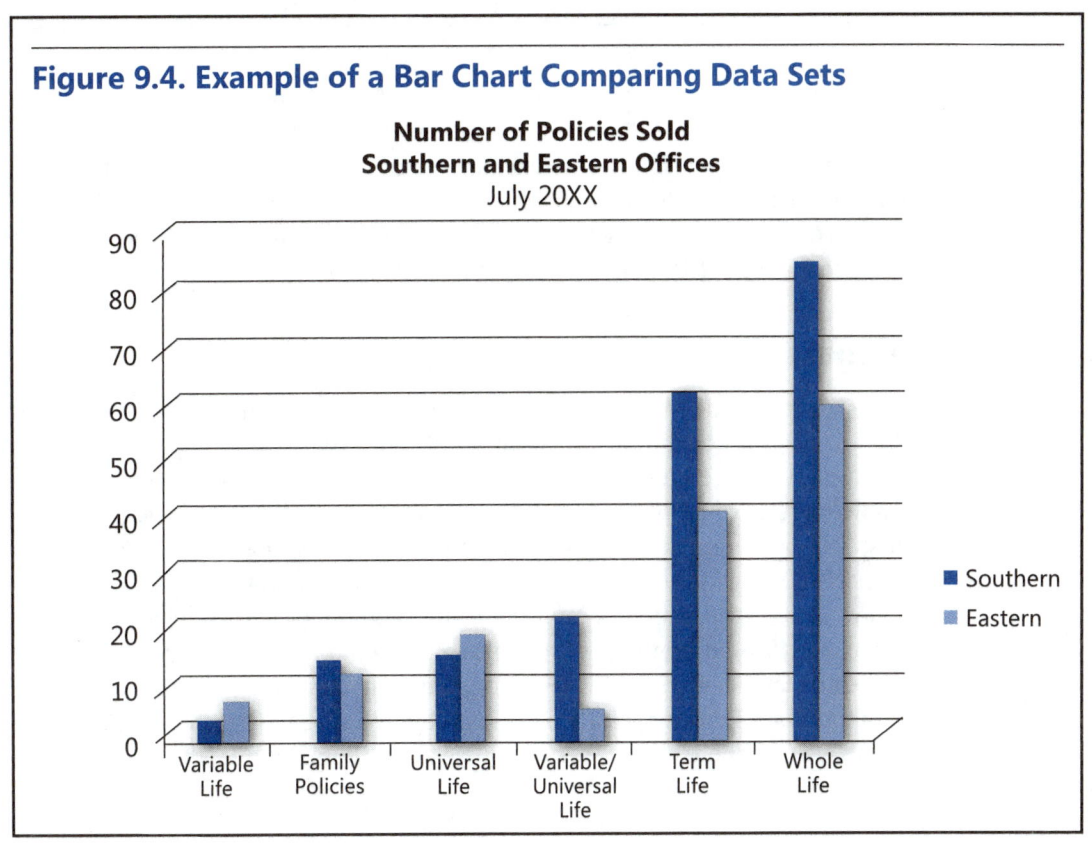

Figure 9.4. Example of a Bar Chart Comparing Data Sets

Number of Policies Sold
Southern and Eastern Offices
July 20XX

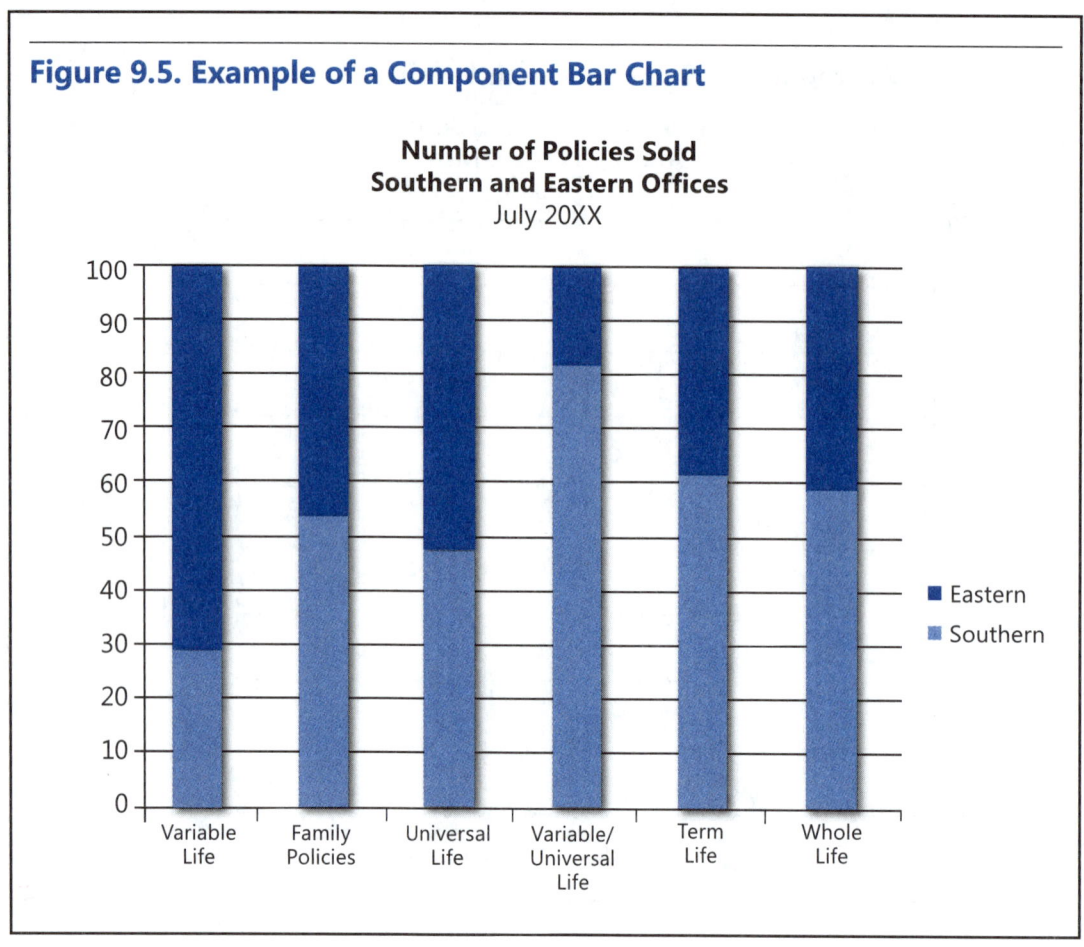

Figure 9.5. Example of a Component Bar Chart

Number of Policies Sold
Southern and Eastern Offices
July 20XX

whole life coverage sold by the Southern field office are distributed. A histogram such as the one in Figure 9.6 would provide this information.

Sometimes, it's possible to increase the visual impact of bar charts by using symbols or pictures, called *pictographs*, rather than bars to represent the data values. For example, a graph showing growth in revenues for a particular insurance product could use stacks of coins instead of bars to show sales amounts.

Pie Charts

Pie charts present data in the shape of a circle (the "pie") that has been cut into pieces. Each piece of the pie represents a different class, or group, into which values are grouped. Pie charts are even more effective than compound bar charts for showing relative proportions or percentages because they allow users to highlight specific groups. Pie charts can be constructed using calculated percentages or numerical values for each segment. Most computer software applications convert raw data into proportions automatically. Figure 9.7 shows what our insurance company's Southern field office sales data would look like presented in a pie chart. Note that the numbers for each policy type have been converted to percentages in the chart. Percentages are calculated by dividing the number of policies in each category by the total number of policies sold. For example, the 84 whole life

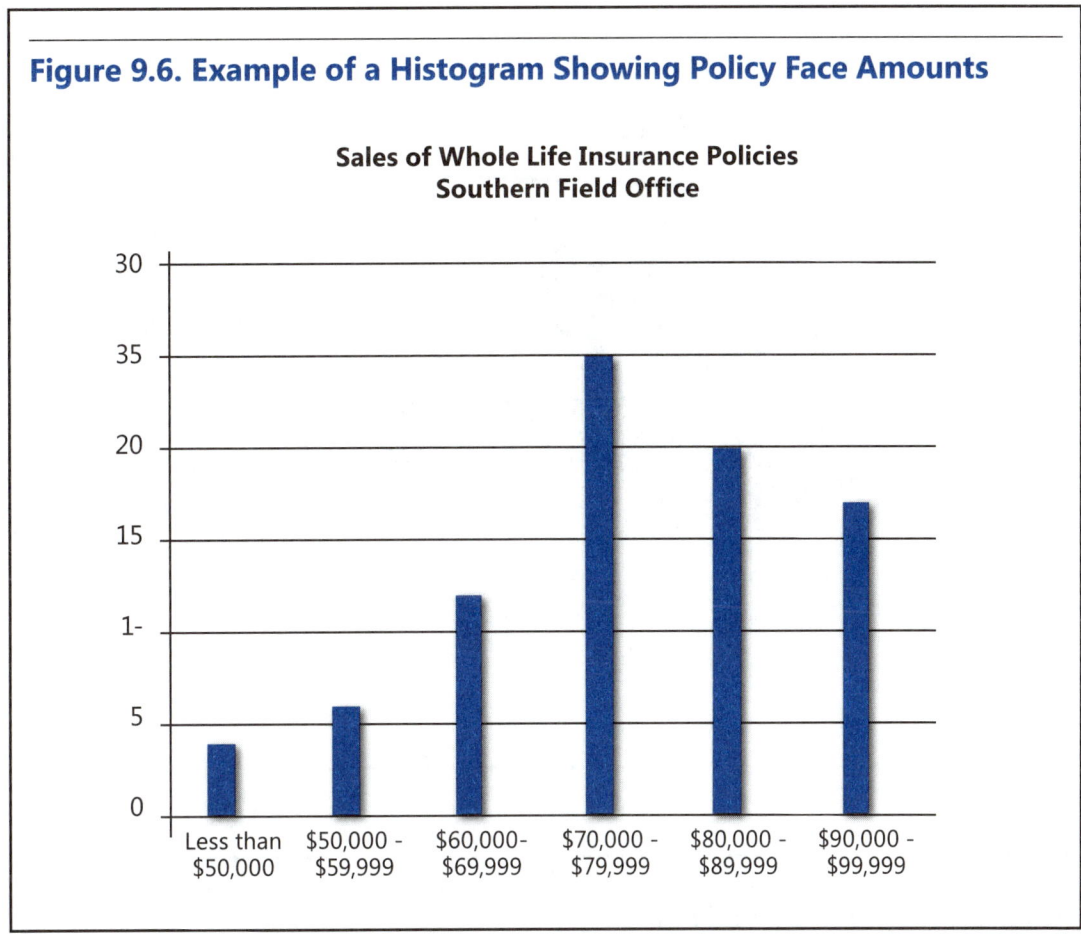

Figure 9.6. Example of a Histogram Showing Policy Face Amounts

Sales of Whole Life Insurance Policies
Southern Field Office

policies sold represent 42% of the 198 policies sold by the field office (84 ÷ 198 = 0.42).

The pie chart in Figure 9.7 is an example of a two-dimensional pie chart. Pie charts can also take a variety of other forms. Figure 9.8 shows additional types of pie charts.

Line Diagrams

Line diagrams, also known as line charts or line graphs, are used to show changes in data over time. For example, companies can use line diagrams to show trends in data, such as a rise or fall in sales volume. Line diagrams can show changes for a single category—such as sales of a single product, total sales of a single field office, or sales for a single year—or for multiple categories, such as sales of multiple products, total sales for multiple field offices, or sales for multiple years. Figure 9.9 includes two different types of line diagrams used to show quarterly sales of whole life insurance for our sample company's two field offices. The first example is a simple line diagram; the second is a three-dimensional line diagram.

Insurance companies frequently use line diagrams to show changes in mortality experience. In this application, a line diagram allows an insurer to identify

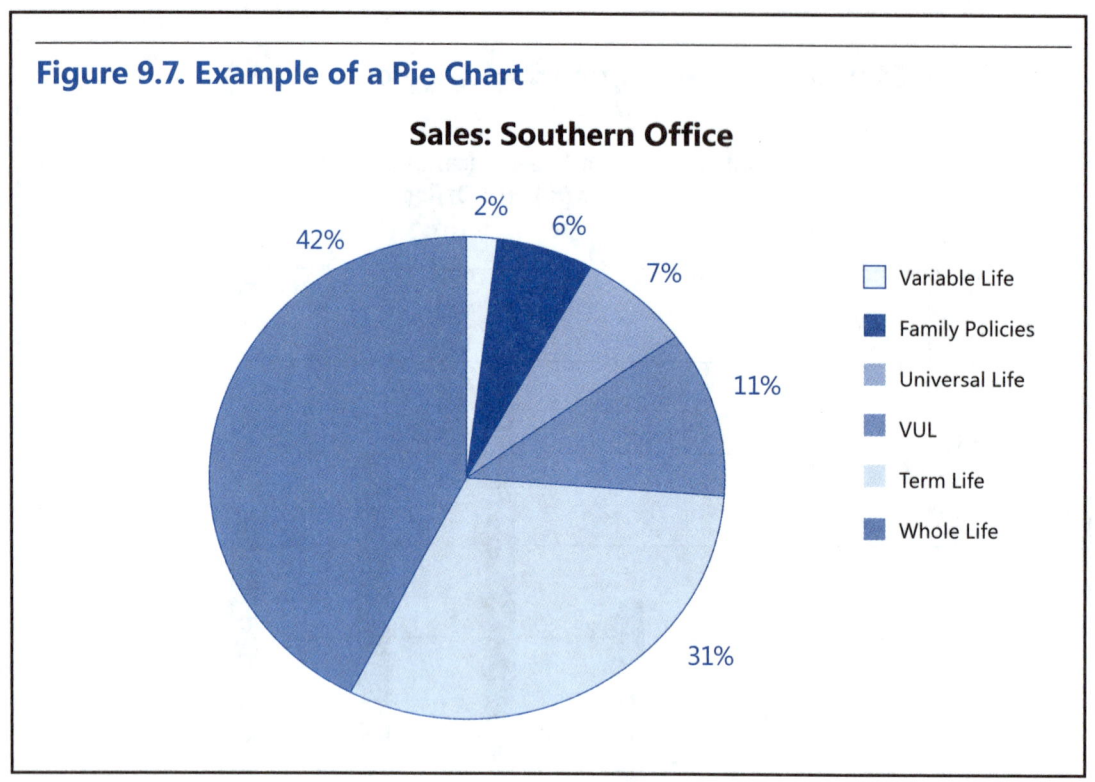

Figure 9.7. Example of a Pie Chart

Sales: Southern Office

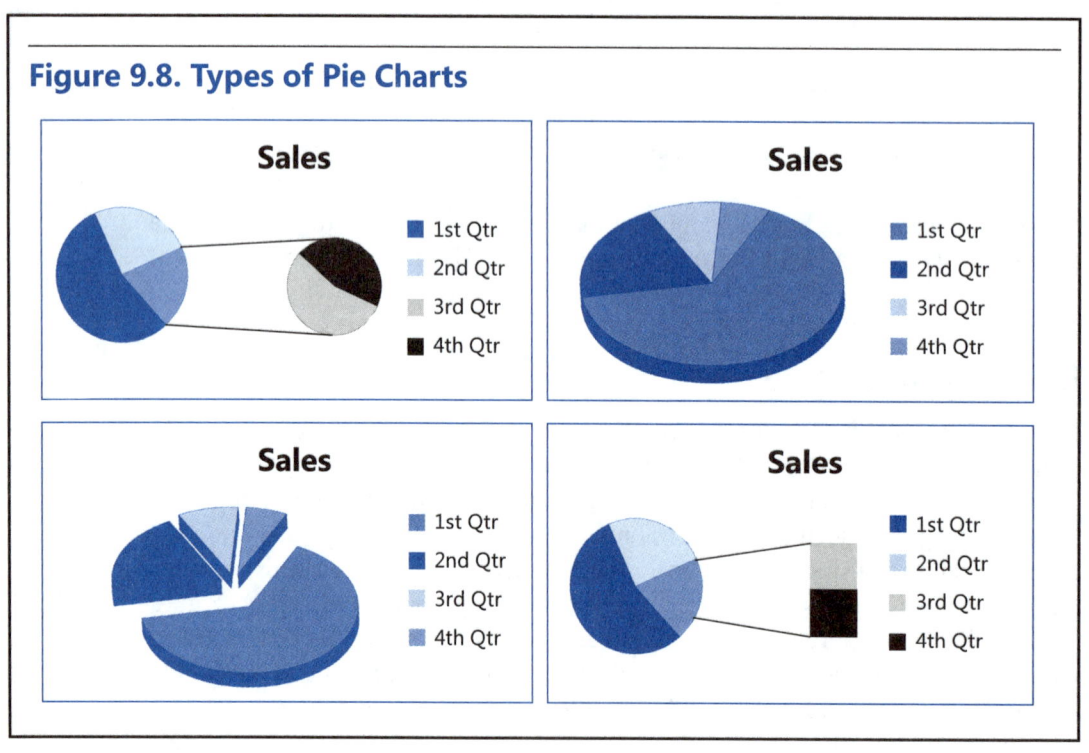

Figure 9.8. Types of Pie Charts

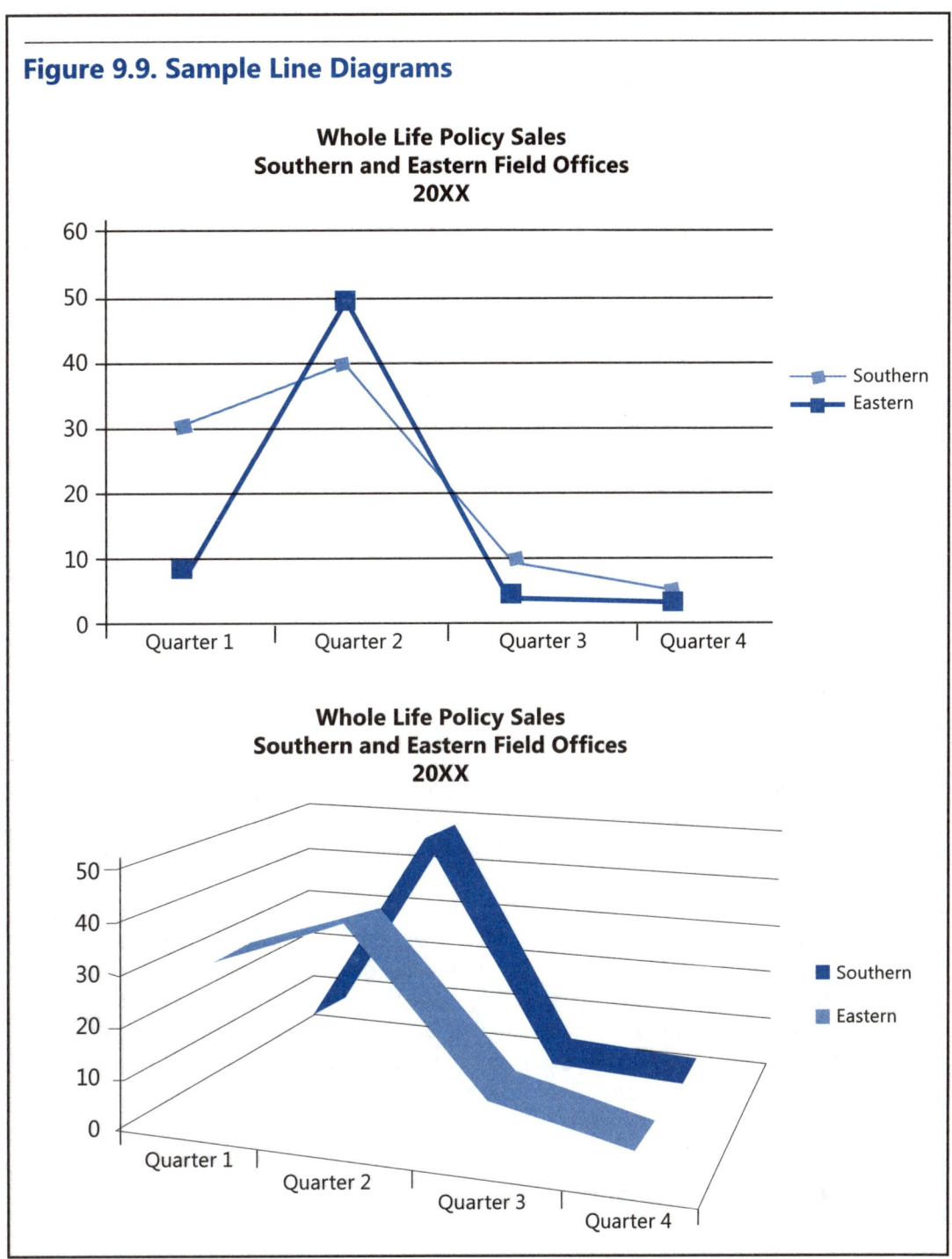

Figure 9.9. Sample Line Diagrams

when changes in mortality occur and whether those changes are positive or negative. Line diagrams can also help identify possible causes for change. For example, an increase in mortality experience during the winter months could be the result of increased deaths caused by flu and other seasonal diseases. Line diagrams can also compare a company's mortality experience from one year to another or compare company mortality experience with the mortality rates shown in mortality tables or with the mortality projections used during product design. In this case, comparative diagrams can identify variances between actual experience and expected experience. Line diagrams provide similar information when used to present data on persistency or claims for a particular product or group of products or from one period to another.

Other Ways to Present Data Visually

Visual presentations don't just provide insurers with a way to order, condense, and display numbers. They also provide companies with a way to plan, organize, and control activities. Three of the most popular graphic tools for these applications are flow charts, Gantt charts, and PERT networks. These displays can be constructed by hand or generated automatically using applications included in most project management software programs.

Flow Charts

A *flow chart* is a graphic representation of a sequence of activities and decisions. A sequence is an arrangement of events or activities in their actual or desired order. Most flow charts consist of a series of ovals, boxes, and diamonds. In general,

- Ovals are used to represent starting and stopping points

- Boxes are used to represent important activities

- Diamonds are used to indicate yes/no decision points

Figure 9.10 shows an example of a flow chart. Although this example shows a simplified picture of the arrangement of critical events in the claim decision process, managers in all divisions and at all levels can use flow charts to identify and sequence important activities and decisions.

Flow charts are valuable tools because they encourage critical thinking. To create a flow chart, a manager needs to consider all the relevant activities in a particular project and to determine the proper sequence of those activities. However, flow charts have disadvantages. For example, flow charts don't indicate the total amount of time necessary to complete a project or the different amounts of time needed to complete individual activities. In addition, flow charts are not always practical for complex projects in which multiple activities take place at the same time. As a result, they have limited value as a scheduling tool.

Project Scheduling Charts

Project scheduling is a critical part of an insurance company's planning process, especially when later steps in a project depend on the successful completion of earlier steps. Schedules help ensure that projects are handled efficiently by providing managers with information about the activities involved in a project, when those activities must be performed, and where resources should be allocated. Schedules also provide managers with a way of monitoring progress on a project and identifying places where corrective action may be needed.

Although projects vary widely in terms of complexity and length, all projects

- Have a beginning point and an end point.

Figure 9.10. Sample Flow Chart

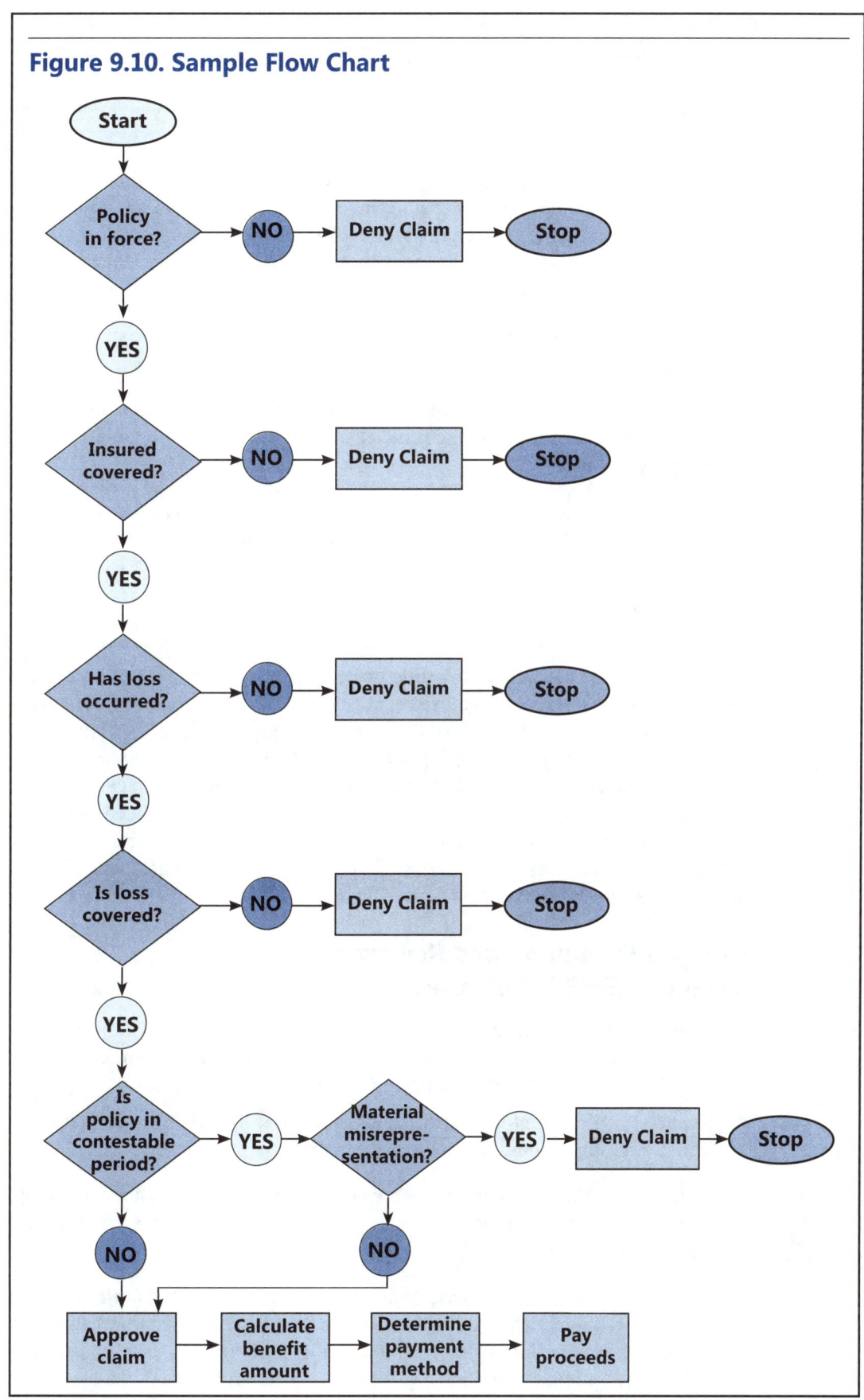

- Include a set of activities and events. An activity is an operation that takes time and requires resources. For example, sending policy forms to regulators for approval is an activity in the product development process. An event, or goal, marks the completion of one or more activities. Receiving regulatory approval is an event.

- Follow a series of steps. Usually, some steps must be completed before other steps can be started. Some steps are independent and can begin while other steps are under way. For example, developing and testing the promotional materials for a new product can usually take place at the same time training materials are developed and tested because they involve different resources.

- Require time to complete. The amount of time required varies from project to project.

- Generally require the efforts of more than one person. For example, the development of a new insurance product involves input from people from all company divisions.

Two of the most effective tools for scheduling insurance projects are Gantt charts and program evaluation and review technique (PERT) networks.

Gantt Charts

A *Gantt chart* is a graphical scheduling tool that separates projects into critical activities and plots starting and ending dates for each activity. Gantt charts are widely used for all types of organizational activities. For example, insurers often use Gantt charts for scheduling activities in large projects. Figure 9.11 provides an example of a Gantt chart showing the activities involved in introducing a new insurance product. Because activities are shown graphically, managers can see immediately which activities have been completed and which still need to be performed. Managers can also track the progress of activities and determine whether corrective action is necessary. Like flow charts, however, Gantt charts can become cumbersome when projects become overly complex.

Program Evaluation and Review Technique (PERT) Networks

A *program evaluation and review technique (PERT) network* is a project scheduling tool that helps shorten the length of time needed to complete large, complex projects. PERT networks include four important elements:

- **Events**. A PERT event is a performance milestone. It marks the completion of an activity and, in some cases, the beginning of another activity.

- **Activities.** A PERT activity is a job that requires time and resources. In most cases, an activity begins and ends with an event. As a result, an activity generally indicates work in progress.

- **Time.** PERT times are estimates of the time needed to complete each PERT activity. PERT times are generally weighted averages of three separate estimates: (1) the **optimistic time** is the least amount of time needed, usually achieved only under optimum conditions; (2) the **most probable time** is the time most

Figure 9.11. Gantt Chart for New Product Introduction Project

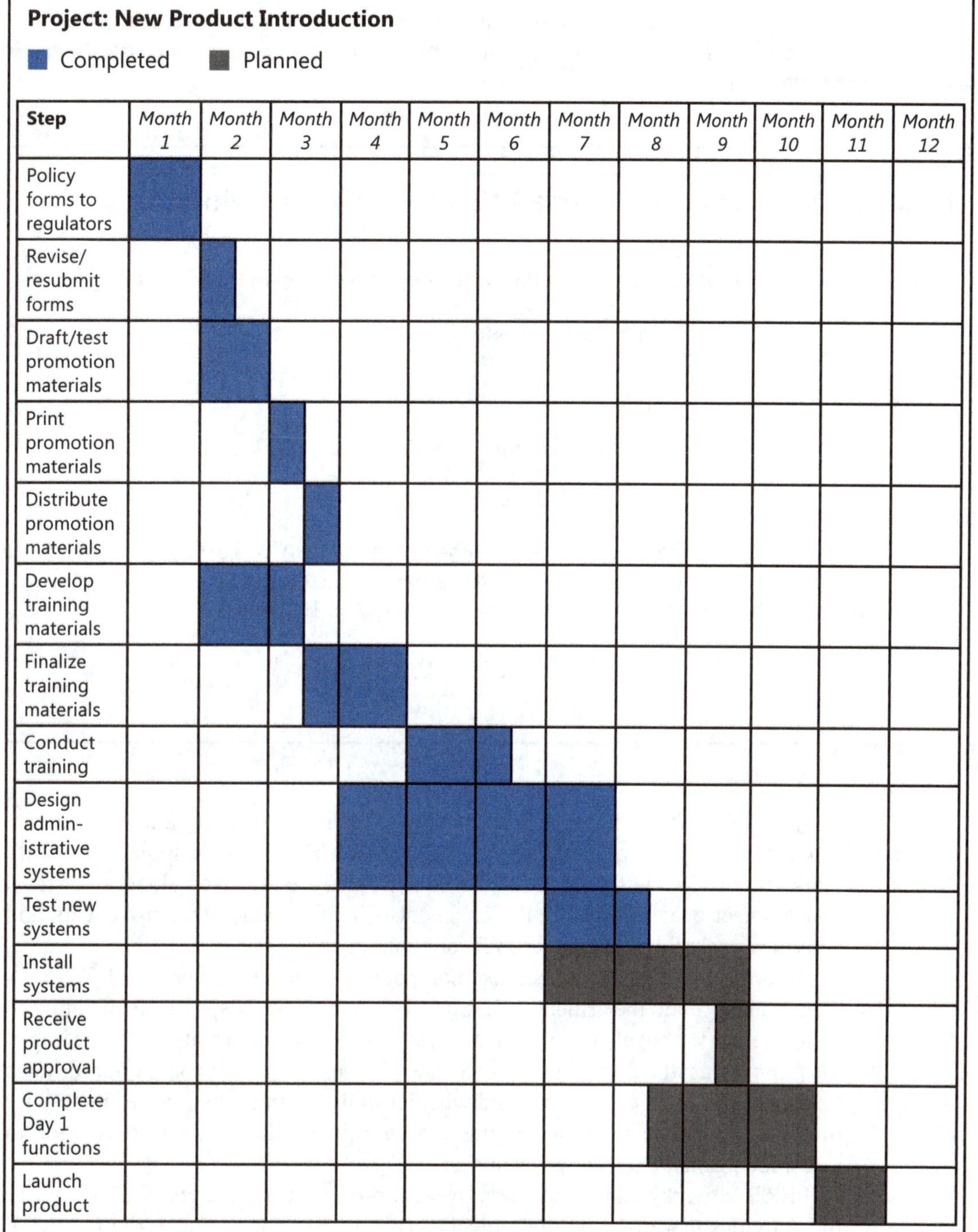

Project: New Product Introduction

■ Completed   ■ Planned

Step	Month 1	Month 2	Month 3	Month 4	Month 5	Month 6	Month 7	Month 8	Month 9	Month 10	Month 11	Month 12
Policy forms to regulators	■											
Revise/ resubmit forms		■										
Draft/test promotion materials		■										
Print promotion materials			■									
Distribute promotion materials			■									
Develop training materials		■	■									
Finalize training materials			■	■								
Conduct training					■	■						
Design admin- istrative systems				■	■	■	■					
Test new systems							■	■				
Install systems								■	■			
Receive product approval									■			
Complete Day 1 functions									■	■		
Launch product											■	

likely needed for completing activities under normal conditions; and (3) the **pessimistic time** is the longest possible time needed, usually the result of the worst possible conditions. The weighted average of these three time estimates produces the **expected time** for each activity. The formula for calculating the expected time needed to complete an activity is shown in Figure 9.12.

■ **Critical path.** The critical path is the most time-consuming chain of activities and events in a PERT network. It may or may not be the chain that includes the most activities and events. Identifying the critical path is important because if any of the activities along the path are delayed, the entire project will be delayed. Delays in activities not on the critical path don't necessarily delay the project.

Figure 9.12. Calculating Expected Times for PERT Activities

The equation for calculating the expected time needed to complete a PERT activity is

$$\frac{Expected}{time} = \frac{(a+4m+b)}{6}$$

where

a = optimistic time

m = most probable time

b = pessimistic time

For example, suppose that the optimistic time for Activity A is 10 days, the most probable time for the activity is 16 days, and the pessimistic time is 20 days. Using the formula above, the expected time to complete Activity A is 15.7 days.

$$\frac{[10+(4\times16)+20]}{6} = 15.7 \text{ days}$$

Figure 9.13 shows how the activities involved in introducing a new insurance product would look if plotted as a PERT network. In this example, events are marked by circled letters, and numbered activities are arranged along the arrows that connect events. Most PERT charts also include tables that list events and activities, including estimated times for completion.

In most cases, managers can use computer software to generate a PERT network and calculate the critical path. Such software not only speeds the creation of PERT networks, but also allows managers to customize information. For example, most programs allow managers to choose whether to specify completion days as business days or calendar days, and whether to use a single time for each activity or to calculate expected times. Using expected times allows managers to build in a cushion against unexpected events.

PERT networks allow managers to see a project in its entirety and to identify the activities that make up the project's critical path. For example, the following table shows the times needed for each sequence of events in the project mapped in Figure 9.13.

Figure 9.13. PERT Network for New Product Introduction

PERT Events	PERT Activities	Times
A. Policy form sent to regulators for review	1. Regulatory review of policy form	25 days
B. Comments back from regulators	2. Revise policy form	15 days
C. Promotion materials drafted	3. Draft and test promotion materials	36 days
D. Training materials drafted	4. Print promotion materials	15 days
E. Design new administrative system	5. Distribute promotion materials	10 days
F. Promotion materials approved	6. Draft training materials	21 days
G. Training materials tested	7. Test training materials	14 days
H. New system tested	8. Finalize training materials	2 days
I. File revised policy form	9. Conduct training	21 days
J. Training materials approved	10. Design new administrative system	60 days
K. New system debugged	11. Test new system	21 days
L. Promotion materials printed	12. Install new system	5 days
M. New system installed	13. Day 1 functionality	14 days
N. Day 1 functionality completed	14. Final product approval	15 days
O. Product introduced to market	15. Product launch	1 day

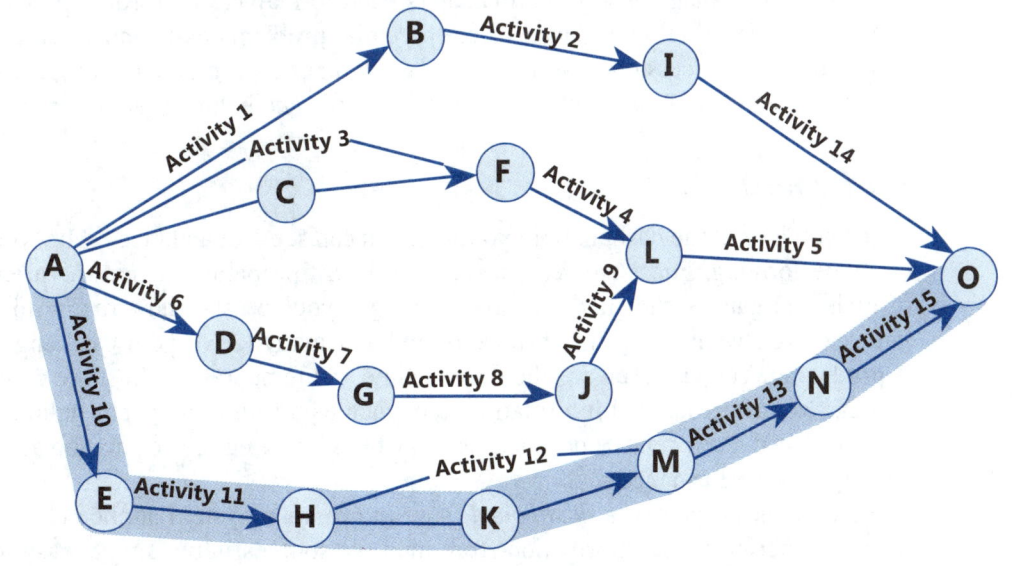

Path	Time to Completion (in days)	Critical Path
A, B, I, O	55	No
A, C, F, L, O	61	No
A, D, G, J, L, O	68	No
A, E, H, K, M, N, O	101	Yes

According to the information in this chart, the critical path for our sample project is the path that goes from Event A to E to H to K to M to N to O, which takes a total of 101 days to complete.

PERT networks also allow managers to see quickly whether any of the activities in the project are falling behind schedule. If delays are identified, the manager can decide whether to (1) spend more resources to make up for lost time, (2) reduce the time—and possibly the quality—of subsequent activities in the path, or (3) accept the delay.

PERT networks and other scheduling tools can provide misleading information if the numbers used to create them are inaccurate. For example, inaccurate assumptions about the timing or sequence of events in the schedule can negate the value of the information the schedule provides. In addition, PERT networks and other project scheduling models must be evaluated and updated periodically to ensure that they reflect any changes that may have occurred in the project.

Performance Management Charts

In addition to managing projects, managers need to manage performance. They need to be able to tell at a glance where potential problems exist and when corrective action is necessary. Two tools that allow managers to collect and display performance information graphically are dashboards and balanced scorecards.

Dashboards

When you look at the dashboard in your car, you can see—at a glance—how your car is performing. For example, your car dashboard probably includes a variety of dials and gauges showing you how much gas you've used, how many miles you've driven, what your current speed is, and how many RPMs your car's engine is producing. You can even see the current time and temperature. In some cases, you can get more detailed information, too, such as average miles per gallon or average speed. Performance dashboards show the same kind of information about a company's performance.

In a business context, a *dashboard* is an information system application that combines performance information from multiple sources into a single, easy-to-read format. Like a car dashboard, a performance dashboard puts all the information managers need to evaluate the performance of the company or of individual business units in one place. Performance dashboards often use some of the same graphic formats used in a car dashboard. For example, an insurance company dashboard might include a

- Pie chart showing the company's premium income, by month

- Pie chart, or "heat map," showing sales by agency office or region. A heat map is a two-dimensional data map in which different values for a given variable appear as different colors.

- Gauge, similar to a gas gauge, with a mark showing the company's sales target and an indicator showing year-to-date sales

- Line diagram tracking sales of particular products

- Bar graph showing total sales by month

- Line diagram or bar chart showing sales trends

Each chart and diagram would also include links to detailed information about performance for individual months, products, or offices. Although dashboards commonly focus on sales, they can be used for other applications, including recruiting, human resources, company operations, project management, and customer relationship management.

Because dashboards capture and report specific data from various departments within a company, they allow management to

- Monitor the contributions of various departments

- Measure operating efficiencies and inefficiencies

- Make informed decisions based on collected business intelligence

- Align company strategies with the company's business goals

- Eliminate the need for multiple runs to produce data

Balanced Scorecards

A *balanced scorecard* is a strategic performance management tool used to monitor a company's performance in key areas. Managers use balanced scorecards to assign target outcomes to a small number of financial or nonfinancial activities and then monitor the actual performance of those activities to see how closely current performance meets expectations. To create a scorecard, management generally

- Translates the company's mission statement into specific operational goals

- Links the identified goals to individual areas of performance

- Sets target performance levels or indexes for each area

- Compares actual performance against targeted performance

Scorecards allow managers to identify potential problem areas and take action where necessary. They also allow managers to feed results back into the planning process to adjust strategies.

Scorecards are often presented as simple tables broken down into major sections with specific objectives, performance measures, trends, and initiatives for each section. Figure 9.14 shows the general format of a balanced scorecard. The four general performance categories used in this example are typical of scorecards and include

- **Financial**, which addresses how the company looks to its shareholders

- **Customer**, which addresses how customers see the company

- **Internal business**, which describes the areas in which the company thinks it should excel

- **Growth and innovation**, which identifies where the company feels it can improve and create value

At the center of the scorecard is the company mission, which is linked to and drives each of the company's performance objectives. Companies can sometimes find published performance measures that can be included in the scorecard, but most companies determine specific measures in-house and use published information as benchmarks for evaluating the company's performance.

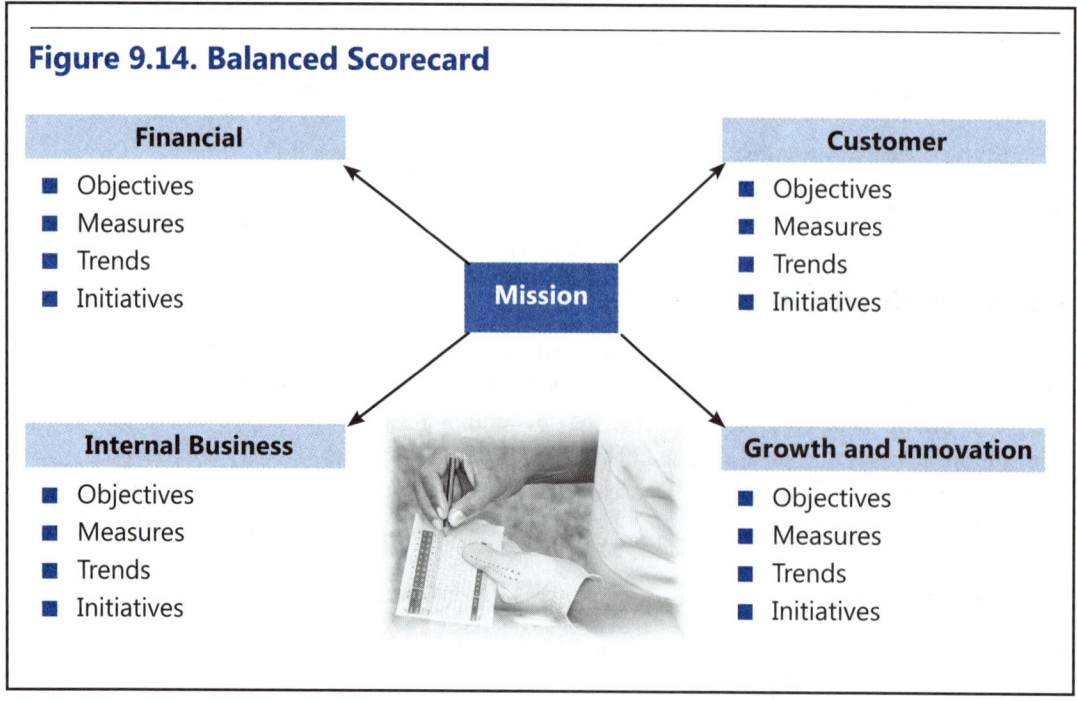

Figure 9.14. Balanced Scorecard

Financial
- Objectives
- Measures
- Trends
- Initiatives

Customer
- Objectives
- Measures
- Trends
- Initiatives

Mission

Internal Business
- Objectives
- Measures
- Trends
- Initiatives

Growth and Innovation
- Objectives
- Measures
- Trends
- Initiatives

Avoiding Deceptive Uses of Visual Presentations

Although tables, charts, graphs, and scheduling tools are effective ways to help users visualize information, they can be deceptive if they aren't constructed carefully. For example, using an inappropriate scale in a graph can make differences seem larger or smaller than they really are. Figure 9.15 shows quarterly sales for a hypothetical product. In this figure, Graph A uses a scale of 0 to 4.5 and Graph B uses a scale of 0 to 45. The actual sales figures are the same in both graphs, but the impression they give is very different. Because Graph B uses a scale 10 times larger than Graph A, sales appear much flatter in Graph B than in Graph A.

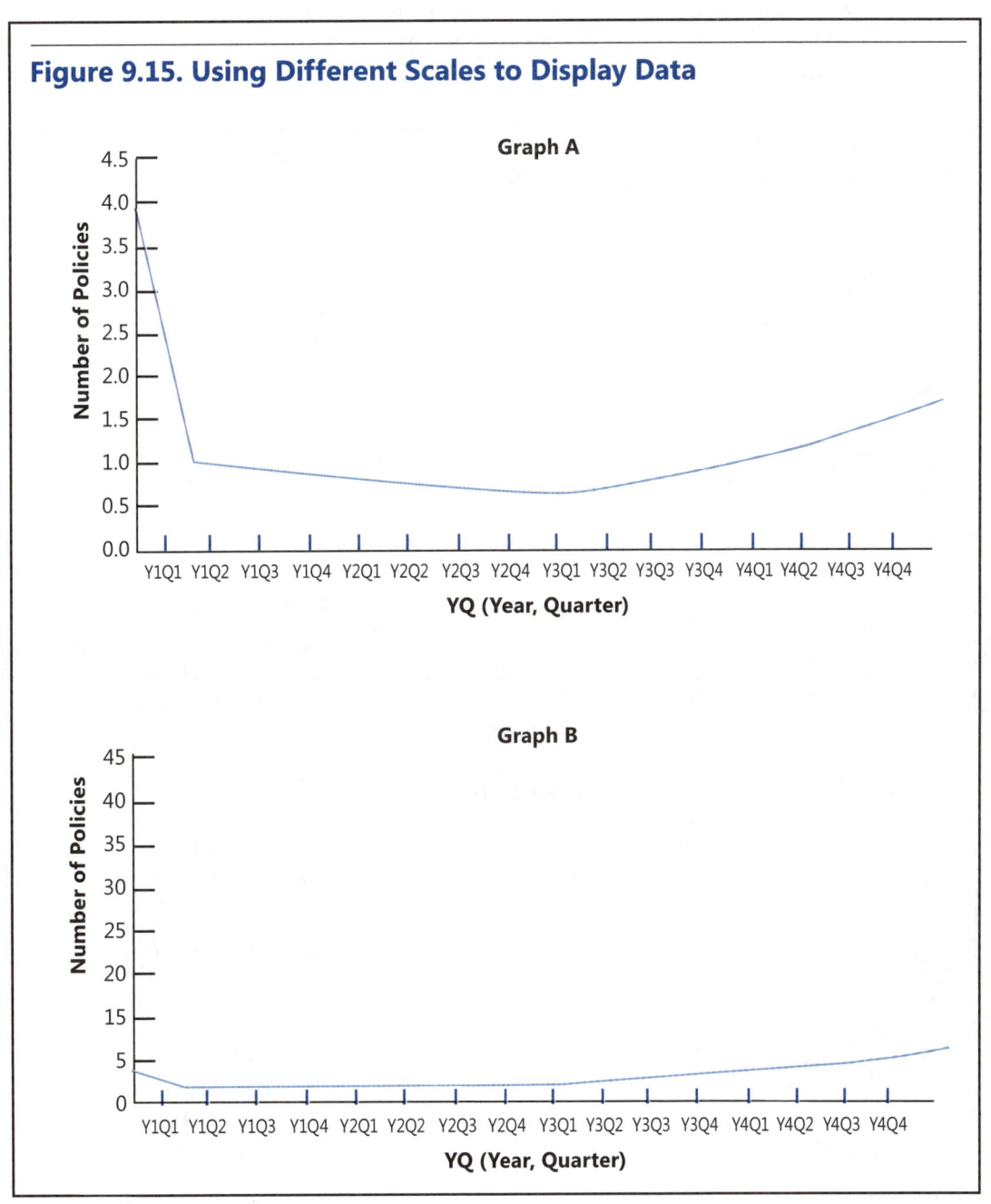

Figure 9.15. Using Different Scales to Display Data

Graphs also create confusion if the quantities used in the scale don't start with 0. For example, sometimes reports have limited space for graphics, so charts or graphs may be cropped to show only the relevant information. Graphs may also be cropped if all of the information falls within a very small range, leaving a large portion of the graph empty.

Figure 9.16 shows two versions of a graph mapping product sales over a period of several years. In Sample C, the scale ranges from 0 to 10, even though all sales fall between 8 and 10. In this graph, sales for the product appear to be flat, and there's a lot of empty space below the graph line. In Sample D, the scale has been cropped so that it begins at 8 instead of 0. This graph focuses on actual sales and eliminates all the wasted space included in Sample C. This presentation provides a clearer picture of the pattern of product sales, but because the range in Sample D starts at 8 and not 0, the sales figures in Sample D appear to be much lower than in Sample C. The changes in sales from one year to the next also appear to be much larger than in Sample C.

Figure 9.16. Using Cropped Scales to Present Data

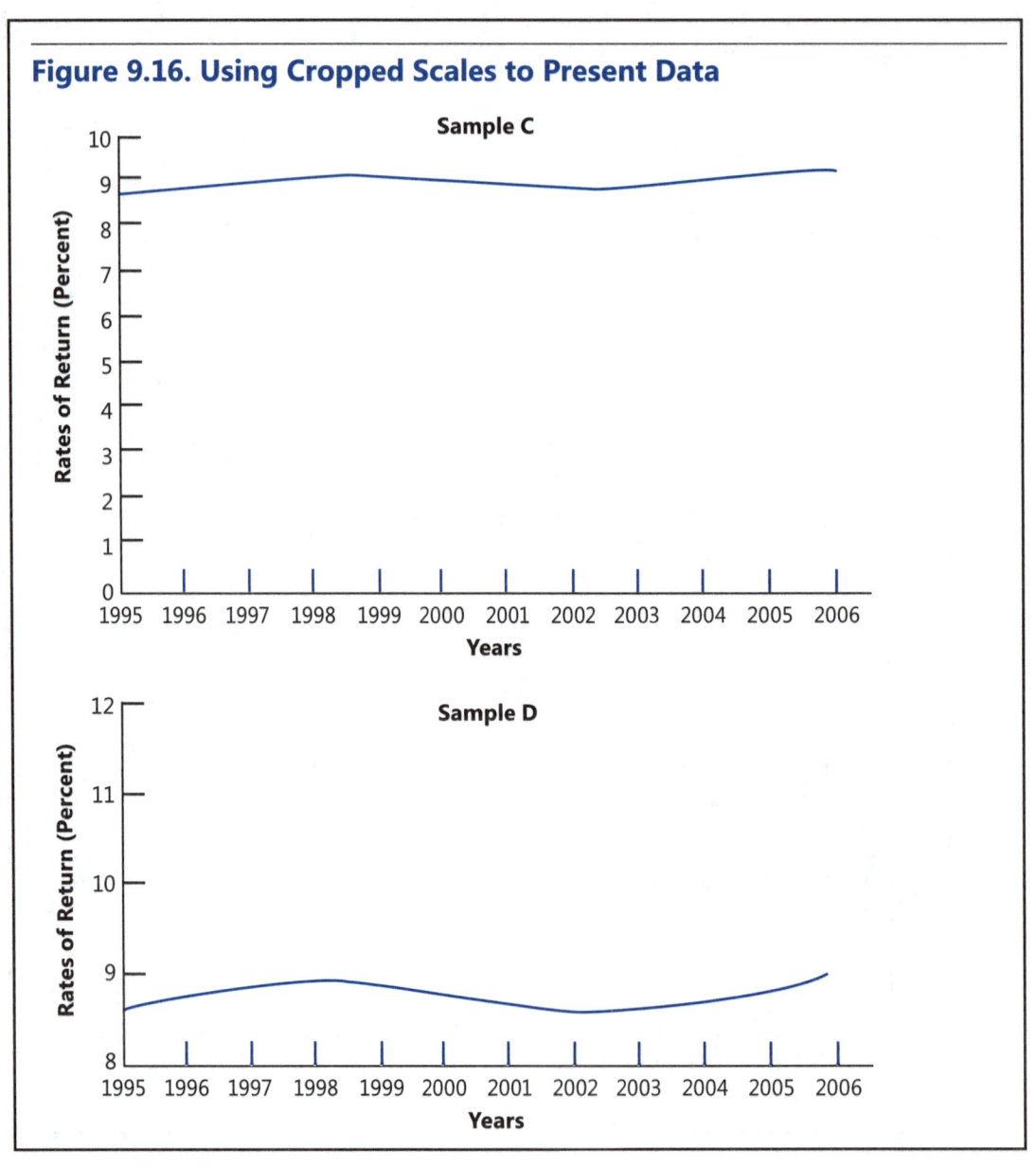

Finally, line diagrams and bar charts showing more than one data set, such as sales figures for multiple years or for multiple products, tend to suggest relationships that might not be accurate. The fact that multiple data sets are included in the same display doesn't prove that they are related or that changes in a variable had the same effect on both data sets. Showing multiple data sets also doesn't prove a cause-and-effect relationship between the data sets. For example, a line diagram showing sales of a particular product over a period of years and total revenue over those same years might imply that changes in product sales caused changes in total revenue, even if the relationship doesn't really exist.

Problems can also arise when pictographs are used to present data. For example, suppose the information in Figure 9.3, showing the numbers of various types of insurance policies sold, had been displayed with symbols of documents rather than bars. Figure 9.17 shows what happens when pictographs are used correctly. In this figure, increases in the number of policies sold are shown by increasing the number of document symbols. Figure 9.18 shows what happens when pictographs are used incorrectly. In this figure, increases in the number of policies sold is shown by a single document symbol that increases in size, making it appear that the size, rather than the number of policies, is increasing.

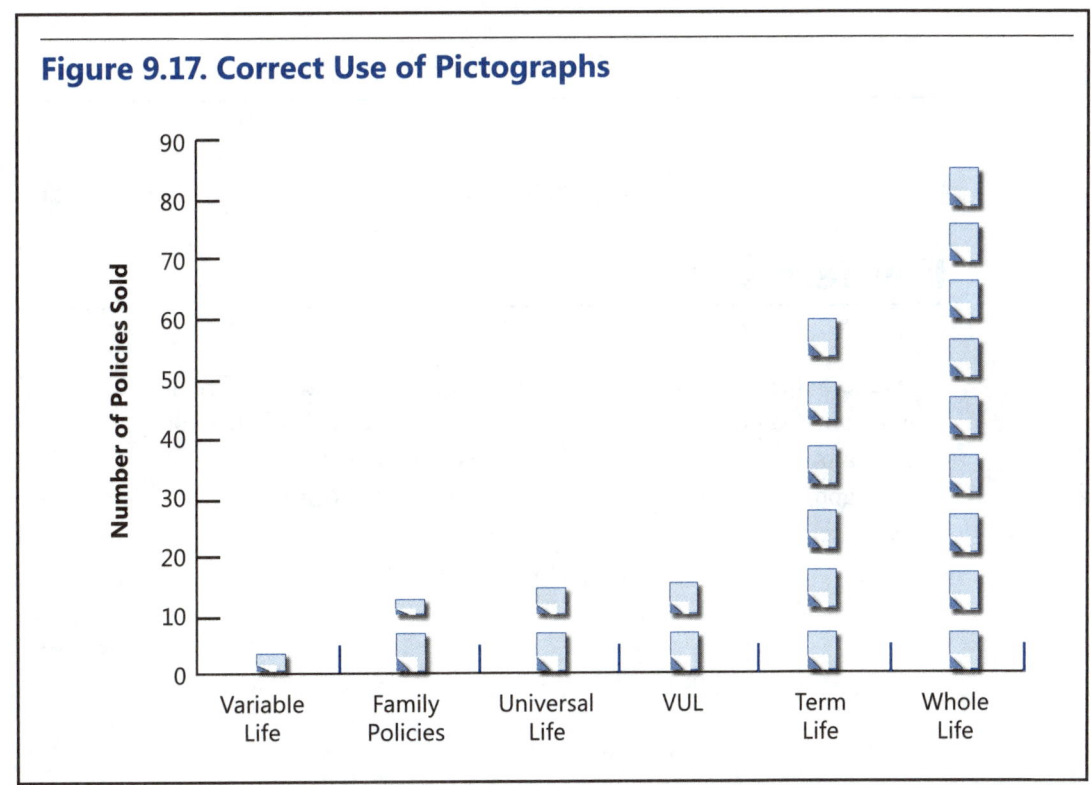

Figure 9.17. Correct Use of Pictographs

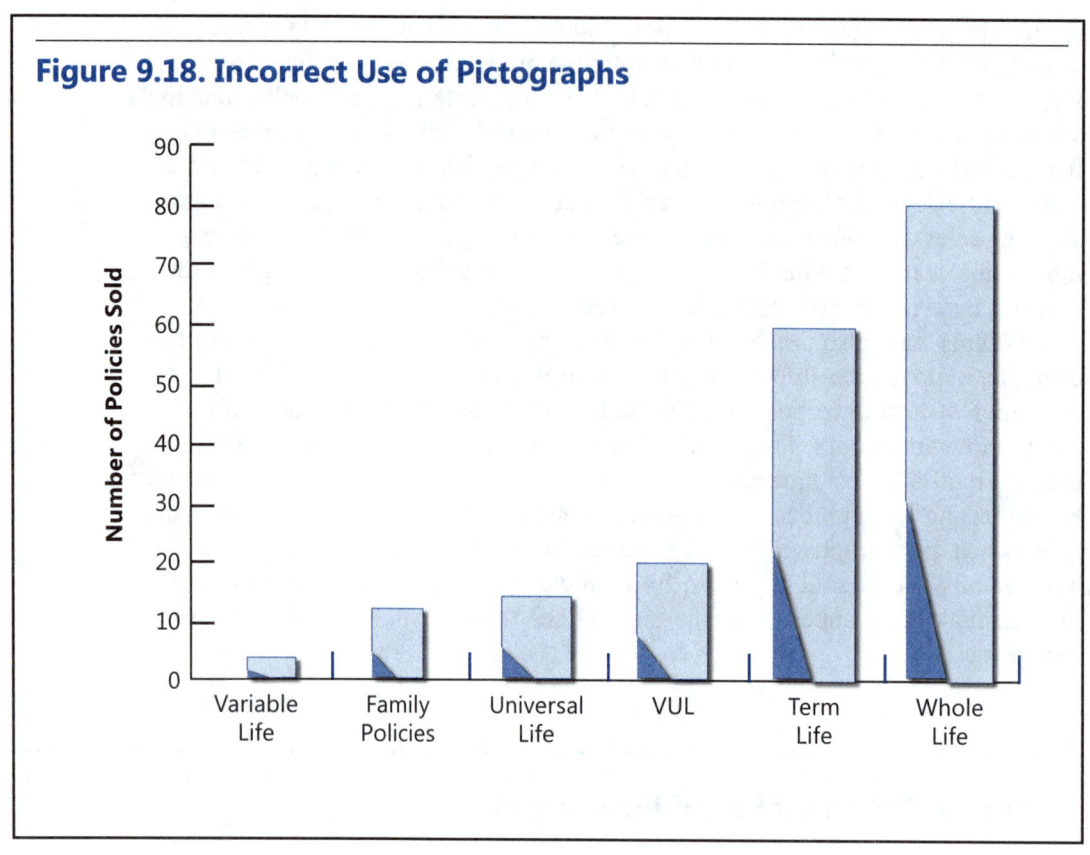

Figure 9.18. Incorrect Use of Pictographs

Key Terms

table

grouped frequency distribution

component bar chart

histogram

pictograph

flow chart

Gantt chart

program evaluation and review
    technique (PERT) network

dashboard

balanced scorecard

Chapter 10

Analyzing Population Data

Objectives:

After studying this chapter, you should be able to

- Define descriptive statistics and describe the primary benefits they provide to managers

- Calculate the three primary measures of central tendency—the mean, the median, and the mode—and describe the strengths and limitations of each measure

- Calculate the three primary measures of dispersion—the range, the variance, and the standard deviation—and explain their importance to insurers and other users

- Distinguish between normal and non-normal distributions and identify insurance situations in which they apply

- Identify the characteristics necessary to ensure data quality

Outline

Measures of Central Tendency
- Mean
- Median
- Mode

Measures of Dispersion
- Range
- Variance
- Standard Deviation

Improving the Value of Descriptive Statistics

Data Distributions
- Normal Distributions
- Non-Normal Distributions

Data Quality

Although tables, charts, and graphs are an effective way to arrange and display large amounts of numerical data, they don't always provide managers with information they can use to make decisions.

Suppose that a life insurance company sent a survey to 10,000 of its customers to find out how satisfied they are with the company's products and services. Customers were asked to indicate their level of satisfaction with each item in the survey on a scale of 1 to 5. At the end of the survey, managers received a set of tables listing each customer's numerical rating for each question on the survey.

Even if only a portion of the customers who received the survey provided answers, these tables would include an enormous amount of data. However, managers would have a difficult time using that data to answer such questions as

- What is the overall level of customer satisfaction with our products and services?

- What proportion of our customers are very satisfied? What proportion are dissatisfied?

- Which products or services have the highest level of satisfaction among customers? Which have the lowest level of satisfaction?

- What is the relationship between the level of satisfaction for a particular product and the level of satisfaction for our products as a whole?

That's where statistical analysis comes in. **Statistical analysis** is the use of mathematical techniques to collect, organize, describe, analyze, and interpret large amounts of numerical data in order to help people make decisions. The numerical data are called **statistics.**

Statistics that summarize or describe a complete set of collected data—known as a **population**, or *data set*—are called **descriptive statistics**. Descriptive statistics, which include measures of central tendency and measures of dispersion, allow managers to

- Reduce large amounts of raw data into a single value that is representative of all the individual values in a population

- Describe how individual values are arranged, or dispersed, around specified representative values

Although most spreadsheet and statistical computer programs have formulas that will compute representative values automatically, knowing what these measures are and how they're calculated is important in understanding how and when to apply them.

Measures of Central Tendency

Measures of central tendency are representative values that describe the values in the middle of a population. The most common measures of central tendency are the mean, the median, and the mode.

Mean

Most people think of the *mean* as the numerical "average" of a series of values. It's calculated by summing all the values in a given population and then dividing the total by the number of values in the population. A mean that is based on population data is often referred to as the *population mean*. Expressed as a formula, the

Mean = Sum of values ÷ Number of values

Knowing the mean value of a large number of observations can be a valuable tool. For example:

The claim manager for the Foremost Life Insurance Company is in the process of evaluating his staffing needs for the coming year. To help him identify whether he needs to hire additional analysts, he gathered data about the number of life insurance claims filed each month over a three-year period. The data he collected are shown in the table below.

Life Insurance Claims

	Year 1	Year 2	Year 3
Jan	360	500	530
Feb	255	270	250
Mar	270	290	230
Apr	285	280	200
May	350	320	420
Jun	350	310	400
Jul	340	350	430
Aug	350	350	450
Sep	320	360	480
Oct	310	340	170
Nov	300	300	126
Dec	290	100	100
Total	**3,780**	**3,770**	**3,785**

Because staffing levels depend on the number of claims the company receives, the manager wants to know how many claims the department receives in a typical month.

To calculate the mean number of claims per month, Foremost's claim manager needs to find the total of all claims received each year and divide that total by the number of months in the year. According to the information in this table, the mean—or average—number of claims received per month by Foremost in Year 1 is equal to 315; in Year 2 the mean is equal to 314.2; and in Year 3 the mean is equal to 315.4.

> Mean = Total number of claims ÷ Number of months
>
> Year 1: 3,780 ÷ 12 = 315.0
> Year 2: 3,770 ÷ 12 = 314.2
> Year 3: 3,785 ÷ 12 = 315.4

Although the mean is easy to calculate, its accuracy as a measure of central tendency can be limited if

■ **The population includes outlier values**. An *outlier* is an extremely high or low value that is not representative of the other values in the population. In our example above, all of the values for Year 1 are relatively close together; there are no unusually high or unusually low values. However, Year 2 has a very low value (100) and a very high value (500). The presence of outliers in Year 2 makes the mean less accurate as a representative value for Year 2 than it is for Year 1.

■ **Values in the population are not evenly distributed**. Most of the values in Year 3 are clustered at either end, with half considerably lower than the mean and half considerably higher than the mean. The mean value of 315.4, therefore, is not representative of all the values in this population either. (Note that the values of 100 and 530 in this case aren't outliers because they aren't significantly different from other values in the population.)

Median

The *median* is the middle value in a set of values that is arranged in numerical order. A median derived from a population is referred to as the *population median*. The median is often used to describe economic characteristics, such as median family income, median household size, or median education level. Knowing median values for a population can help an insurer gain insight into its customers' lifestyles and potential product needs.

Finding the median is fairly simple. There are only two requirements: (1) the values in the population must be arranged in numerical order and (2) the manager must know how many values are in the population. If the population contains an odd number of values, then the median is the middle value and has an equal number of values above and below it.

> If Foremost's manager wanted to get a generalized picture of the mean values he calculated, he could look at the median of the three yearly means. In this case, the three numbers were
>
> Year 2: 314.2
> Year 1: 315.0
> Year 3: 315.4
>
> Because he had an odd number of values, the median value was the middle value, or 315.

If the population has an even number of values, the median is determined by calculating the average of the two middle values.

Foremost's manager also wanted to know the median value for each year. The first step was to put the data in numerical order, as shown below:

Year 1	Year 2	Year 3
255	100	100
270	270	125
285	280	170
290	290	200
300	300	230
310	**310**	**250**
320	**320**	**400**
340	340	420
350	350	430
350	350	450
350	360	480
360	500	530

In this case, each of the three yearly data sets has 12 values—one for each month of the year. Because 12 is an even number, the manager needed to find the average of the two middle values—value #6 and value #7. For Year 1 and Year 2, the two middle values are 310 and 320, making the median 315.

$$(310 + 320) \div 2 = 315$$

In Year 3, the two middle values are 250 and 400, so the median for that year is 325.

$$(250 + 400) \div 2 = 325$$

Unlike the mean, the median is not an arithmetic average of all the values in a population. It is simply the value that falls in the middle. When a population contains an odd number of values, the median is one of the values in the population. When a population contains an even number of values, the median is a calculated value.

The primary drawback of using the median as a measure of central tendency is that it ignores all the values in a population except the middle values. If the values in a population are evenly distributed, the median can be an accurate measure of central tendency. However, if the population contains outliers or if values are unevenly distributed, as they are in our example, then the median won't accurately represent all the values in the population.

Mode

Sometimes it's important to know the most common value in a population rather than the mean or median value. The statistical measure that identifies the value that appears most often in a population is the **mode**, or *population mode*. To find the mode, it isn't necessary to list the values in order, but it definitely makes the process easier.

The mode can be a valuable tool for identifying baseline values. For example, an insurer might want to know the most common amount of coverage its life insurance policies provide or the most common age at which people apply for life insurance coverage. Knowing this information could help the insurer focus its marketing efforts on the types of products and customers that are most likely to generate new business for the company.

The mode can also be used to identify patterns in a population that might require attention. For example, Foremost's claim manager could get a reasonably accurate picture of whether his current staff of analysts is sufficient to handle the work load by knowing the most common number of claims filed per month. If the modal number is consistent over several years, it could even be used to determine the optimum number of claim analysts for the department.

In our example, it's fairly easy to see that 350 appears more often in Year 1 (3 times) and Year 2 (2 times) than any other value. The mode for these two years, therefore, is 350. There isn't a mode for Year 3, because no number in the data set appears more than once.

Life Insurance Claims		
Year 1	**Year 2**	**Year 3**
255	100	100
270	270	125
285	280	170
290	290	200
300	300	230
310	310	250
320	320	400
340	340	420
350	**350**	430
350	**350**	450
350	360	480
360	500	530
Total 3,780	3,770	3,785
Mean 315.0	314.2	315.4
Median 315.0	315.0	325.0

The mode in our example isn't any more useful than the mean or median for making decisions. For example, the mode (350) is well above the means for Year 1 (315.0) and Year 2 (314.2). The mode is also higher than the medians for Year 1 (315) and Year 2 (315). As a result, it's more representative of values at the high end of the population than at the low end. The presence of outliers in Year 2 makes the mode even more unreliable as a measure of central tendency for that year. The mode fails completely as a measure of central tendency if a population contains more than one mode or, as happens in Year 3, there is no mode because no number in the population appears more than once.

If our manager based staffing decisions solely on the mean, the median, or the mode, the department would be overstaffed the majority of the time and understaffed a considerable part of the time. Our manager can reduce the risk of making decisions based on inaccurate or inappropriate data, however, by looking at more than one measure of central tendency or by evaluating measures of central tendency in conjunction with measures of dispersion.

Figure 10.1 provides a summary of the strengths and limitations of the mean, median, and mode as measures of central tendency.

Measures of Dispersion

Measures of dispersion are representative values that describe the distribution of data around specified central values. In most cases, the central value is the population mean. The three most common measures of dispersion are the range, variance, and standard deviation. Together, these measures provide managers with information about how data in a population are distributed.

Range

The simplest measure of dispersion is the *range*, which is the difference between the highest and lowest values in a particular population. For example, let's look again at Foremost's claim data.

Figure 10.1. The Strengths and Limitations of Measures of Central Tendency

Measure	Calculated as	Strengths	Limitations
Mean	Average of all values in the population	Easy to calculate Considers all values in the population	Accuracy affected by the presence of outliers and distribution of values within the population
Median	Middle value (for odd number of values) or average of two middle values (for even number of values)	Identifies the center of the population	Considers only middle values Accuracy limited if data do not cluster around the mid-point of the population
Mode	Value that occurs most frequently in the population	Can provide insight about common practices	Considers only most common value A population may contain more than one mode or no mode at all

---

Life Insurance Claims		
Year 1	**Year 2**	**Year 3**
255	100	100
270	270	125
285	280	170
290	290	200
300	300	230
310	310	250
320	320	400
340	340	420
350	350	430
350	350	450
350	360	480
360	500	530
Total **3,780**	**3,770**	**3,785**
Mean **315.0**	**314.2**	**315.4**
Median **315.0**	**315.0**	**325.0**
Range **105**	**400**	**430**

Because values in this sample are listed in numerical order, from lowest to highest, it's easy to calculate the range: simply subtract the lowest number from the highest number. In our example, the range for Year 1 is 105 (360 – 255); for Year 2, the range is 400 (500 – 100); for Year 3, the range is 430 (530 – 100).

Assuming that Foremost's claim manager knows how many claims a single analyst can process each day, he could use the range to identify the department's lower and upper staffing limits. However, because the range varies considerably from year to year, even that information isn't very helpful. In addition, because the range considers only two values—the lowest and the highest—in the population, it doesn't really provide very much additional information. For example, it doesn't indicate whether there are outliers or whether values are clustered at one or more points within the range. It also doesn't indicate whether there are any patterns in the data.

Variance

Users can get a better understanding of how values are dispersed throughout a population by calculating the distances between individual values and the mean value of the population. The **variance** is the average squared distance between the population mean and each individual item in population. The distance between the mean and each item is the difference between the value of an individual item and the population mean (the arithmetic average of all values in the population). The squared distance is the calculated distance between the item and the mean multiplied by itself. To find the variance, it's necessary to

1. Calculate the mean
2. Find the distance between each item of data and the mean and then square each distance (that is, multiply each distance by itself)
3. Add all the squared values
4. Divide the total by the number of items in the population

For example, consider the values from Year 1 of Foremost's claim data:

Yr. 1	255 270 285 290 300 310 320 340 350 350 350 360

Earlier, we determined that the mean value for year 1 was equal to 315 (3,780 ÷ 12 = 315). The results of variance calculations for these numbers are summarized in the table below. Negative numbers in the center column indicate values that are below the mean; positive numbers indicate values above the mean.

Item Value	Distance from Mean	Squared Distance
255	−60 (255 − 315)	3,600
270	−45 (270 − 315)	2,025
285	−30 (285 − 315)	900
290	−25 (290 − 315)	625
300	−15 (300 − 315)	225
310	−5 (310 − 315)	25
320	+5 (320 − 315)	25
340	+25 (340 − 315)	625
350	+35 (350 − 315)	1,225
350	+35 (350 − 315)	1,225
350	+35 (350 − 315)	1,225
360	+45 (360 − 315)	2,025
Total of squared distances	=	13,750.0
Variance (13,750 ÷ 12)	=	1,145.8

Although the variance includes all the values in the population, it isn't necessarily an accurate measure of the dispersion of values within the population. For example, because the variance is based on squared distances, it doesn't provide information about the actual distance between different data items or between individual data values and the mean. That's because the variance is not on the same numerical scale as the raw data. To resolve the difference, it's necessary to look at the standard deviation.

Standard Deviation

The *standard deviation* of a population is the square root of the variance of the population. The square root of a number is the value that, when multiplied by itself, produces the number. For example, the square root of 25 is 5, because 5 × 5 = 25. Similarly, the square root of 100 is 10, because 10 × 10 = 100. In effect, calculating the standard deviation of a population reverses the process used to calculate the variance and thus puts the results back in the same numerical scale as the raw data.

The square root of a number is represented mathematically by the symbol $\sqrt{}$ above the number. The square root of 25, then, can be written as $\sqrt{25}$, the square root of 100 can be written as $\sqrt{100}$, and the square root of the variance in our example can be written as $\sqrt{1,145.8}$.

Calculating the square root of 1,145.8 is clearly more complex than calculating the square root of 25 or 100. However, most calculators and computers have applications that will calculate square roots automatically, eliminating the need to do calculations by hand. The standard deviation for our population is equal to 33.85.

In general, the larger the standard deviation, the farther the values are from the mean. In other words, the larger the standard deviation, the more dispersed the values in the population. Smaller standard deviations indicate that values in the population are closer to the mean and less dispersed. Figure 10.2 shows two distribution curves, one showing wide dispersion and one showing narrow dispersion.

Insurance companies frequently use the standard deviation to evaluate risk factors such as mortality risk, market risk, interest-rate risk, or customer behavior risk. For example, by using the standard deviation to identify how customers in various age groups are distributed around the mean and comparing results to the mortality information in standard mortality tables, insurers can gain insight into their likely claim experience.

Even though the standard deviation provides important information, it has limits. For example, the standard deviation serves as a measure of dispersion only if the data are normally distributed. Data are normally distributed if values are distributed throughout the population so that half of the values are below the mean

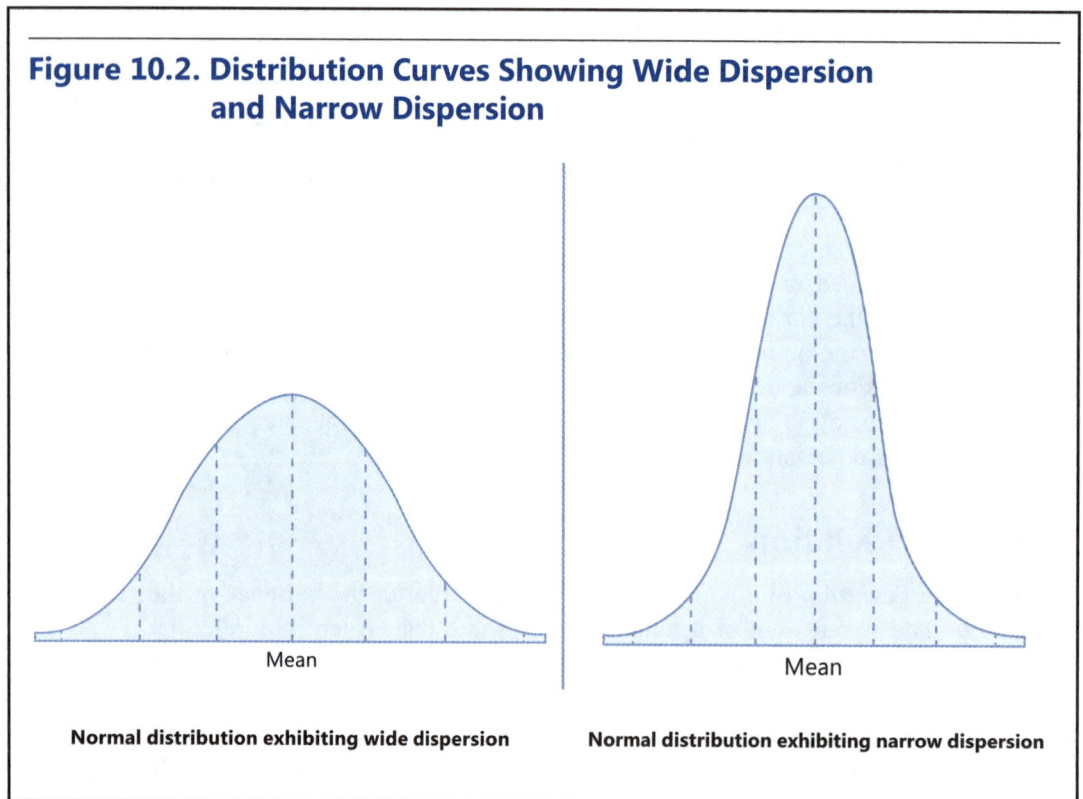

Figure 10.2. Distribution Curves Showing Wide Dispersion and Narrow Dispersion

Mean

Mean

Normal distribution exhibiting wide dispersion

Normal distribution exhibiting narrow dispersion

Figure 10.3. The Strengths and Limitations of Measures of Dispersion

Measure	Calculated as	Strengths	Limitations
Range	Difference between the highest and lowest value in the population	Easy to calculate Identifies the limits of distribution within the population	Considers only the end points of the population Relationship among data values is unclear
Variance	Average of squared distances of data values from the mean	Considers all values in the population	Value is not on the same numerical scale as the data
Standard Deviation	Square root of the variance of the population	Value is on the same numerical scale as the data Describes the distribution of values in the population	Assumes that values follow normal probability distribution patterns

and half of the values are above the mean. Unfortunately, a lot of real-world values aren't distributed normally. In fact, most financial values are not distributed normally. Figure 10.3 summarizes the strengths and limitations of the range, variance, and standard deviation as measures of dispersion.

Improving the Value of Descriptive Statistics

An important point to remember about the descriptive statistics calculated here is that they're based on a very small number of values. It's not surprising, therefore, that the calculated values aren't completely representative of all the values in the population. Most real populations are much larger. For example, an insurance company's customer database or its expense records can include thousands of individual values. The mortality rates included in mortality tables are usually based on 100,000 or more individual values.

In general, the more values in a population, the more representative central values such as the mean, median, and mode are likely to be. For example, suppose our manager combined the data from Year 1, Year 2, and Year 3 into a single expanded population, as shown below:

Life Insurance Claims

100	290	350
100	290	350
125	300	350
170	300	360
200	310	360
230	310	400
250	320	420
255	320	430
270	340	450
270	340	480
280	350	500
285	350	530

The total of all the values in this expanded population would be equal to 11,335 (3,780 + 3,770 + 3,785) and the number of values would be equal to 36. The mean, therefore, would be equal to 314.86 (11,335 ÷ 36 = 314.86). This is approximately the same mean value our manager got from looking at each year separately. The median value of the expanded population—315 [(310 + 320) ÷ 2]—and the mode (350) are the same, too. These results aren't surprising because the numbers are all the same and are all arranged in order.

The difference is that there are no outliers in this expanded population and the values are evenly distributed throughout the population rather than being clustered at either end. As a result, the summary values are much more representative of the expanded population than they were of the individual yearly populations. Even more important, any staffing decision our manager might make based on the expanded population values is likely to be more accurate.

Increasing the size of the population also changes the measures of dispersion. For example, the range for the expanded population is equal to 430 (530 − 100), which is much larger than the individual ranges for Year 1 and Year 2, and indicates that the data in the expanded population are more widely dispersed than the data in the individual yearly populations. This result is confirmed by the values for the variance and standard deviation. As you recall, the variance for Year 1 was equal to 1,145.8 and the standard deviation for Year 1 was equal to 33.85. If we round the mean of the expanded population from 314.86 to 315, then the total of the squared distances for all 36 values is equal to 354,625, which means that the variance—the total of the squared distances divided by the number of values—is equal to 9,850.7 (354,625 ÷ 36 = 9,850.7). The standard deviation—$\sqrt{9,850.7}$ —is equal to 99.25.

Data Distributions

A data distribution is a listing of all the values in a population. When plotted on a graph, the values in a data distribution form a curve. The height, width, and shape of the curve depend on whether the data distribution is a normal distribution or a non-normal distribution.

Normal Distributions

A data distribution that includes both data values and the probability of observing each value is called a probability distribution. *Probability* is the likelihood that a given event, observation, or result will occur. A *normal distribution*, in which the number of values that are less than the mean is the same as the number of values greater than the mean, is the most common form of probability distribution. Normal distributions describe a wide variety of everyday data such as

- Heights and weights of individuals

- Test scores on an examination

- Times required to complete a task

- Regular monthly expenses, such as rent, car payments, and mortgage payments

  For insurers, normal distributions describe such variables as the

- Number of insurance policies sold by individual producers

- Number of customer calls handled by call center staff

- Amount of time needed to complete transactions

- Amount of expenses for underwriting, issuing, and maintaining policies

- Commissions paid on sales of insurance policies

An insurer's total claim data would likely follow a normal distribution pattern as well.

The variables in a normal distribution are considered *discrete variables* because they include a finite, or limited, number of values. Most discrete variables have only one value.

The values in a normal distribution create a bell-shaped curve in which the midpoint of the bell is the mean value. Because values are distributed normally, the mean, median, and mode are all the same. The shape of the bell—whether it is short and wide or tall and narrow—depends on the size of the standard deviation. A large standard deviation generally produces a short, wide curve, such as the one shown on the left in Figure 10.2. A small standard deviation generally produces a tall, narrow curve, such as the one on the right in Figure 10.2.

Regardless of dimensions, all normal curves share the following characteristics:

- 68.27% of the data in the distribution falls within one (plus or minus) standard deviation of the mean. In other words, about 68% of all data are between one standard deviation less than the mean and one standard deviation greater than the mean.

- 95.45% of the data in the distribution falls within two (plus or minus) standard deviations of the mean.

- 99.73% of the data in the distribution falls within three (plus or minus) standard deviations of the mean.

Figure 10.4 illustrates the relationships among the data values in a normal curve that has a standard deviation equal to 4. In this curve, the mean is located at "0," and standard deviations are located at ±4, ±8, and ±12. The portions of the curve that extend beyond three standard deviations from the mean on either side are called "tails." In a true normal curve, the probability of a value being in one of the tails is extremely small—approximately 0.003, or 0.30%.

Non-Normal Distributions

Non-normal distributions are asymmetrical distributions in which the number of values on one side of the mean is greater than the number of values on the other side of the mean. An example of a non-normal distribution curve is shown in Figure 10.5. Unlike normal distribution curves, non-normal distribution curves often have a tail at only one end.

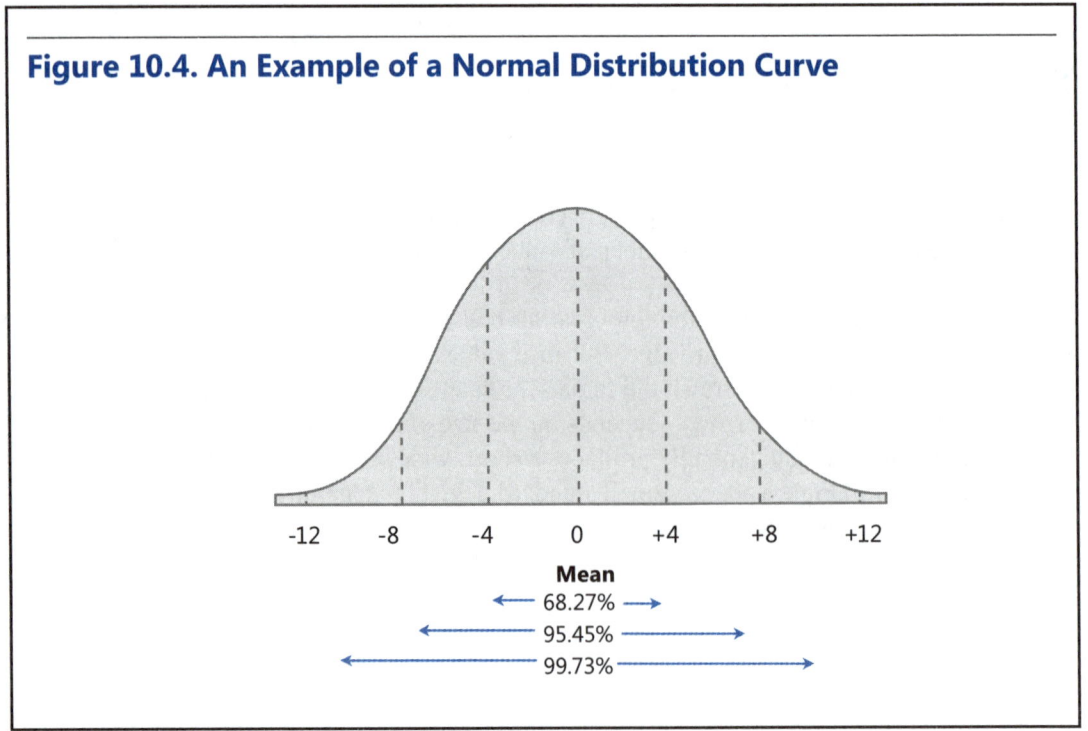

Figure 10.4. An Example of a Normal Distribution Curve

-12   -8   -4   0   +4   +8   +12

Mean

← 68.27% →

← 95.45% →

← 99.73% →

Business and Financial Concepts for Insurance ProfessionalsChapter 10: Analyzing Population Data | 219

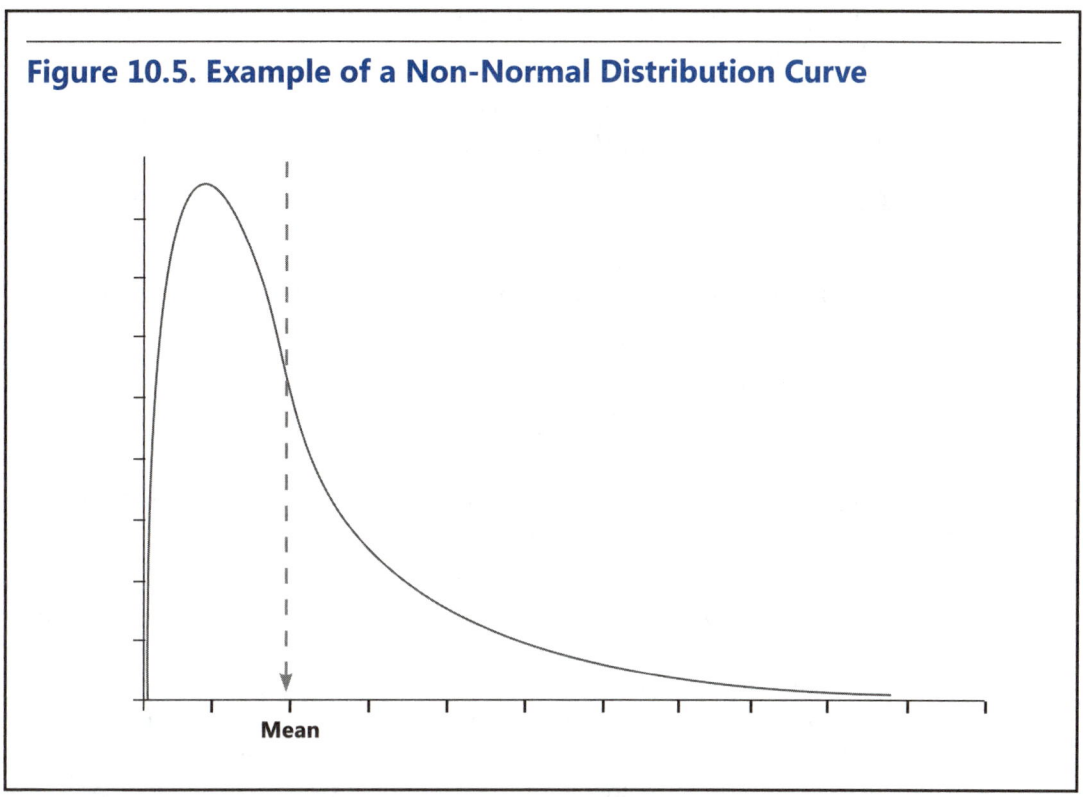

Figure 10.5. Example of a Non-Normal Distribution Curve

The variables in non-normal distributions are generally random rather than discrete variables. A ***random variable*** is a variable whose values represent all possible outcomes. Financial values such as stock values are often distributed non-normally because they are affected by a variety of market factors. For insurance companies, many of the variables used in the financial design of insurance products are also random variables, including

- Investment earnings, which depend on market conditions

- Mortality costs and other costs of benefits

- Product expenses

- Lapse rates, withdrawal rates, changes in premium allocations, and benefit utilization choices, which depend on customer behavior

- Product shelf-life, which is an estimate of the length of time a policy will remain in force

Insurers generally use financial modeling to account for the multiple outcomes generated by random variables.

Data Quality

The quality of any decision based on statistical information depends on the quality of the data being analyzed. In general, data quality is measured in terms of the data's

- **Appropriateness.** The degree to which data meet the requirements of their intended applications.

- **Accuracy.** The degree to which data correctly describe the real-world phenomena they are designed to measure.

- **Relevance.** The degree to which information derived through data analysis meets the needs of users.

- **Timeliness.** A measure of the delay between the reference date for the data and the date the analysis is published.

- **Interpretability.** The ease with which data can be correctly interpreted.

- **Accessibility.** The ease with which needed data can be obtained.

- **Coherence.** The degree to which data can successfully be integrated with other statistical information over time.

Ideally, the data used for statistical analysis should have all the attributes of quality data. In reality, trade-offs are often necessary. For example, ensuring data timeliness may require sacrificing the degree of data accuracy, and ensuring maximum accuracy may require sacrificing timeliness. Similarly, increasing accessibility often limits the relevance of the data to end users, and increasing relevance often limits data accessibility. For example, obtaining detailed information about a product's costs requires searching through multiple systems over a long period of time. Although detailed information is useful for an insurance company's actuaries or accountants, it is generally not needed for senior management, who are more interested in seeing the "big picture." Limiting data to summary values would simplify data collection and make the information more accessible to senior management, but it would not meet the needs of actuaries or accountants.

Key Terms

statistical analysis	mode
statistics	measures of dispersion
population	range
descriptive statistics	variance
measures of central tendency	standard deviation
mean	probability
outlier	normal distribution
median	discrete variable
	random variable

Analyzing Sample Data

Objectives:

After studying this chapter, you should be able to

- Describe how the law of large numbers affects the value of conclusions based on sample data

- Describe the three primary forms of probability sampling and identify the strengths and limitations of each form

- Describe situations in which nonprobability sampling is, and is not, appropriate for insurers

- Identify some of the actions insurers can take to reduce various forms of sampling bias

- Describe how sample values differ from population values and explain how insurers can improve the statistical validity and accuracy of sample results

- Explain how identifying trends in population data can help insurance companies make decisions about products and markets

- Describe the three primary elements of a financial model and explain how insurers can use modeling to forecast future financial conditions

Outline

Law of Large Numbers

Sampling
- Probability Sampling
- Nonprobability Sampling
- Avoiding Sampling Bias

Using Sample Data to Estimate Population Characteristics
- Calculating Sample Values
- Fitting Sample Values to the Population

Using Sample Data to Forecast Behavior
- Trend Analysis
- Modeling

An insurance company's information systems are filled with company-specific data about the company's expenses, underwriting decisions, mortality experience, and past and current policyowners. Some of these complete data sets—or populations—are enormous. Using descriptive statistics to make predictions about a given population by analyzing every data value in the population can be time consuming and expensive.

Imagine how much it would cost and how long it would take an insurer to sift through data about every person who owns an insurance policy it issued. Examining every member of a large population can also be impractical. For example, by the time an insurer has collected data about every person over age 65 in a particular geographical area, the number of people in the population may have changed. Some of the original members of the population would have died in the interim, and people who had been excluded at the beginning because they were under the age limit would now be included. In these situations, analyzing a sample is easier and more economical than examining the entire population.

Basing decisions on sample data, however, can be risky because conclusions drawn from sample values are not facts, but inferences. A *fact* is a piece of objective information that can be proven to be true. An *inference* is a conclusion based on facts and other information. An inference can be right, but it can also be wrong. Inferential statistics can help reduce this risk. *Inferential statistics* are methods that allow people to make predictions about a population on the basis of data gathered from only a sample, or portion, of the population.

Law of Large Numbers

The accuracy of conclusions based on sample data depends, in large part, on whether the sample is representative of the population. The more representative the sample data, the more accurate the conclusions drawn from sample data are likely to be.

An important concept that helps ensure the accuracy of sample data is the law of large numbers. The *law of large numbers* is a mathematical concept which states that, under normal circumstances, the more times a particular event is observed, the more likely it is that the observations will approximate the "true" probability that the event will occur. The classic example of the effect of the law of large numbers is the probability that a coin tossed repeatedly into the air will land with the "head" side face up half of the time and with the "tail" side face up half of the time. Here's how it works:

> Suppose a coin tossed into the air landed with the head side up. You would have a 50% chance of seeing this result, because a head or a tail are the only two options. Now suppose you toss the coin four more times. Like the first toss, each additional toss has a 50% chance of landing head side up. The overall results of the five tosses, however, might be 4 heads and 1 tail. Even 10 or 20 tosses might not result in an equal number of heads and tails.
>
> However, if you tossed the coin 1,000 times, the likelihood that you would have an approximately equal number of heads and tails would be fairly high. In fact, the more times you toss the coin, the more likely it is that you will see an approximately equal number of heads and tails and the more likely it is that your findings will approximate the "true" probability of the event.

According to the law of large numbers, the larger the sample, the higher the probability that the sample will accurately represent the population. And the more representative the sample is, the more likely it is that the results of analyzing sample data will be representative of the results obtained by analyzing population data.

The law of large numbers has important applications in insurance. For example, insurance companies rely on the law of large numbers when they use mortality tables, which project the number of deaths that are likely to occur within a given group of people during a given time period. Individual insurance companies typically have years of recorded data about how many of their insureds have died and how old they were when they died. Countries generally collect similar information about the population as a whole and record their findings in publications such as Census reports. Combining individual company mortality data with population mortality data has allowed insurers to estimate with great accuracy how many people in a large group (usually 100,000 or more) are likely to die at each age. Insurers use similar tables—called morbidity tables—to estimate the probability, or incidence, of sickness and accidents among a given group of people of a given age. Mortality and morbidity tables are an important tool that insurers use to establish premium rates that will be adequate to pay the insurer's claims.

Sampling

Researchers can select samples from a population in one of two ways: probability sampling or nonprobability sampling. Which technique is most appropriate depends on the situation.

Probability Sampling

Sometimes, it's essential that the values included in a sample be representative of all the values in the population. For example, insurers often survey a sample of their customers to determine how satisfied they are with the company's products and services. These insurers need to know that the sample customers answer the survey questions in a way that is representative of all customers.

Generally, insurers also use probability sampling in situations where the intent is to demonstrate that a company is consistently following documented or required procedures. For example, insurers in most jurisdictions are required to submit a sample of their financial and nonfinancial records to auditors and insurance regulators for examination. To ensure that the reports prepared by examiners are accurate, insurers need to be sure that the records they submit are representative of all the company's records. The best way to ensure that sample data accurately represent the population is to select sample data from the population at random.

Probability sampling, or *random sampling*, is a technique in which each member of a population has a determinable chance, or probability, of being selected. The three most common types of probability sampling are simple random sampling, systematic random sampling, and stratified random sampling.

Simple Random Sampling

In *simple random sampling*, every member of a population has an *equal* probability of being in the sample. If a population is well defined and the number of elements needed for a sample is relatively small, sampling can be done by hand, using a table of random numbers or a random number generator. A *random number generator* is a software application that automatically identifies a pattern of values that would be produced by sampling a probability distribution.

> Suppose an auditor has been assigned to evaluate the accuracy of an insurance company's underwriting practices. Instead of examining each of the 1,000 insurance applications processed during the past month, the auditor selected a sample of 200 records. To generate the sample group, the auditor numbered the records from 0001 to 1,000 and then put those numbers through a random number generator. The auditor then pulled the 200 records whose numbers matched the numbers produced by the random number generator.

Systematic Random Sampling

Another way of producing a random sample is to use systematic random sampling. *Systematic random sampling* involves selecting items from the population at a uniform interval, which is generally measured by time, order, or space. For example, a call center manager evaluating the performance of customer service representatives might monitor one call every 15 minutes. In this case, the interval would be measured by time. A claim manager who evaluates the accuracy of claim processing by examining one claim from each face value amount would be using an interval measured by order. An auditor who examined every fifth record in the underwriting department's application file would be using an interval measured by space.

Researchers can use any size interval and can start sampling at any point in the population. As an example, let's look at the systematic random sample drawn by our auditor.

> If the auditor started at the beginning of the application file and examined every fifth record, she would select record #5, record #10, record #15, and so on. When she reached the end of the file, she would have selected all 200 records needed for her sample (200 × 5 = 1,000).

> If the auditor began sampling with record #12, she would select record #12, record #17, record #22, record #27, and so on. Because she started with record #12, she would have selected only 198 records when she reached the end of the file. The auditor would need to go back to the beginning of the file to select the last two records for her sample of 200.

Systematic random sampling is often the most convenient way to select random samples, because it doesn't require the use of a random number generator. In addition, as our example illustrates, if the sample size is sufficiently large relative to the size of the population and the interval used is appropriate, systematic random sampling ensures that the entire population is sampled, regardless of where sample selection begins.

If the sample size is small relative to the size of the population, then interval size, starting point, and order (numerical or alphabetical) are important.

> Suppose our auditor sampled 200 of the 1,000 records in the application file by selecting every other record. In this case, the auditor would have selected 200 records well before she reached the end of the file. In fact, she would have selected 200 records from the first 400 records in the file (200 × 2 = 400). If the records were filed in alphabetical order, those at the beginning of the alphabet would be over-represented, and those at the end of the alphabet would be ignored. If the auditor had begun selecting records near the middle of the file, she would have ignored records at the beginning and the end of the alphabet. The same imbalance would be created if the records in the file were arranged according to face amount.

To increase the likelihood of selecting a representative sample, researchers such as our auditor should

■ Select an appropriate sample size

■ Select a random interval size

■ Choose a random starting point for sampling

■ Proceed through the entire population

Stratified Random Sampling

Simple random sampling and systematic random sampling are usually most effective when population elements are homogeneous—that is, when the elements in the population are similar. Insurance applications and underwriting procedures are good examples of homogeneous data. If the population is varied or clearly segmented, simple random sampling and systematic random sampling are generally not appropriate. For example, suppose an insurer has 3,000 producers spread among four separate locations.

Location	Number of Producers
Home office	1,800
Region A	300
Region B	800
Region C	100
Total	**3,000**

If the insurer used simple random sampling to survey 100 of its producers, mere chance could cause a disproportionate number of producers from Region C to be included in the sample. The views of these producers would have a disproportionate effect on the final data, even though they may or may not represent the view of the other producers. Even systematic random sampling is likely to result in a larger proportion of elements from some segments than from others.

To address the problems created by segmented populations, companies often use stratified random sampling. *Stratified random sampling* divides the population into subgroups, or strata, and then selects a proportional number of items from each stratum at random. To determine the number of items from each stratum to include in the sample, the researcher would first determine the ratio of items in the sample to the total number of items in the population. In our example, the ratio is 100/3,000, or 1/30. Next, the researcher would multiply the number of items in each stratum by the ratio. The example below shows the number of producers that would be selected from each stratum.

Location	Number of Producers				Number in Sample
Home office	1,800	×	1/30	=	60
Region A	300	×	1/30	=	10
Region B	800	×	1/30	=	27
Region C	100	×	1/30	=	3

Note that multiplying the number of producers in Region B and Region C by 1/30 produces fractions: $800 \times 1/30 = 26.67$ and $100 \times 1/30 = 3.33$. Because our insurer can't select fractions of producers, the fraction was rounded to the nearest whole number. The total number of producers in the sample is equal to 100.

The specific producers from each stratum would then be selected at random. Each producer, in this case, has a *weighted* rather than an *equal* probability of being included in the sample, and all strata are represented fairly in the final sample.

Figure 11.1 summarizes the characteristics of these three probability sampling techniques.

Figure 11.1. Strengths and Weaknesses of Probability Sampling

Method	Sample selected	Strengths/Weaknesses
Simple Random Sampling	Mechanically, using a random number table or random number generator	+ All population members have an equal probability of selection − Not useful for varied or segmented populations − Sampling process often time-consuming
Systematic Random Sampling	At predetermined intervals	+ Doesn't require user to assign numbers to elements + Ensures that entire population is sampled − Interval size and order of elements important in small samples
Stratified Random Sampling	Proportionally from individual segments according to ratio of sample to population; individual elements in each segment selected at random	+Useful for varied or clearly segmented populations − Requires additional calculations

Nonprobability Sampling

Unlike probability sampling, nonprobability sampling makes no attempt to randomize sample selection by using random number generators, sampling intervals, or strata. Instead, *nonprobability sampling* bases sample selection on specific, personally selected criteria. For example, a researcher might sample only home office employees or employees in specific organizational units. Similarly, a researcher might limit a sample of customers to those within a specified age range, those who live in a specified geographical area, or those who pay a specified policy premium.

Because using specific selection criteria excludes some members of the population, not every member has an equal or even a predetermined probability of being selected. As a result, nonprobability sampling is less reliable than probability sampling for predicting the characteristics of a population based on the characteristics of the sample.

However, these limitations don't mean that nonprobability sampling can't be useful. Insurance companies often use nonprobability sampling when there is reason to believe that examining only a few clearly defined members of a population can identify a "typical" member.

> The Basic Insurance Company is developing a new life insurance product targeted to men and women ages 18 to 35. Management believes the new product will be especially attractive to customers between the ages of 18 and 24. To confirm that belief, Basic surveyed a sample of individuals between the ages of 18 and 24 from the total market for the product.

Insurers also use nonprobability sampling when they specifically select repeat customers to participate in a customer service survey, or when they sample the top 5% of producers. In these examples, samples are selected according to pre-determined criteria rather than probability.

Avoiding Sampling Bias

No matter how carefully a company selects a sample, the information the company obtains from the sample may not be representative if the method used to collect data is flawed.

- **Response bias** occurs when the way questions are asked distorts the data. For example, a question that begins with "Don't you agree that..." or "Wouldn't you prefer that..." encourages sample members to provide particular answers. Unclear questions can also create problems. Even the order in which choices are presented can bias answers because sample members are more likely to select the first choice in a list than the last choice in the list.

- **Nonresponse bias** occurs when certain sample members are more likely to provide information than other members. For example, studies show that middle-income people are more likely to respond to mail surveys than are upper- or lower-income people. As a result, responses to a mail survey tend to over-represent the middle-income population, even though all income levels were included in the sample. Similarly, customer service surveys tend to generate more responses from customers who have had extremely positive or extremely negative experiences than from customers who have had more neutral experiences.

- **Selection bias** occurs when the way data are collected systematically excludes certain members of the sample. For example, a survey of customers conducted by calling customers at home between 9:00 am and 5:00 pm would systematically exclude customers who work outside the home during regular business hours. In this case, information from certain sample members is excluded because the sample members weren't contacted, not because they were contacted and chose not to respond.

Making sure that surveys don't include questions that lead to specific answers and varying the order of questions can usually reduce the effects of response bias. Sending reminders or additional surveys to nonresponders can often reduce nonresponse bias. Expanding the hours during which calls are made and following up on missed calls can reduce selection bias.

Using Sample Data to Estimate Population Characteristics

The first step in using sample data to estimate population characteristics is to calculate sample values. The next step is to compare sample values to population values.

Calculating Sample Values

Inferential statistics provide users with the same basic types of information about samples that descriptive statistics provide about populations: measures of central tendency and measures of dispersion. The difference is that inferential statistics provide fewer of these measures. For example, the only measure of central tendency that describes sample data is the sample mean. The median and the mode have little, if any, meaning when applied to samples. The primary measures of dispersion for sample data are the variance and standard deviation. Because samples represent only a portion of the population, the range isn't helpful.

Sample Mean

The sample mean, like the population mean, is calculated by summing all the values in the sample and dividing the total by the number of values in the sample. In other words,

> **Sample mean = Sum of sample values ÷ Number of sample values**

To see how this works, let's go back to the three-year claim data collected by Foremost's claim manager from Chapter 10. We'll assume, for this discussion, that the data were arranged in ascending order rather than by year.

Suppose that instead of analyzing the population, Foremost's claim manager decided to analyze a sample of the claim data. He constructed his sample by selecting every other value in the population. The sample values are highlighted below:

Life Insurance Claims

100	250	290	320	350	420
100	**255**	**290**	**320**	**350**	**430**
125	270	300	340	350	450
170	**270**	**300**	**340**	**360**	**480**
200	280	310	350	360	500
230	**285**	**310**	**350**	**400**	**530**

The total of these 18 values is 5,565. The sample mean, therefore, is equal to 309.17 (5,565 ÷ 18 = 309.17), which is smaller than the population mean value of 315.

Sample Variance and Standard Deviation

The calculations used to determine sample variance and sample standard deviation are similar, but not identical, to the calculations used to determine the variance and standard deviation for a population. For example, the first three steps in calculating a sample variance are the same as the steps in calculating a population variance:

■ Calculate the sample mean

■ Find the distance of each value in the sample from the mean and then square each distance

■ Sum all the squared distances

The fourth step, however, is slightly different. Instead of dividing the total squared distances by the number of values, sample variance calculations require you to

■ Divide the total squared distances by the number of values **minus one**. Subtracting one from the number of values is designed to correct for sampling bias.

As is the case with population standard deviation calculations, finding the sample standard deviation requires finding the square root of the sample variance.

> After calculating the sample mean, Foremost's claim manager calculated the variance and standard deviation of the sample data.
>
> To calculate the sample variance, he squared the distance between each value and the mean, and then summed all the squared distances. In this sample, the sum of all the squared distances was equal to 173,725.
>
> The manager then divided the total by the number of values in the sample *minus 1*. Dividing 173,725 by 17 (the number of values in the sample *minus 1*) produced a sample variance of **10,219**.
>
> To calculate the sample standard deviation, the manager calculated $\sqrt{10,219}$. The result was a sample standard deviation of approximately **101**.

These sample values, like the sample mean, are slightly different than the population variance of 9,850.7 and the population standard deviation of 99.25. These differences aren't surprising. In fact, values derived from sample data are usually different from population values.

The differences between population values and the values derived from a sample of the population are called *sample errors*. Sample errors are caused by chance and are unavoidable. However, it is possible to reduce sampling errors by using appropriate sampling techniques and selecting a sufficiently large sample size. If a manager takes into account the possibility of sampling errors, then the likelihood that decisions based on sample data are right increases.

Fitting Sample Values to the Population

As our previous example proved, it's impossible to guarantee that analyzing a sample will produce the same results as analyzing the entire population. It's also impossible to guarantee that different samples from a given population will produce the same results. Here's what happens if Foremost's claim manager starts sampling with the second value rather than the first value in the data set.

The sample in this case would include the values highlighted below:

Life Insurance Claims

100	250	290	320	350	420
100	**255**	**290**	**320**	**350**	**430**
125	270	300	340	350	450
170	**270**	**300**	**340**	**360**	**480**
200	280	310	350	360	500
230	**285**	**310**	**350**	**400**	**530**

This sample contains the same number of elements as the first sample, but the sample mean for this group of values—320.55 (5,770 ÷ 18= 320.55)—is higher than both the original mean value of 315.00 and the first sample mean of 309.17.

The variance and standard deviation for this sample would also be different from those in the first sample.

Statistical Validity

It's possible to improve the accuracy of results drawn from sample data by ensuring that the observed results are statistically valid. *Statistical validity* is the degree to which an observed result, such as a difference between two measurements, can be relied upon and not attributed to random error in sampling or measurement. For example, the differences between the means, variances, and standard deviations our claim manager derived by analyzing a sample of the data and the values derived by analyzing the population tell us that the sample data don't accurately represent the population. As a result, the sample results are not statistically valid and shouldn't be relied upon for making decisions. Statistical validity of sample results depends, in large part, on the sample size. To determine the appropriate number of values to include in a sample, an insurer needs to consider the following factors:

- **The number of data values in the population.** In general, the larger the population, the larger the sample must be to represent the population accurately.

- **The desired degree of confidence required to make a decision.** The degree of confidence used in inferential statistics is an indicator of the likelihood that a calculated value is accurate. For example, a 95% degree of confidence means that there is a 95% likelihood that calculated results are accurate. In general, the larger the sample size, the higher the degree of confidence. If the risk involved with a decision based on sample data is low, managers may be able to select a relatively small sample. If the risk involved with a decision is high, managers may need to increase the size of the sample to increase the degree of confidence.

- **The acceptable margin of error.** The margin of error indicates how accurately a given sample represents the population. In most cases, the larger the sample size, the smaller the margin of error. A margin of error of 3% is considered acceptable for most samples. If the margin of error is larger than 3%, it may be necessary to increase the size of the sample.

Using Sample Data to Forecast Behavior

In addition to predicting population characteristics, sample data can provide important information about future conditions. For insurance companies, being able to estimate the future behavior of key risk factors over the lifetime of insurance products is critical to the companies' long-term financial success.

Sometimes, an insurer can use the patterns that emerge from analyzing historical data to forecast the future behavior of that data. In other cases, insurers use modeling to produce estimates of future conditions.

Trend Analysis

Trend analysis forecasts the future movement of specified factors based on historical patterns. Insurers often use trend analysis to identify patterns in population characteristics. For example, analysis of the demographic data included in periodic census reports has identified a number of population trends that could have a significant impact on the insurance industry. These trends include changes in

- **Population growth.** Census information published in 2000 predicted that the populations in most countries would increase between 2000 and 2010, but at a decreasing rate. Figure 11.2 shows the expected growth rates for a sample of countries. The expected growth rate of 8.91% for the United States is significantly lower than the growth rates for such countries as India (15.21%), the Philippines (20.62%), and Saudi Arabia (38.69%). In addition, U.S. Census Bureau statistics indicate that much of the growth in the United States comes from immigration. These trends are indicators of potential future markets for insurance products.

- **Age.** Overall the world's population is growing older. According to 2000 census information, the median age in the United States in 1970 was 28 years; in 2000 it had increased to 35 years; and by 2050, it is expected to reach 42 years. Certain population segments are growing at an even faster rate. For example, Baby Boomers—people born between 1946 and 1964—represent the largest segment of the U.S. population in terms of age. In addition, the number of people over age 65 is increasing steadily. The aging of the population is likely to have a significant impact on the demand for insurance products. Seniors and older members of the Baby Boom segment represent a significant market for annuities, long-term care insurance, and health insurance. People in younger age groups, who are often faced with caring for both children and parents, represent an important market for life insurance products.

- **Household structure.** In demographic terms, a household is any single person who lives alone or any group of people, related or not, who share the same residence. In the United States and Canada, households are increasing in number, decreasing in size, and changing in composition. For example, the proportion of family households and the proportion of married couple families in the United States have declined, while the proportion of nonfamily households have increased dramatically. These changes are important for insurance companies because the demand for insurance products is linked to consumers' need to provide support for dependents if the main wage earner dies prematurely. Families with only one wage earner generally need a larger amount of

---

Figure 11.2. Population Growth by Country

Population (in millions)

Country	2000	2010 (Projected)	Percentage Change
Australia	19,165	20,925	9.18%
Brazil	172,860	186,823	8.08%
Canada	31,278	35,253	9.51%
China	1,261,832	1,359,141	7.71%
Germany	82,797	84,616	2.20%
India	1,014,004	1,168,205	15.21%
Indonesia	224,784	259,743	15.55%
Japan	126,550	127,252	0.55%
Philippines	81,160	97,898	20.62%
Saudi Arabia	22,024	30,546	38.69%
United Kingdom	50,508	60,602	1.84%
United States	275,563	300,118	8.91%

---

insurance protection than families with two incomes. In addition, single-person households represent a significant market for disability income, medical expense, and long-term care coverage.

■ **Household income.** In recent years, three emerging income segments have gained special attention from insurance companies. The mass affluent segment, which includes individuals with total household assets worth between $100,000 and $1 million, currently holds more than 50% of total market assets and is growing at a rate 5 times greater than that of the general population. Members of the high-net-worth segment hold between $1 million and $25 million in household assets. Ultra-high-net-worth individuals hold more than $25 million in household assets. Although this segment is small, it accounts for more than 15% of total market assets. High-income segments are a prime market for asset accumulation as well as asset protection products.

Although trend analysis can be a valuable tool for forecasting the kinds of characteristics discussed here, it generally doesn't provide accurate estimates for factors whose behavior is more volatile. For example, market interest rates, which are an important factor in pricing insurance products, can vary widely from year to year, depending on prevailing conditions in the economy. To determine the future behavior of factors that fall outside the range of observed values, insurers generally rely on modeling.

Modeling

Insurers often use financial models to generate estimates of future financial conditions such as future cash inflows, future cash outflows, and future values for assets, reserves, capital, and expenses. Most financial models consist of three primary elements:

- **Input** generally takes the form of *variables*, which are items of data whose value varies over time. The input variables used in financial models are independent variables. An *independent variable* is a variable that influences the behavior of another variable. Independent variables can be drawn from historical or real-world observations or they can be randomly selected from a data distribution.

- **Processes** usually simulate the behavior of known values and use those behaviors to identify how unknown values are likely to behave over time. For example, insurers can use computer-generated simulations to assess the impact of different levels of economic activity, such as market interest rates and economic growth, on the company's future financial condition. The objective of modeling is not to produce a single forecast of future conditions, but to identify a number of "what if" situations, or scenarios, that describe financial and economic conditions.

- **Output** represents the projected future values produced by processing input variables through the model. Output variables are considered *dependent variables* because they react to outside influences. In particular, dependent variables react to changes in independent variables. The outputs created by financial models can be single values or a listing of all possible values in a data set.

The estimates of future financial values generated by models usually take one of three forms:

- Probability distributions

- Point estimates

- Range estimates

Earlier, we discussed the characteristics of normal distributions and non-normal distributions. In general, normal distributions follow established patterns and, as a result, future values can be estimated with a relatively high degree of accuracy. Non-normal distributions are used to evaluate factors, such as reserve requirements or rates of return, that don't follow regular patterns. In particular, non-normal distributions identify "tail" values—those values that have a very low probability of occurring, but that carry very high risk.

A *point estimate* is an estimate that is assigned a single value. Point estimates have a number of applications for insurance companies. For example, Foremost's claim manager could model the claim data he collected to produce a point estimate of the number of claims processed. He could then use the point estimate to identify the optimum number of analysts to maintain on staff. He could also use a point estimate to forecast future claim volume.

Another important application of point estimates for insurance companies is calculating product profitability based on interest earnings.

> Suppose an insurer used a pricing model to estimate the profitability of a proposed life insurance policy. The insurer ran the model using an assumed 6% interest rate. The model produced a point estimate of the product's earnings at the assumed rate. To see how the product's profitability would be affected if interest rates differed from the assumed 6% rate, the insurer reran the model, using multiple possible interest rates. The insurer then examined the point estimates of the product's earnings at each interest rate to determine the range of possible outcomes.

As an alternative to using modeling to produce a point estimate, an insurer could specify a range of values for modeling outcomes. An estimate that provides a range of possible outcome values is called a ***range estimate***.

> Suppose that our insurer programmed the model to produce estimates of the product's earnings that fell into the following ranges:
>
> Between 5% and 7%
> Between 3% and 9%
> Between 2% and 10%
>
> By analyzing the output values in these ranges, the insurer can identify what interest rate should be used during product design to provide a cushion if actual interest rates are unfavorable or to capitalize on favorable rates.

Insurers can improve the accuracy and value of range estimates by assigning specified probabilities to various ranges.

When insurers use models to produce data distributions, point estimates, and range estimates, they use a single modeling run to produce a single scenario of results. Using multiple iterations of a financial model produces multiple scenarios. By analyzing multiple scenarios, insurers can often determine the amount and timing of changes in output variables created by changes in input variables.

> Suppose our insurer modeled several separate input values instead of a single value. The model, in this case, would produce a different estimate for each input value. By making changes to the input variable and then running separate model runs for each new value, the insurer could determine whether outcomes represented favorable conditions or unfavorable conditions as well as the likelihood of each of the outcomes.

In all cases, statistics play a critical role in helping insurers interpret and use information to make decisions.

Key Terms

fact
inference
inferential statistics
law of large numbers
probability sampling
simple random sampling
random number generator
systematic random sampling
stratified random sampling
nonprobability sampling
sample errors
statistical validity
trend analysis
variable
independent variable
dependent variable
point estimate
range estimate

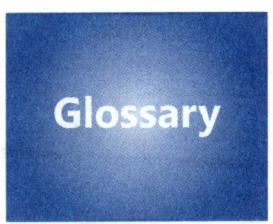

Glossary

accumulated value. For a fixed deferred annuity, the net amount paid for the annuity, plus interest earned, less the amount of any withdrawals or fees. [6]

acquisition expense. An expense an insurer incurs to obtain and issue new business. [5]

activity ratio. A ratio that measures the rate at which a company's various assets are converted (turned over) into sales or cash. Sometimes called an *operating efficiency ratio* or a *turnover ratio*. [8]

adverse deviation. In product operations, a difference between actual and assumed product values that produces a decrease in actual product profitability relative to assumed product profitability. *Contrast with* **favorable deviation**. [4]

ALM. *See* **asset-liability management**.

amortization. The reduction of a debt by regular payments of principal and interest that result in full payment of the debt by the maturity date. [3]

annual report. A document that a company's management sends to interested parties—such as stockholders and investors—to report on the company's financial performance during the past year; helps users assess a company's profitability. *Contrast with* **Annual Statement**. [7]

Annual Statement. A financial report that every insurer in the United States must file annually, as well as on a quarterly basis, with the National Association of Insurance Commissioners (NAIC) and the insurance regulatory organization in each state in which the insurer conducts business; helps regulators assess a company's solvency. *Contrast with* **annual report**. [7]

annuity. For the purposes of financial analysis, any series of equal payments made at regular intervals over a specified period of time. [4]

annuity due. An annuity in which the periodic payments are made at the beginning of each payment period. *Contrast with* **ordinary annuity**. [4]

asset. Any item of value owned by a company. [3]

asset accumulation product. A product that enables customers to increase the amount and/or value of their assets over time. [1]

asset-based commission schedule. For annuity sales, a commission schedule in which commissions are calculated as a percentage of the accumulated value of a deferred annuity contract's funds. *Contrast with* **deposit-based commission schedule**. [5]

asset concentration risk. The risk of the excessive concentration of assets in any single category. [3]

asset-liability management (ALM). The practice of coordinating the administration of an insurer's asset portfolio (its investments) with the administration of its liability portfolio (its obligations to customers) so as to manage risk and still earn an adequate level of return. *See* **asset portfolio** and **liability portfolio**. [3]

asset portfolio. In asset-liability management, the portfolio which holds the insurer's securities and other invested assets. *See* **portfolio** and **asset-liability management**. *Contrast with* **liability portfolio**. [3]

asset protection product. A product that protects owners against the risk of financial loss from unforeseen events such as natural disasters, theft, accidents, illnesses, and death. [1]

audit. A systematic examination and evaluation of a company's records, procedures, and controls. [2]

authority. The right an employee has to make decisions, take action, and direct others. [2]

balance sheet. A financial document that lists the values of a company's assets, liabilities, and capital and surplus as of a specific date. *See* **asset, liability, capital**, and **surplus**. Also known as a *statement of financial position* or a *statement of financial condition*. [7]

balanced scorecard. A strategic performance management tool used to monitor a company's performance in key areas. [9]

basic accounting equation. An equation which states that a company's assets equal the sum of its liabilities and its capital and surplus. *See* **balance sheet, asset, liability, capital**, and **surplus**. [7]

basis point (bp). 1/100th of a percent, or 0.0001. [4]

benchmarking. A process which consists of (1) identifying the best outcomes that other companies have achieved for a specific activity or process and the practices that produced those outcomes, and (2) implementing the best practices to equal or surpass the best outcomes. [5]

board of directors. Elected by a company's owners, this group of individuals serves as the company's primary governing body. [2]

bond. A security that represents a debt that the borrower (the issuer of the bond) owes to the bondholder (the person or company that buys the bond). [1]

boom. *See* **expansion**.

bottom-up budgeting. A budgeting approach that starts at the bottom of a company, with lower-level managers generating budgets for their areas, which are then presented in the form of recommendations to senior management. *Contrast with* **top-down budgeting**. [7]

bp. *See* **basis point**.

BPR. *See* **business process reengineering**.

budget. A financial plan of action expressed in monetary terms that covers a specified time period. [2]

budget deficit. In fiscal policy, a budget in which government expenditures exceed government revenues in a given time period. *See* **fiscal policy**. *Contrast with* **budget surplus**. [6]

budget surplus. In fiscal policy, a budget in which government revenues exceed government expenditures in a given time period. *See* **fiscal policy**. *Contrast with* **budget deficit**. [6]

budgeting. An accounting process that includes creating a financial plan of action designed to help an organization achieve its goals. [7]

business cycle. A recurring pattern of fluctuations in the economic activity of a nation over a specified period of time, generally a year or more. *See* **expansion, contraction, recession, recovery**, and **depression**. [6]

business process reengineering (BPR). A comprehensive and systematic analysis and redesign of an organization's work processes. Also known as *reengineering*. [5]

business risk. The risk that changes in a company's external environment will affect its operations. Also known as *marketplace risk*. [3]

capital. In the context of minimum capital standards, refers to the excess of an insurer's assets over its liabilities. On a balance sheet, refers to the amount of money invested in a company by its owners, usually through the purchase of the company's stock. [3, 7]

capital and surplus. On a balance sheet, the amount remaining after liabilities are subtracted from assets. *See* **capital** and **surplus**. [7]

capital and surplus ratio. A solvency ratio that describes the relationship between a company's capital and surplus and its liabilities. [8]

capital appreciation. An increase in the value of invested assets. [1]

capital budget. A budget which shows a company's plans for the financial management of its long-term, high-cost investment proposals. [7]

capital budgeting. The process that companies undertake to analyze decisions about investing in long-term projects or assets. [7]

capital market. *See* **financial market**.

cash. The amount of currency on hand or on deposit at an insurer's bank. [3]

cash budget. A budget which projects a company's beginning cash balance, cash inflows, cash outflows, and ending cash balance for a specified accounting period, typically by quarter. [7]

cash disbursements budget. A schedule showing the timing and amount of all cash disbursements (cash outflows) expected during an accounting period. [7]

cash equivalent. A short-term asset that is not cash but can be converted to cash within 90 days with little or no risk of losing value. [3]

cash flow statement. A financial statement that provides information about a company's cash receipts (cash inflows), cash disbursements (cash outflows), and net change in cash during a specific accounting period. Also called a *statement of cash flows*. [7]

cash receipts budget. A schedule of cash receipts (cash inflows) expected during an accounting period. [7]

chain of command. The structure of authority that travels downward through an organization from higher levels to lower levels. [2]

circular flow diagram. A diagram that illustrates the flow of funds through an economy. [1]

CMO. *See* **collateralized mortgage obligation**.

coincident indicator. A statistical variable that tends to change about the same time that gross domestic product (GDP) changes. *See* **gross domestic product**. [6]

collateralized mortgage obligation (CMO). A bond secured by a pool of residential mortgage loans. *See* **residential mortgage**. [3]

commercial mortgage. A loan secured by commercial real estate, such as shopping centers, office buildings, hospitals, factories, and retail stores. [3]

commercial paper. A financial instrument that consists of short-term, unsecured promissory notes issued to businesses or governments by corporations as an alternative to short-term bank loans or other forms of borrowing. [1]

commission. Payment for services rendered; usually calculated as a percentage of the transaction amount. [1]

committee. A group of people chosen to consider, investigate, or act on specified issues. [2]

common cost. *See* **indirect expense**.

common stock. Stock that entitles its owner to share in the issuing corporation's dividends and provides its owner with the right to vote on certain matters, such as voting for the company's board of directors. *See* **stock**. *Contrast with* **preferred stock**. [3]

competition risk. Any risk posed by direct competitors of a company, changes in an industry's structure, or changes in an industry's standards for the use of technology. [3]

component bar chart. A bar chart that combines the component values from two or more data sets into a single set of bars and indicates the percentage of the total attributable to each set. [9]

compound interest. Interest earned on both the principal and accumulated interest. *Contrast with* **simple interest**. [4]

comprehensive budget. *See* **master budget**.

concurrent control. A control that addresses a company's current activities and systems by continuously monitoring activities as they are performed. [2]

conditionally vested commission. A commission that becomes vested only after a producer reaches a certain age or number of years of service with the company. [5]

Consumer Price Index (CPI). A measurement that compares the average price of a market basket of goods and services at a stated point in time to the average price of the same market basket at a different point in time. [6]

contraction. The phase in the business cycle in which unemployment begins to rise and real GDP decreases from an earlier quarter. Also known as a *downturn*. *See* **business cycle** and **real GDP**. [6]

contractionary fiscal policy. The type of fiscal policy that is used to decrease aggregate demand in order to slow down the economy. Also known as a *restrictive fiscal policy*. *See* **fiscal policy**. *Contrast with* **expansionary fiscal policy**. [6]

contractual reserve. A liability which represents the amount that, together with future premiums and investment earnings, the insurer estimates it needs to pay benefits on in-force policies as they come due. [3]

contractual savings institution. A financial institution that acquires funds at periodic intervals on a contractual basis. [1]

control. The process of monitoring, evaluating, and regulating how effectively and efficiently a company and its employees are performing the activities necessary for achieving the company's goals. [2]

control cycle. A repetitive process designed to ensure that all areas of a company adhere to the company's performance standards. [2]

controllable expense. A cost over which a specified manager or organizational unit has power and influence. *Contrast with* **noncontrollable expense**. [5]

corporate bond. A bond issued by a corporation. [3]

corporate budget. *See* **master budget**.

corporate objective. A statement of a long-term result a company plans to achieve. [2]

corporate strategy. A long-term method that a company intends to use to achieve its objectives. [2]

corporation. A legal entity, separate from its owners, that is created by the authority of a government and that continues beyond the death of any or all of its owners. [2]

cost accumulation. The process of capturing all of a company's costs and categorizing them in meaningful ways. [5]

cost of benefits. For an insurance or annuity product, the value of the contractually required benefits that the product promises to pay. Also known as the *cost of insurance*. [4]

cost of insurance. *See* **cost of benefits**.

coupon rate. For a bond, the interest rate that determines the amount of the periodic interest payments made to the bondholder. [3]

CPI. *See* **Consumer Price Index**.

credit risk. The possibility that a borrower could be late with payments or could entirely fail to pay its obligations. Sometimes called *default risk*. [3]

currency risk. The risk arising from changes in currency exchange rates. [3]

current interest-crediting rate. For a fixed deferred annuity, the rate of interest that an insurer declares and pays; this rate of interest is generally higher than the guaranteed minimum interest-crediting rate. *See* **guaranteed minimum interest-crediting rate**. [6]

current ratio. A solvency ratio that compares a company's current assets to its current liabilities. [8]

customer behavior risk. *See* **policyholder behavior risk**.

cyclical variation. A variation that results from changes that affect more than one phase in the business cycle over a period of several years. *See* **variation**. [6]

dashboard. In a business context, an information system application that combines performance information from multiple sources into a single, easy-to-read format. [9]

data set. *See* **population**.

debt-to-equity ratio. A type of leverage ratio that compares long-term debt to owners' equity. [8]

default. A failure to meet a financial obligation. *See* **credit risk**. [3]

default risk. *See* **credit risk**.

deflation. A fall in the general price level. *Contrast with* **inflation**. [6]

demutualization. The conversion of a mutual insurance company to a stock insurance company. [2]

dependent variable. A variable that reacts to outside influences. *Contrast with* **independent variable**. [11]

deposit-based commission schedule. For annuity sales, a commission schedule that pays commissions only on premium payments made by annuity owners. *Contrast with* **asset-based commission schedule**. [5]

depository institution. A financial institution that specializes in accepting deposits and making loans. [1]

depression. An economic condition in which real GDP declines drastically and, for a period of at least two years, unemployment is unusually high, prices for most goods and services are unusually low, and there is a general inability to purchase goods and services relative to the amount that could be produced using current resources and technology. *See* **business cycle** and **real GDP**. [6]

descriptive statistics. Statistics that summarize or describe a complete set of collected data, known as a population, or data set. *Contrast with* **inferential statistics**. [10]

development expense. An expense an insurer incurs in designing, testing, and implementing a new product or product line. [5]

direct expense. A product expense incurred for or physically traceable to a specified life insurance or annuity product. Also known as a *traceable cost. Contrast with* **indirect expense**. [5]

discrete variable. A variable that includes a finite, or limited, number of values. *Contrast with* **random variable**. [10]

disinflation. A decrease in the rate of inflation. *See* **inflation**. [6]

disintermediation. A process in which large numbers of people withdraw funds from financial intermediaries, such as banks, savings and loan associations, and insurance companies, in order to directly invest in instruments yielding higher returns. *Contrast with* **intermediation**. [6]

diversifiable risk. A risk that is specific to an individual asset or issuer. Also known as a *nonsystematic risk*. *Contrast with* **nondiversifiable risk**. [3]

diversification. A technique for spreading risk by investing in different assets with different characteristics. [3]

dividend. A share of a company's profits payable to owners of the company's stock. [1]

downsizing. *See* **rightsizing**.

downturn. *See* **contraction**.

early-warning financial ratio tests. In Canada, a set of ratios used by regulators to analyze insurers' financial statements. [8]

economic indicator. A statistical variable that demonstrates the direction of an economy. *See* **leading indicator, coincident indicator**, and **lagging indicator**. [6]

economics. The study of how societies and individuals allocate limited resources among competing, unlimited wants. *See* **want**. [1]

economy. The part of the environment that includes all of the elements affecting the production, distribution, and consumption of goods and services. [1]

effective interest rate. The type of interest rate that includes the effects of compounding. *Contrast with* **nominal interest rate**. [4]

end-to-end processing. *See* **straight-through processing**.

enterprise risk management (ERM). A system that identifies and quantifies risks from both potential threats and potential opportunities and manages these risks in a coordinated approach that supports the organization's strategic objectives. [3]

equity risk. Market risk that applies to the stock market. *See* **market risk**. [3]

ERM. *See* **enterprise risk management**.

exception report. A report produced automatically by an insurance company's management information system (MIS) when certain predetermined conditions or exceptions in operating performance occur. *See* **management information system (MIS)**. [2]

exchange. A transaction in which one party gives something of value to another party and receives something of value in return. [1]

expansion. The phase in the business cycle in which unemployment is low and real GDP rises for two or more consecutive quarters. Also known as a *boom*. *See* **business cycle** and **real GDP**. [6]

expansionary fiscal policy. The type of fiscal policy that is used to increase aggregate demand in order to increase the pace of the economy. *See* **fiscal policy**. *Contrast with* **contractionary fiscal policy**. [6]

expense. An amount that a company spends in the course of conducting business. *See* **income statement**. *Contrast with* **revenue**. [5]

expense budget. A type of operational budget that presents a schedule of expenses expected during an accounting period. *See* **expense** and **operational budget**. [7]

expense risk. The risk that actual expenses will be higher than expectations, causing the insurer to lose money on its products; a type of pricing risk. [3]

expenses for contractual benefits. The total amount that an insurer must pay to fulfill the terms of its insurance and annuity contracts. [5]

face value. *See* **par value**.

fact. A piece of objective information that can be proven to be true. [11]

FAST. *See* **Financial Analysis and Solvency Tracking System**.

favorable deviation. In product operations, a difference between actual and assumed product values that produces an increase in actual product profitability relative to assumed product profitability. *Contrast with* **adverse deviation**. [4]

Federal Reserve System (the Fed). In the United States, the central banking system and monetary authority. [6]

feedback control. A control that is used to compare actual performance or output with established standards. [2]

feedforward control. *See* **steering control**.

fiduciary. A financial institution that holds a special position of trust or confidence when handling the affairs of others and who must put the interests of others ahead of its own interests. [1]

final good. A good that is consumed rather than a good used to produce another product. *See* **gross domestic product**. [6]

Financial Analysis and Solvency Tracking (FAST) System. In the United States, a system used to evaluate the solvency of insurers; based on (1) ratio analysis of an insurer's most recent financial statements and (2) analysis of a five-year history of specific aspects of the insurer's financial statements. [8]

financial (capital) market. A market in which money is transferred from savers to borrowers. [1]

financial audit. An evaluation of whether a company's financial information, financial statements, and source documents comply with accounting standards and are a fair and consistent depiction of the company's financial condition and performance. [2]

financial design. *See* **technical product design**.

financial institution. A business that owns financial assets, such as stocks and bonds, rather than fixed assets, such as equipment and raw materials. [1]

financial reporting. The process of presenting financial data about a company's financial position, its operating performance, and its flow of funds during a specified period of time. [7]

financial statement. A report that summarizes a company's financial situation or major monetary events and transactions. [7]

first-year commission. For a life insurance policy, a commission equal to a stated percentage of the amount of the premium an insurer receives during the first policy year. *Contrast with* **renewal commission**. [5]

fiscal policy. In economics, the use of government spending and taxation to change aggregate demand—indicated by the level of spending—in the economy. [6]

fixed expense. An expense amount that remains relatively constant regardless of the number of policies sold or some other measure of the level of operating activity. *Contrast with* **variable expense**. [5]

flow chart. A graphic representation of a sequence of activities and decisions. [9]

foreign exchange market. A market that converts currencies used by buyers into currencies acceptable to the sellers. [1]

fraternal benefit society. An organization formed to provide social and insurance benefits to its members. [2]

future value (*FV*). For a sum of money, the amount that an original sum is expected to be worth at a specified future date, given a specified interest rate. *Contrast with* **present value**. [4]

future value interest factor (*FVIF*). The future value of $1.00 at a given interest rate for a stated number of periods. [4]

FV. See **future value**.

FVIF. See **future value interest factor**.

Gantt chart. A graphical scheduling tool that separates projects into critical activities and plots starting and ending dates for each activity. [9]

GDP. *See* **gross domestic product**.

general and administrative expenses. The expenses that result from undertaking normal business activities to generate sales of products and to support products. [5]

government bond. A bond issued by a national, state, provincial, or city government. [3]

gross domestic product (GDP). The market value of all final goods and services produced within a country in a given time period, usually a year. *See* **market value** and **final good**. [6]

grouped frequency distribution. A table that displays the number of times observed grouped data fall within specified classes. [9]

guaranteed minimum interest-crediting rate. For a fixed deferred annuity, the minimum rate that an insurer must credit to the contract's accumulated value. *See* **accumulated value**. [6]

heaped commission schedule. For life insurance sales, a commission schedule that features a relatively high first-year commission and lower renewal commissions. [5]

histogram. A bar chart showing grouped data; each bar represents a different class of data. [9]

hyperinflation. An out-of-control inflationary spiral. *See* **inflation**. [6]

income statement. A financial document that lists an insurer's revenue and expenses over a specific period, such as a year, and shows whether the insurer experienced a profit or a loss during that period. Also known as a *statement of operations* or a *profit and loss statement (P&L)*. *See* **revenue**, **expense**, and **net income**. [7]

independent variable. A variable that influences the behavior of another variable. *Contrast with* **dependent variable**. [11]

indirect expense. A product expense that cannot be traced to or that is not incurred for one specific product. Also known as a *common cost*. *Contrast with* **direct expense**. [5]

industrial production. A coincident indicator that measures the raw volume of goods produced by industrial firms, such as factories, mines, and electrical utilities. *See* **coincident indicator**. [6]

inference. A conclusion based on facts and other information. [11]

inferential statistics. Methods that allow people to make predictions about a population on the basis of data gathered from only a sample, or portion, of the population. *Contrast with* **descriptive statistics**. [11]

inflation. A rise in the general level of prices in an economy over a period of time. *Contrast with* **deflation**. [6]

insolvency. A condition in which a company is unable to meet its financial obligations on time. *Contrast with* **solvency**. [3]

insurance. A mechanism for transferring some or all of the risk of a financial loss from an individual or entity to an insurance company. [1]

insurance leverage ratio. A leverage ratio that compares a company's contractual reserves to its capital and surplus. [8]

Insurance Regulatory Information System (IRIS). In the United States, a ratio-based analysis of insurance companies that uses 12 standardized financial ratios to identify insurance companies that are most likely to experience financial difficulty. [8]

interest. A fee that individuals and financial institutions pay (or charge) for the use of borrowed money. [1]

interest margin. *See* **interest spread**.

interest rate. The percentage by which an amount of money is multiplied to derive the amount that is paid for the use of that money. [4]

interest-rate risk. The uncertainty arising from fluctuations in market interest rates. [3]

interest spread. Represents the element of profit that insurers hope to earn from their investment operations; found by subtracting the interest-crediting rate from the interest rate earned. Also known as an *interest margin*. [4]

intermediation. The transfer of funds from savers to borrowers through the services of a financial intermediary. *Contrast with* **disintermediation**. [1]

investment. Any use of a company's resources that is intended to generate a positive return of some type. [3]

investment expenses. The costs associated with investing a company's assets. [5]

IRIS. *See* **Insurance Regulatory Information System**.

kaizen. The Japanese word for continuous improvement; refers to improving a system by constantly improving the little details. [5]

labor market. A market in which households offer their labor to businesses and governments in exchange for wages or other compensation. [1]

lagging indicator. A statistical variable that tends to change after gross domestic product (GDP) changes. *See* **gross domestic product**. [6]

law of large numbers. A mathematical concept which states that, under normal circumstances, the more times a particular event is observed, the more likely it is that the observations will approximate the "true" probability that the event will occur. [11]

leading indicator. A statistical variable that tends to change before gross domestic product (GDP) changes. *See* **gross domestic product**. [6]

lean management. A quality improvement method that emphasizes teams or "cells" that process work with fewer hand-offs, greater speed, and better communication. [5]

leverage. *See* **leverage effect**.

leverage effect. A measure of the impact of fixed costs—either operating costs or financing costs—on a company's potential risks and returns to company owners. Also known as *leverage*. [8]

liability. A debt or future obligation of a company. [3]

liability portfolio. In asset-liability management, the portfolio which represents the insurer's obligations to customers. Also known as a *product portfolio*. *See* **portfolio** and **asset-liability management**. *Contrast with* **asset portfolio**. [3]

license. A document issued by a regulatory agency that grants an insurer the legal authority to conduct insurance business in a specific jurisdiction. [2]

life expectancy. The average number of years of life remaining for a group of people. [6]

liquidity. In the context of financial products, the ease with which an asset can be converted to cash for an approximation of its underlying value. [1]

liquidity risk. The risk of not having adequate liquidity to meet obligations as they come due. *See* **liquidity**. [3]

maintenance expense. A product-related expense an insurer incurs while a contract is in force. Also known as a *renewal expense*. [5]

management. The process that companies use to plan, organize, and control operations effectively and efficiently. [2]

management information system (MIS). A computerized system that provides information about a company's daily operations. [2]

market risk. The risk arising from movements in the direction of an entire financial market. [3]

market value. The price that people would be willing to pay for a good or service, rather than the cost of producing it. *See* **gross domestic product**. [6]

marketplace risk. *See* **business risk**.

master budget. A budget which shows the overall operating and financing plans for a company during a specified accounting period; formed by combining all of the individual budgets for each department. Also known as a *comprehensive budget,* a *corporate budget*, or a *performance plan*. [7]

maturity date. For a bond, the date on which the bond issuer must pay the bondholder the bond's par value. [3]

maturity value. *See* **par value**.

mean. The numerical "average" of a series of values. Also known as a *population mean*. [10]

measure of central tendency. A representative value that describes the values in the middle of a population. *See* **population**. [10]

measure of dispersion. A representative value that describes the distribution of data around specified central values. [10]

median. The middle value in a set of values that is arranged in numerical order. Also known as a *population median*. [10]

medium of exchange. A standardized method of making and receiving payments for goods and services. [1]

MIS. *See* **management information system**.

mission statement. A written statement that describes a company's fundamental purpose or reason for being. [2]

mode. The statistical measure that identifies the value that appears most often in a population. Also known as a *population mode*. [10]

model. A system that simulates something else—in product design, a system that simulates an insurance or annuity product. [4]

monetary policy. The strategy a country's monetary authority uses to increase or decrease the money supply in an effort to stabilize the economy. [6]

mortality. The incidence of death in a specified group of people. [4]

mortality risk. The risk that actual mortality will differ from expectations, causing the insurer to lose money on its products; a type of pricing risk. [3]

mortgage. A loan, typically long term, secured by a pledge of specified real estate. [3]

mutual fund. An investment company that pools the funds of customers and uses the funds to buy stocks, bonds, and other financial instruments. [1]

mutual insurance company. An insurance company that is owned by its policyowners. [2]

mutualization. The conversion of a stock insurance company to a mutual insurance company. [2]

NAIC. *See* **National Association of Insurance Commissioners**.

National Association of Insurance Commissioners (NAIC). In the United States, an association of state insurance commissioners designed to promote consistent insurance regulation. [7]

need. A condition that must be satisfied by a product or service in order for individuals, businesses, and governments to survive and function properly. *Contrast with* **want**. [1]

net gain. Positive net income; results when an insurer's revenue is greater than its expenses. *See* **net income**. *Contrast with* **net loss**. [7]

net income. The difference between an insurer's revenue and its expenses. *See* **net gain** and **net loss**. [7]

net loss. Negative net income; results when an insurer's expenses are greater than its revenue. *See* **net income**. *Contrast with* **net gain**. [7]

net profit margin. A profitability ratio which shows how much after-tax profit is generated by each dollar of total revenue. Also known as a *return on revenue ratio*. [8]

nominal interest rate. The named interest rate for a particular investment. *Contrast with* **effective interest rate**. [4]

noncontrollable expense. A cost over which no specified manager or organizational unit has power or influence. *Contrast with* **controllable expense**. [5]

nondiversifiable risk. A risk that affects all assets in an economy and is therefore not specific to an individual asset or issuer. Also known as a *systematic risk*. *Contrast with* **diversifiable risk**. [3]

nonprobability sampling. A sampling technique that bases selection on specific, personally selected criteria. [11]

nonsystematic risk. *See* **diversifiable risk**.

nonvested commission. A commission that is payable to a producer only if the producer still represents the company when the commission becomes due. *Contrast with* **vested commission**. [5]

normal distribution. A type of probability distribution in which the number of values that are less than the mean is the same as the number of values greater than the mean. [10]

operating efficiency ratio. *See* **activity ratio**.

operating expenses. The costs of operations other than expenses for contractual benefits. *See* **expenses for contractual benefits**. [5]

operational budget. A budget that includes all of a company's core business operations; shows the revenue and expenses that a company expects during a specified accounting period. [7]

operational risk. The risk of financial losses resulting from (1) inadequate or failed internal processes and controls, people, or systems, or (2) external events. [3]

ordinary annuity. An annuity in which the periodic payments are made at the end of each payment period. *Contrast with* **annuity due**. [4]

organizational chart. A visual display of the various jobs and the formal lines of authority and reporting within a company. [2]

outlier. An extremely high or low value that is not representative of the other values in a population. [10]

outsourcing. The practice of hiring an external vendor to perform specified operations. [5]

overhead expense. A cost an insurer incurs during normal business operations that is not directly connected to a specific product or service. [5]

owners' equity. The owners' financial interest in the company. Also known as *capital and surplus*. [7]

par value. For a bond, the amount owed on the bond's maturity date. Also known as *face value* or *maturity value*. [3].

pension fund. A contractual savings institution that provides retirement funds for individuals covered by pension plans. [1]

pension plan. An arrangement under which a plan sponsor provides plan participants with a lifetime income benefit that begins at retirement. [1]

per capita GDP. Gross domestic product divided by a country's population. *See* **gross domestic product**. [6]

performance plan. *See* **master budget**.

performance standard. A previously established level of performance against which actual performance can be measured. [2]

persistency bonus. In producer compensation, a bonus that provides extra earnings for favorable persistency results; can be used as an alternative to a production bonus. [5]

persistency rate. The percentage of an insurer's business in force at the beginning of a specified period that remains in force at the end of the period. [2]

personal consumption expenditures (PCE). A coincident indicator that contains figures on how much money people are spending on goods and services. *See* **coincident indicator.** [6]

PERT network. *See* **program evaluation and review technique (PERT) network.**

pictograph. A picture or symbol that is used instead of bars to represent the data values in a bar chart. [9]

planning. The process of evaluating business opportunities, assessing resources, determining goals, and developing strategies for implementation and control. [2]

point estimate. In modeling, an estimate that is assigned a single value. *Contrast with* **range estimate.** [11]

policy dividend. The portion of a mutual company's operating profits that is distributed to policyowners. [2]

policyholder behavior risk. The risk that a company faces as a result of the choices made by policyholders; a type of pricing risk. Also known as *customer behavior risk.* [3]

population. In statistical analysis, a complete set of collected data. *See* **statistical analysis** and **descriptive statistics.** Also known as a *data set.* [10]

population mean. *See* **mean.**

population median. *See* **median.**

population mode. *See* **mode.**

portfolio. A collection of various risky assets, usually assembled to meet a defined set of goals. [3]

preferred stock. Stock that entitles its owner to certain privileges that common stockholders do not have. For example, preferred stockholders have the first right in receiving dividends. *See* **stock.** *Contrast with* **common stock.** [3]

present value (*PV*). For a sum of money, the amount that, if invested at a specified interest rate on a specified date, would grow to equal a specified future amount. *Contrast with* **future value.** [4]

present value interest factor (*PVIF*). The present value of $1.00 discounted at a given interest rate for a stated number of periods. [4]

pricing risk. The risk that an insurer's actual experience will be significantly worse than expectations, causing the insurer to lose money on its products. [3]

prime rate. The interest rate that commercial banks charge their best corporate customers. [6]

principal. The original amount of money upon which interest is calculated. [4]

privately held company. A company in which ownership is restricted to specified individuals. *Contrast with* **publicly held company.** [2]

probability. The likelihood that a given event, observation, or result will occur. [10]

probability sampling. A sampling technique in which each member of a population has a determinable chance, or probability, of being selected. Also known as *random sampling*. [11]

process. A series of ongoing activities directed toward achieving a goal. [5]

product design. *See* **technical product design**.

product (output) market. A market in which businesses supply finished goods and services to households, other businesses, and governments. [1]

product portfolio. *See* **liability portfolio**.

profitability. A company's overall success in generating returns to its owners and increasing the value of the company. [3]

profitability ratio. A ratio that provides insurers with a relative measure of their overall success by comparing the company's profits, or gains from operations, to the resources used to generate those profits. [8]

program evaluation and review technique (PERT) network. A project scheduling tool that helps shorten the length of time needed to complete large, complex projects. [9]

publicly held company. A company that sells ownership shares to the public. *Contrast with* **privately held company**. [2]

PV. *See* **present value**.

PVIF. *See* **present value interest factor**.

QC circle. *See* **quality control circle**.

quality circle. *See* **quality control circle**.

quality control circle. A voluntary problem-solving group of 5 to 10 employees from the same work area who meet regularly to discuss quality improvement and ways to reduce costs. Also known as a *QC circle* or a *quality circle*. [5]

random number generator. A software application that automatically identifies a pattern of values that would be produced by sampling a probability distribution. [11]

random sampling. *See* **probability sampling**.

random variable. A variable whose values represent all possible outcomes. *Contrast with* **discrete variable**. [10]

random variation. A variation that results from changes that are either unexpected or are one-time occurrences. *See* **variation**. [6]

range. The difference between the highest and lowest values in a particular population. [10]

range estimate. In modeling, an estimate that provides a range of possible outcome values. *Contrast with* **point estimate**. [11]

rating agency. An independently owned, private organization that evaluates the financial condition of insurers and provides information to potential customers of and investors in insurance companies. [8]

ratio. A comparison of two numeric values expressed in the form of a fraction or percentage. [8]

ratio analysis. The study of the relationships between various financial statement amounts. [8]

RCA. *See* **root-cause analysis**.

real GDP. Gross domestic product that has been adjusted for changes in price levels. *See* **gross domestic product**. [6]

real rate of interest. The difference between the nominal, or stated, rate of interest and the expected inflation rate. [6]

recession. A significant decline in economic activity spread across the economy, lasting more than a few months. During a recession, unemployment is generally high and real GDP usually falls for two or more quarters. Also known as a *slump*. *See* **business cycle** and **real GDP**. [6]

recovery. The phase of the business cycle in which real GDP increases for two or more quarters after a recession or depression. *See* **recession, depression, business cycle**, and **real GDP**. [6]

reengineering. *See* **business process reengineering**.

refinance. To make new borrowing arrangements, usually because of a drop in market interest rates. [6]

regulatory risk. The risk that arises from changes in the regulatory environment. [3]

reinvestment-rate risk. The risk that a decline in interest rates will lead to lower income when bonds are paid off and the insurer must reinvest the funds. [3]

renewal commission. A commission on life insurance policies that remain in force that is equal to a stated percentage of each premium paid for a specified number of years after the first policy year. *Contrast with* **first-year commission**. [5]

renewal expense. *See* **maintenance expense**.

required rate of return. For a given investment, the sum of the risk-free rate of return and the risk premium. *See* **risk-free rate of return** and **risk premium**. [3]

residential mortgage. A loan secured by a single-family home. [3]

restrictive fiscal policy. *See* **contractionary fiscal policy**.

return. Any reward, profit, or compensation an investor hopes to earn in exchange for taking a risk. [3]

return on assets ratio (ROA). A profitability ratio which provides companies with information about a company's success in using assets to earn a profit. [8]

return on equity ratio (ROE). A profitability ratio which measures the return to a company's owners by relating profits to owners' equity. [8]

return on invested assets ratio (ROIA). A profitability ratio which compares a company's net income to its average invested assets. [8]

return on revenue ratio. *See* **net profit margin**.

revenue. An amount that a company earns from its business operations. *See* **income statement**. *Contrast with* **expense**. [7]

revenue budget. A type of operational budget that indicates the amount of income from operations that a company expects in the coming budget period. *See* **revenue** and **operational budget**. [7]

rightsizing. The elimination of nonessential employees or jobs within an organization. Also known as *downsizing*. [5]

risk. The possibility that results will be different than expected; generally associated with the possibility of loss. [1]

risk-free rate of return. The return on a risk-free investment. *See* **required rate of return** and **risk premium**. [3]

risk management. The practice of systematically identifying, assessing, and minimizing the negative impact of risk. [3]

risk premium. The compensation that investors demand for taking on the risk associated with a specific investment. *See* **required rate of return** and **risk-free rate of return**. [3]

risk-return trade-off. The interplay between risk and return; according to this interplay, in general, the greater the risk associated with an investment, the greater the expected return on the investment; conversely, the lower the risk associated with an investment then, generally, the lower the expected return on the investment. [3]

risk tolerance. From an individual investor's perspective, that individual's comfort level with risk. [1]

ROA. *See* **return on assets ratio**.

ROE. *See* **return on equity ratio**.

ROIA. *See* **return on invested assets ratio**.

root-cause analysis (RCA). A set of problem-solving methods and tools that attempts to determine the actual causal factors that led to an incident so that these factors can be corrected or removed. [5]

sample errors. The differences between population values and the values derived from a sample of the population. [11]

SBU. *See* **strategic business unit**.

seasonal variation. A variation that results from routine patterns that typically occur in the course of one year. *See* **variation**. [6]

SEC. *See* **Securities and Exchange Commission**.

Securities and Exchange Commission (SEC). In the United States, a federal government agency that regulates the investment industry. [7]

security. A document or certificate that represents an ownership interest in a business (stock) or an obligation of indebtedness owed by a business, government, or agency (bond). [1]

shared service. A functional area that performs specified business processes for multiple strategic business units (SBUs) and that shares accountability for the costs, timing, and quality of those processes with the SBUs. *See* **strategic business unit**. [2]

simple interest. Interest that is applied only to the principal amount of an investment. *Contrast with* **compound interest**. [4]

simple random sampling. A type of probability sampling in which every member of a population has an equal probability of being in the sample. [11]

Six Sigma. A disciplined approach for improving quality by reducing process defects or correcting problems so that results fall within customer specifications. [5]

slump. *See* **recession**.

solvency. An insurance company's ability to meet its financial obligations on time. *Contrast with* **insolvency**. [3]

span of control. The number of people who report directly to a manager. [2]

spread compression. The narrowing of an insurer's interest spread. *See* **interest spread**. *Contrast with* **spread expansion**. [6]

spread expansion. The widening of an insurer's interest spread. *See* **interest spread**. *Contrast with* **spread compression**. [6]

stagflation. A combination of inflation, slow economic growth, and high unemployment. *See* **inflation**. [6]

standard deviation. For a population, the square root of the variance of the population. *See* **variance** and **population**. [10]

statement of cash flows. *See* **cash flow statement**.

statement of financial condition. *See* **balance sheet**.

statement of financial position. *See* **balance sheet**.

statement of owners' equity. A financial statement that provides information about changes in owners' equity between two sequential balance sheets. *See* **owners' equity** and **balance sheet**. [7]

statistical analysis. The use of mathematical techniques to collect, organize, describe, analyze, and interpret large amounts of numerical data in order to help people make decisions. [10]

statistical validity. The degree to which an observed result, such as a difference between two measurements, can be relied upon and not attributed to random error in sampling or measurement. [11]

statistics. The numerical data used in statistical analysis. *See* **statistical analysis**. [10]

steering control. A control that is established in advance and that describes the company's expectations. Also known as a *feedforward control.* [2]

stock. A security that represents an ownership interest in a company. [1]

stock insurance company. An insurance company that is owned by the people and organizations that purchase shares of the company's stock. [2]

straight-through processing. The automation of the steps in industry-specific transactions electronically, with little or no manual intervention. Also known as *end-to-end processing.* [5]

strategic business unit (SBU). An area of business distinct from other areas within a company in that it generates its own profits, has its own separate set of customers and competitors, has its own management, and is capable of having its own goals and strategies. [2]

stratified random sampling. A type of probability sampling that divides the population into subgroups, or strata, and then selects a proportional number of items from each stratum at random. [11]

surplus. The cumulative amount of money—calculated as an insurance company's assets minus its liabilities and its capital—that remains in the company over time. *See* **asset, liability,** and **capital**. [7]

surrender. When the owner of a cash value life insurance policy or deferred annuity contract chooses to receive the contract's monetary value before the contract reaches maturity. [3]

SWOT analysis. In planning, an analysis in which a company weighs company strengths and weaknesses against environmental opportunities and threats. [2]

systematic random sampling. A type of probability sampling that involves selecting items from the population at a uniform interval, which is generally measured by time, order, or space. [11]

systematic risk. *See* **nondiversifiable risk**.

table. An orderly listing of data. [9]

technical product design. The phase in the product development process in which a product's financial structure is created. Also known as *financial design* or *product design.* [4]

telecommuting. A remote work arrangement that gives employees the flexibility to determine their working location and hours. [5]

time value of money. A concept which states that the value of a sum of money will change over time as a result of the effects of interest. [4]

top-down budgeting. A budgeting approach that begins at the top of a company and is passed down to lower-level management. *Contrast with* **bottom-up budgeting**. [7]

total asset turnover ratio. A type of activity ratio which indicates how efficiently a company is using its cash, investments, and other assets to support income-producing activities. [8]

total quality management (TQM). The process of creating an organizational culture committed to continuous improvement. [5]

TQM. *See* **total quality management**.

traceable cost. *See* **direct expense**.

transfer payment. A payment made by a government for which no goods or services are given in return. [1]

trend. A movement in a specific direction, either upward or downward. [6]

trend analysis. A type of analysis that forecasts the future movement of specified factors based on historical patterns. [11]

turnover ratio. *See* **activity ratio**.

unemployment rate. The percentage of people in the labor force who are without jobs but who are actively seeking jobs. [6]

unit of account. In an economy, the monetary unit in which value is expressed. [1]

unity of command. A principle which states that each employee should be under the authority of and be accountable to only one person. [2]

U.S. Treasury bill. An obligation issued by the U.S. Treasury as part of its ongoing process of funding the national debt. [3]

variable. An item of data whose value varies over time. [11]

variable expense. An expense amount that varies in direct proportion to some variation in a specified level of operating activity. *Contrast with* **fixed expense**. [5]

variance. The average squared distance between the population mean and each individual item in a population. [10]

variation. A change or fluctuation in a trend. *See* **seasonal variation, cyclical variation**, and **random variation**. [6]

vested commission. A commission that is guaranteed payable to a producer whether or not the producer represents the company when the commission becomes due. *Contrast with* **nonvested commission**. [5]

want. A desire for a particular product or service. *Contrast with* **need**. [1]

weighted value. A value that has been multiplied by a percentage. [8]

ZBB. *See* **zero-based budgeting**.

zero-based budgeting (ZBB). A budgeting approach in which a company begins with the premise that no resources will be allocated for the next accounting period unless and until each expense is shown to be in accord with the company's strategic and operational goals. [7]

A

accumulated value, 136
acquisition expenses, 104–105
activity ratios, 168–170
actuaries, 76, 185. *See also* product
    development, financial aspects of
administrative charge, 79
adverse deviation, 81–82, 83
age, trends in, 232
ALM. See asset-liability management
A. M. Best, *180*
amortization, 64
annual report, 153–155, *157, 163*
Annual Return, 178
Annual Statement, 147, 153, *157, 163*, 178
annuities, 33, 90–91, *92*
    annuity due, 91, *92*
    commissions for, 113–114, *115*
    fixed deferred annuities, 136
    ordinary annuities, 91, *92*
annuity due, 91, 92, *96*
asset accumulation products, 30–32
asset-based commission schedule, 114, *115*
asset concentration risk, 70
asset distribution, 33
asset-liability management, 71
asset-liability portfolio, 71
asset portfolio, 71
asset protection products, 32
assets, 61, 150–152, 174
assuming company, 60
audit committee, 49
audits, 54
authority, 51
automobile insurance, as asset
    protection product, 32

B

balanced scorecard, 199–200
balance sheet, 150–152, *153, 163, 170*
bank, commercial, *26*
bar charts, 186–188, 203
basic accounting equation, 150
basis point, 80
benchmarking, 51, 115–116, *117*
benefits, cost of, 77–78
black belts, 119
board of directors, 48

bondholder, 62
bonds, 27, 28, 62–63
    market values of, inversely related to market
        interest rates, 138–140, 141, 142
    prices of, 138–139, 141
bonuses, for production, 113
boom (economic), 130
bottom-up budgeting, 158, *159*
bp. *See* basis point
BPR. *See* business process reengineering
brokerage accounts, *31*
broker/dealers, 27
budget deficit, 142
budgeting, 156
    approaches to, 158–59
    reasons for, 156–58
budgets, 53–54, *163*
    types of, 160–163
budget surplus, 143
budget variances, 54
business cycles, 130–133
businesses
    financial needs of, 28–33
    as market participants, 22, 23
business process reengineering, 122–123
business process risk, 68, *73*
business risk, 69

C

capital, 61–62, 151
capital appreciation, 30
capital budget, 162
capital budgeting, 162
capital market. *See* financial market
capital standards, 61–62
capital and surplus, 151–152, 175
capital and surplus ratio, *173*, 175
cash, 64
cash budget, 160–162
cash disbursements, *162*
cash disbursements budget, 161
cash equivalents, 64
cash flow statement, 152, *163*
cash management account, 29
cash management products, 29–30
cash receipts, *162*
cash receipts budget, 161
catastrophic risk, 72
CDs. *See* certificates of deposit

ceding company, 60
central banks, 143–144
certificates of deposit, *31*
chain of command, 51
charts, 186–192
checking account, *29*
circular flow diagram, 23
CMOs. *See* collateralized mortgage obligations
coincident indicators, 133
collateralized mortgage obligations, 64
commercial bank, *26*
commercial mortgages, 64
commercial paper, 27, *28*
commissions
    or annuities, 113–114, *115*
    for asset accumulation products, 32
    for life insurance, 112–113
committees, 49
common costs, 106–107
common stock, 63
competition risk, 69, *73*
component bar chart, 186, *188*
compounding periods, 88
compound interest, 84–85, *87*
comprehensive budget, 160
comprehensive business analysis, 77
concurrent controls, 52, 53, 54
conditionally vested commission, 113
confidence, degree of, 231
Consumer Price Index, 135
consumption, 128
continuous-flow processing, 121, 122
continuous improvement, 116, 118, *119*
contraction, 130
contractionary fiscal policy, 143
contractual benefit payments, 148
contractual benefits, 77–78
contractual reserves, 61, 150–151
contractual savings institutions, 25–27
control, 51
    mechanisms for, 53–55
    process of, 51–52
    span of, 49–50
control cycle, 52, *53*
controllable expenses, 106
controlling, of company operations, 42, 51–55
corporate bonds, 63
corporate budget, 160
corporate objectives, 43, *44*
corporate planning, 42–45
corporate strategies, 44
corporations, 36–38
cost accumulation, 103
cost of benefits, 77–78
cost of insurance, 77–78
coupon payments, 62
coupon rate, 62
CPI. *See* Consumer Price Index
credit products, 29–30

credit ratings, 178–179
credit risk, 66, 67, *73*
credit unions, *26*
critical path, 196
cropped scales, 202
currency risk, 66, 67–68, *73*
current assets, 174
current liabilities, 174
current ratio, *173*, 174
customer behavior risk, 70
customer-centered, 117
customer service performance, 51
customer type, organization by, 47
cyclical variations, 132

D

dashboards, 198–199
data, 182–183
    quality of, 219–220
data distributions, 217–219
data set, 206
debt-to-equity ratio, 175–176
default, 67
default risk, 66, 67
defects, 118
deferred annuities, *31*
deflation, 137
demographic data, trends in, 232
demutualization, 39
dependent variables, 234
deposit-based commission schedule, 113, 114, 115
depository institutions, 25
    forms of, 26
depression, 132
descriptive statistics, 206
    improving the value of, 215–216
    measures of central tendency, 207–211
    measures of dispersion, 211–215
design phase, of BPR, 123
development expenses, 104
deviations, in product design, 81–82, *83*
direct exchange, 22
direct expenses, 106, *107*
direct writer, 60
disability income insurance, as
    asset protection product, *32*
discounting, 93
discrete variables, 217
disinflation, *138*
disintermediation, 136–137
distribution risk, *73*
diversifiable risk, 71
diversification, return and, 70–71
dividends, 30, 38, 63. *See also* policy dividends
DMAIC (define, measure, analyze, improve,
    controls), 120
"do it right the first time," 116–117

required rate of return, 66
research phase, of BPR, 123
reserve requirements, 61
residential mortgages, 64
response bias, 228
restrictive fiscal policy, 143
return, 62
    on assets, 30. *See also* return on assets
      ratio
    diversification and, 70–71
    required rate of, 66
    risk-free rate of, 66
return on assets ratio, *171*, 172
return on equity ratio, *171*, 173
return on invested assets ratio, *171*, 172
return on revenue ratio, 171
revenue budget, 160, *161*
revenues, 148
rightsizing, 108–109
risk, 31
    accepting, 59–60
    asset concentration, 70
    avoiding, 59
    business, 69
    business process, 68, *73*
    competition, 69, *73*
    controlling, 59, 60
    credit, 66, 67, *73*
    currency, 66, 67–68, *73*
    customer behavior, 70
    default, 66, 67
    distribution, 68, *73*
    diversifiable, 71
    equity, 67, *73*
    event, *73*
    expense, 69, *73*
    human resources, 68, *73*
    interest-rate, 66, 67, *73*, 137–142
    liquidity, 66, 68, *73*
    managing, for profitability, 62–73
    market, 66, 67–68, *73*
    marketplace, 69, *73*
    mortality, 69, *73*
    nondiversifiable, 71, 137–138
    nonsystematic, 71
    operational, 68–69, *73*
    policyholder behavior, 70, *73*
    pricing, 69–70, *73*
    regulatory, 69, *73*
    reinvestment-rate, 67, *73*
    retaining, 59–60
    systematic, 71
    systems, 68, *73*
    technology, 68, *73*
    transferring, 60–61
    types of, 66–73
risk committee, 49
risk control process, 72–73

risk-free rate of return, 66
risk management, 58
    techniques for, 59–61
risk management culture, 72
risk premium, 66
risk-return trade-off, 64–65
risk tolerance, 31
ROA. *See* return on assets ratio
ROE. *See* return on equity ratio
ROIA. *See* return on invested assets ratio
root-cause analysis, 120
Rule of 72, 85–86

S

sales charges, 32
sample data
    used to estimate population characteristics, 229–231
    used to forecast behavior, 232–233
sample errors, 230
sample mean, 229
sample standard deviation, 229–230
sample variance, 229–230
sampling, 223
    avoiding bias in, 228
    nonprobability sampling, 227–228
    probability sampling, 223–227
    simple random sampling, 224, *227*
    systematic random sampling, 224–225, *227*
savings accounts, *31*
savings and loan associations, *26*
SBU. See strategic business unit
seasonal variations, 132
secondary sector (of an economy), 19, *20*
securities, 27, *28*
Securities and Exchange Commission, 154
selection bias, 228
Service Report (U.S.), 133
services, 19, *20*
share draft account, *29*
shared service, 48
Sigma, 118
simple interest, 84, 85
simple random sampling, 224, *227*
Six Sigma, 118–121
slump (economic), 131
Social Security, 27
sole proprietorships, 36, *37*
solvency, 58
    evaluation of, 178
solvency ratios, 173–175
span of control, 49–50
spread, 139
spread compression, 139–140, 141
spread expansion, 141
stagflation, *138*